T0352569

Aboard the Democracy Train

Aboard the Democracy Train

A Journey through Pakistan's Last Decade of Democracy

NAFISA HOODBHOY

ANTHEM PRESS

LONDON · NEW YORK · DELHI

Anthem Press
An imprint of Wimbledon Publishing Company
www.anthempress.com

This edition first published in UK and USA 2011
by ANTHEM PRESS
75-76 Blackfriars Road, London SE1 8HA, UK
or PO Box 9779, London SW19 7ZG, UK
and
244 Madison Ave. #116, New York, NY 10016, USA

Copyright © Nafisa Hoodbhoy 2011

The moral right of the author has been asserted.

All rights reserved. Without limiting the rights under copyright reserved
above, no part of this publication may be reproduced, stored or introduced
into a retrieval system, or transmitted, in any form or by any means
(electronic, mechanical, photocopying, recording or otherwise),
without the prior written permission of both the copyright
owner and the above publisher of this book.

British Library Cataloguing in Publication Data
A catalogue record for this book is available from the British Library.

Library of Congress Cataloging in Publication Data
Hoodbhoy, Nafisa.
Aboard the democracy train : a journey through Pakistan's last decade
of democracy / Nafisa Hoodbhoy.
        p. cm.
Includes bibliographical references and index.
ISBN-13: 978-0-85728-967-4 (pbk. : alk. paper)
ISBN-10: 0-85728-967-5 (pbk. : alk. paper)
1. Pakistan–Politics and government–1988- 2. Press and politics–
Pakistan. 3. Democracy–Pakistan–History–20th century. 4. Pakistan–
Social conditions–20th century. 5. Pakistan–Ethnic relations. 6. Terrorism–
Pakistan. 7. Women journalists–Pakistan--Biography. 8. Hoodbhoy,
Nafisa. I. Title.
DS389.H3966 2011
954.9105'3–dc22
        2011007392

ISBN-13: 978 0 85728 967 4 (Pbk)
ISBN-10: 0 85728 967 5 (Pbk)

This title is also available as an eBook.

CONTENTS

LIST OF FIGURES

PREFACE

This is a book about politics and journalism in Pakistan, told through first-hand experiences. It is one I have long wanted to write because of my access to people, places and events that are normally hidden from public view. By relating my personal experiences, I hope to give an original insight to Pakistan and reveal who *really* rules the country, as well as expose the enormous effects that being in the US's orbit of influence has had.

In 1984, I began my career at *Dawn* newspaper as its only female reporter, just as Benazir Bhutto made her bid to become Pakistan's first woman prime minister. That year, I had come back from the US, armed with a master's degree in history and a dream, not only to work for the nation's most established newspaper, but to also effect change while working within the bounds of its staid but reliable coverage. As an energetic, young, Western-educated woman, my editor bypassed senior male reporters and deputed me to cover Benazir and her Pakistan Peoples Party (PPP).

That decade of tumultuous democracy, which marked the onset of civilian rule and the end of 11½ years of military dictatorship, would reveal to me why Pakistan has stubbornly resisted change. As an insider, my experience informs the reader on how the establishment – acting in collusion with feudal lords, tribal chiefs, ethnic and mafia groups – has worked against untidy civilian rule.

As a journalist in Pakistan, I constantly walked a tightrope, informing readers about the machinations of corrupt and dishonest military and government leaders, all the while working for a newspaper that often depended on the goodwill of the establishment. In attempting to get the "inside story," I often found myself skating on thin ice and this book relates some of the narrow escapes I had from violently enforced censorship.

My status as a female journalist in a Muslim society inadvertently defined my career. In a society already laden with archaic customs, I covered Islamic legislation that aimed to tie women to medieval ways. The laws were supposedly meant to protect women, yet all around me women were raped and murdered, without recourse to justice. This only motivated me further to use my influence as an insider journalist.

The book focuses primarily on the decade of democratic rule (1988–99) when as a political reporter I had a front seat on history. Again, as a US-based academic and journalist from 2000 to the present, I have shared my unique perspective on Pakistan's politics since it partnered with the US. Whilst the post-9/11 alliance opened the door for Benazir's PPP to return to power, it culminated in her murder and exposed the conspiracies and intrigue that are woven into the nation's political fabric.

This book carries the reader through the issues that face a complex society like Pakistan, in which the population spins out of control, violence breeds because of the total collapse of judicial institutions and the situation for women is one of the most difficult in the world. Indeed, the region is a ticking time bomb – and one that teems with conspiracies that threaten it, not only internally, but also on a global scale.

I was only in my late twenties when I began an exciting career as a journalist in Pakistan. As a young, idealistic woman I began with a clean slate and without any preconceived notions of the complex interplay between politics and society. Back then, I worked according to the news industry's modus operandi to cover breaking news. Given that journalism is often described as "literature in a hurry," and I was too busy gathering facts to form a proper narrative at the time, this book is an attempt to unpack the message.

In essence, I hope to give a human face to a region associated with stereotypical images of Muslim women and terrorists. In offering a nuanced picture of Pakistan, I want readers to appreciate the fascinating kaleidoscope of its recent history. It is a nation riddled with contradictions, where the past and present live side-by-side and where the more things change, the more they remain the same.

It is with the intent of sharing a nuanced perspective that I invite the reader to better understand Pakistan, by sharing in the exciting and dramatic times that I have spent with the nation's politicians and people.

Map 1 Map of Pakistan.

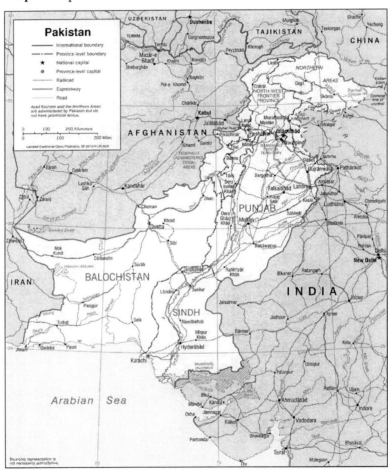

Source: University of Texas.

INTRODUCTION

The Effects of Partition

British Influences

I was born in the young Muslim state of Pakistan, which was carved by the British from India in 1947. My infant memory of the deep quiet that once pervaded Garden East – our residential neighborhood in Karachi in the 1960s – still remains.

Karachi was still a cosmopolitan city. Located along the Arabian Sea in the southern province of Sindh, the port city has always attracted immigrants. At the time, I was too small to know that we were on the threshold of a massive transformation, ushered in by wave upon wave of Muslim migrants arriving from India.

I grew up in a colonial-style two-storied bungalow with a towering fortress and a red bridge connecting two separate living units. Although the Garden zoo was about a mile away, the roar of the lions often shattered the night's silence and made me bolt up startled in my crib. My mother would assure me that the lion was actually quite far away before I could fall back to sleep.

Defying the ravages of the continuously growing port city of Karachi, spurned on by the influx of India's migrants (Mohajirs) and arrivals from across Pakistan and the region, our family bungalow remains the oldest on the block. Although it has been partitioned, it still towers above the newer constructed apartments.

Although the giant banyan tree, which once embraced our bungalow with its muscular branches, was felled long ago, the gentle swoosh of its small diamond-shaped green leaves brushing the top floors – where my uncle's family once lived – is etched in my memory.

Even after a decade of Pakistan's existence, we lived in a mosaic of cultures. Our neighbors in Garden East were not only Ismailis – the tiny Muslim sect to which we belong – but also Christians, Hindus and Zoroastrians. I considered our Christian neighbors, who lived along Pedro D'souza Road, as part of our extended family. It never struck me as odd that they were called the Pintos, Pereiras and D'souzas or even that further down the block lived the tall, imposing, red-faced Englishman, Daddy Patterson – a senior officer in the Karachi police.

The British exited India just as Pakistan was carved out of it in 1947. As a child in the 1960s, I grew up in the bubble they left behind. Being a well-off new Pakistani, my father was among the select few to become a member of the Karachi Gymkhana. The gymkhana was part of a chain of exclusive clubs left by the British. It had red Spanish roof tiles, lush green lawns and had, up until partition, displayed the sign:

"Indians and Dogs not allowed."

We were seeped in Western culture, wearing shorts and frocks to the clubs, which were frequented by European families. It was at the Karachi Gymkhana that I saw blond and blue-eyed kids for the first time. I was fascinated: they looked just like the golden-haired dolls my mother brought back from Europe. And yet times were changing, as we locals with darker hair and eye color began to inherit their privileges.

In those days, Karachi was dotted with bookstores and lending libraries. The exposure to English literature would open up new and exciting worlds. As a teenager, I came across D. H. Lawrence's *Lady Chatterley's Lover*, with its vivid descriptions of sexuality. The expression of shame on my relative's face as he took the book from me made me aware of the high premium society placed on female chastity. Indeed, in a rapidly Islamizing society in which women joined the ranks of the veiled and unseen, it was difficult to believe that men did not obsess about female sexuality in the recesses of their minds.

My earliest memories of Karachi are of a city developed in 1843 by the British from a sleepy fishing village to a seaport and a well-planned city center with theaters, clubs, hotels, coffee shops and bookstores. By the 1960s, the Mohajirs had completed their major migrations from India to the newly created Pakistan. Still, it was a relatively calm period in which the refugees arrived with smaller families and fanned out to rural Sindh in search of job opportunities.

The creation of Pakistan had been a symbol of immense hope for India's Muslim refugees. They arrived from all parts of India: young and old, rich and poor, by train and by bus. Those who crossed the border by foot hoped to achieve the prosperity that they never dreamed of attaining in the predominantly Hindu India. In a short time, they would give up hopes of finding job opportunities in the rural areas of Sindh and begin to converge on Karachi.

Twenty years later, I saw how the convergence of ethnic groups, fighting over a shrinking economic pie, would stoke the fires of intolerance and political instability. Until such a time, Karachi was a clean and quiet city. We took leisurely walks at night around the city's showpiece, Frere Hall, enjoying the cool summer breeze from the Arabian Sea.

We could not have predicted that the well-planned British-built city of Karachi would grow into a sprawling, unplanned metropolis and a hotbed for ethnic and sectarian violence. Nor could we foresee that the US consulate located across Frere Hall would become a repeated target of bomb attacks, with its fortified presence becoming symbolic of anti-American sentiment.

Back then, as my father's antique Austin car inched its way through the city, I sat up and watched for new titles of English movies screened at Rex, Palace, Odeon and Lyric cinema houses. Perched on top of the Bambino cinema house, owned by Hakim Ali Zardari – father of President Asif Ali Zardari – was the object

that made me sit up with special interest: a flashing blue neon
sign with the image of a woman dancer gyrating her hips.

Inside, wide-eyed audiences watched classic movies like
Toby Tyler and *Gone with the Wind*. It did not matter that the
crowds did not understand English. Through the movies came
the images of Western culture – where women mixed freely
with men – and one saw the trappings of great material wealth
and progress.

Roots in Pakistan

My late father came from a large Sindhi Ismaili business family
of 14 brothers and sisters. For decades, he conducted the family
business: traveling through the barren hills of Balochistan and
Sindh to buy wool and goat hair, which he exported as raw
material for the carpet industry in Europe and the Middle East.
His business brought him into contact with the Western world
and his narratives fired my interest in foreign lands.

My father was 41 years old when I was born, the youngest of
five children. I grew close to him when he had already seen much
of the world. At the same time, age never got in the way of his
tremendous zest for life. Being highly sociable, outgoing and a
humanist, he confided to me that he should never have become
a businessman. Instead, as he later saw me enjoy my profession,
where I traveled, met people and got published every day, he told
me that he wished that he too had been a journalist.

As a young man, my father used his business opportunities to travel
abroad, at times taking my mother with him. Back home, we saw
pictures of him aboard the Queen Elizabeth ocean liner, smiling
in a felt hat and tie as he shared a meal with Europeans. His deep
admiration for the West was reflected in the black and white
movies of New York and Europe in the 1950s that he brought back
from his travels, of which he held special viewings for the family.

Despite my father's skeptical distance from the Ismaili
community and his irreverent attitude toward organized religion,
it had a profound influence on us. To begin with, my paternal

grandfather was a religious elder within the Ismaili community. The Aga Khans, who lead the Ismailis, intermarried with Europeans and lived in the West. This would make our family even more open to Western influence.

My maternal grandparents were Sindhi landowners in a small village, Jhirk, a dusty landscape from which they moved to Hyderabad city in Sindh. My grandfather, an honorary magistrate under the ruling British, represented the giant banking and mercantile firm, David Sassoon & Company, in India – which traded with Europe. Although my grandfather wore Western clothes – a suit, bow tie and hat – his life's work showed that his heart lay with his own people.

In the early twentieth century, the British handed over hundreds of acres of fertile agricultural land some 200 km north of Karachi, along the Hyderabad-Mirpurkhas road to Aga Khan 111, Sultan Mohammed Shah. The Aga Khan entrusted the land to my grandfather, who in turn gave it to members of the Ismaili community to become tenant landlords and plant fruit and vegetables in a community known as Sultanabad.

Today, in the center of Sultanabad the Ismaili prayer house, the Jamatkhana, has preserved my grandfather's memory. A photograph depicts him in felt hat and bow tie, his soft, unsmiling eyes exuding concern. Thousands of people from all over Sindh gather every year for *majlis* (prayer services) to pay tribute to the work he created for the community.

My two eldest siblings, Samir and Naseem were born in Karachi before 1947, when it was still a part of British India and had a population of only 400,000 people. But despite top careers in the US, both returned to Pakistan and immersed themselves in professions that also contributed to nation-building. My middle sister, Nargis devoted herself to running a recycling business in Karachi.

My middle brother, Pervez, a nuclear science professor, travels the world on invitation to speak his forthright mind on global issues – prominently nuclear disarmament and world peace.

At the end of the day, we inherited a severely stressed infrastructure. It would only whet our appetite to work for change. Even while I lived in America and visited it scores of times, my head always carried a map of home, family and the people with whom I grew up, along with the prospect of bringing about positive change.

Western Education vs. Culture

My parents enrolled us in British schools in Karachi – then open only to a privileged few – in order to prepare us for further education in the West. It was the education that only the ruling classes of Pakistan – ambassadors, diplomats, politicians, army personnel and feudal lords – were able to afford for their children.

Indeed, British education was meant to groom future rulers of Pakistan. The best-known political family in Pakistan, headed by late Prime Minister Zulfikar Ali Bhutto and the daughter who succeeded him, Prime Minister Benazir Bhutto, were educated in these schools.

My parents sent me and my two sisters to St Joseph's Convent School for girls in Karachi. My school's aloof, imposing marble cathedral and statue of Jesus erected next to severe sandstone buildings bore a stark contrast to the unruly traffic and enormous crowds that gradually grew around it.

St Joseph's Convent School was then run by Catholic nuns, many of whom were British. Each morning, we gathered in our starched gray frocks in front of Christ's statue and chanted the Catholic prayer: "In the name of the Father, the Son and the Holy Ghost – Amen." Our school anthem, "Honor and Glory to Our School," sparked my imagination as our voices rose in crescendo:

> *Here we are taught the Golden Lesson*
> *How to sift out wrong from right*
> *How to bear our crosses bravely*
> *And to keep our goal in sight.*

From the start, I knew that I would have a different life compared to my female friends who, in a Pakistani context, were primed for arranged marriages and motherhood. Being a voracious reader of Jane Austen's novels, I found a striking similarity between her nineteenth-century characters and my schoolmates. While my peers gorged on romantic novels by Georgette Heyer, being girls, they were subject to enormous cultural pressures.

A Kashmiri girl friend of mine with a radiant white complexion, luminous brown eyes and soft brown hair was the first to be coaxed into an arranged marriage. Her family had received a proposal from an older, rich businessman. The problem was that – like other women in this traditional Muslim society – she had never met her husband-to-be.

My friend was in tears as her mother agreed to the match. Still, she'd philosophize to our group that the marriage would finally make her free. To me, her ideas seemed absurd and I was characteristically blunt within our inner circle of friends: "Listen, your husband isn't someone you can lock away in a box and forget for life."

Twenty years later, when I ran into my childhood friend at a gas station, I recognized her – older and more sober – with her head covered. She knew I worked as a journalist and it didn't surprise her. "You're not the sort of person to sit still," she told me as a backhanded compliment.

Apart from bringing up her two daughters, my old friend was increasingly devoted to caring for her ailing husband. Our lives were poles apart: I had set my sights on great challenges, while she now prepared for the marriage of her own 18-year-old daughter.

Karachi Loses its Religious Diversity

My father spent 32 years of his life in the Karachi that was part of British-ruled India. It nurtured his tolerance to other religions. As the captain of a multi-religious cricket team, he had spent a carefree childhood playing with Hindu, Christian and Zorastrian friends. There was a picture of him on the wall – the only cocky Muslim youth in a white cap – heading a team of Hindu players. At the back stood my father's teacher, K. D. Advani, the father of Indian politician, L. K. Advani.

As India's Muslims prepared to migrate to the newly created Pakistan, my father's Hindu friends in Garden East handed the keys of their palatial homes over to him. "They begged me to occupy their homes or buy it for a song," he told us.

But, skeptical that Pakistan would survive and apprehensive of taking advantage of their tragic circumstances, my father declined. Instead, he ardently clung to the hope that his Hindu friends might return to Pakistan some day.

That, as history shows, was a foregone conclusion. Even the first address by the founder of Pakistan, Mohammed Ali Jinnah, to Pakistan's first constituent assembly in 1947 – often quoted by secularists – could not convince non-Muslims to stay in the newly-created Pakistan. In it, Jinnah had said:

> You may belong to any religion or caste or creed; that has nothing to do with the business of the State. You will find that in course of time Hindus will cease to be Hindus and Muslims would cease to be Muslims, not in the religious sense, because that is the personal faith of each individual, but in the political sense as citizens of the State.

The partition of India triggered the biggest massacres between Muslims and Hindus in recent history. It convinced millions of Hindus to flee the newly-created Pakistan. Fearful that Muslim refugees would retaliate in return for the massacre of Muslims in India, our Hindu neighbors in Karachi left in a hurry.

The newer Muslim arrivals from India took over vacant homes in Sindh and Karachi as "evacuee property." False and exaggerated property claims by the newer arrivals became the order of the day as Pakistan – rapidly turning into a majority Muslim state – split on the basis of ethnic affiliations and groups lobbied to bend practices in their favor.

It left non-Muslims the most vulnerable and afraid. In the '60s, Christians evacuated our Garden East neighborhood in droves. Our British neighbor, Daddy Paterson was long gone. The Pereiras sold their picture-perfect bungalow down the road, across from

St Lawrence School, and left. Our neighbors, Anthony and Norbert, who lived in humble quarters next to our bungalow, vanished too. Apparently they were fearful that Pakistan – which translated as "Land of the Pure" – would treat non-Muslims as second-class citizens.

One evening, I saw my father pause momentarily from his favorite pastime of watering the plants in the badminton court. He had straightened his back to peer over the boundary wall at our neighbor, Frankie as the young man poked around his garden. Frankie and his sister, Coral had inherited the bungalow from their grandmother – the last of the palatial houses owned by Christians in our neighborhood.

My father asked in a tone, which to me sounded friendly: "So Frankie, when are you selling your house?"

Our neighbor apparently misunderstood the intent of the question when he replied belligerently, "When are *you* selling your house?"

"Oh, I have no intention of going anywhere," my father replied.

That was the word my father kept until his death in 1997. He had been deeply saddened by the exodus of his Hindu friends. Now, the flight of large numbers of Christians convinced him that the neighborhood was changing for good. It was a taste of things to come.

India's Migrants Flood Karachi

The most wide-ranging transformation of Karachi began outside our privileged enclave as the Mohajirs settled in concentric circles around the heart of Karachi. They had arrived in a region where everyone already had their own ethnic identity – Sindhis, Baloch, Pashtuns and Punjabis. Even though the term, "Mohajir" means refugee, the newcomers would use the term in contradistinction, to assert themselves politically as a fifth identity.

As Urdu-speakers flooded Karachi, my Sindhi parents prepared to become an ethnic minority. Indeed, by the 1960s, Karachi had become a predominantly Mohajir city and Urdu was ingrained into the lingua franca. Like more privileged families, we grew up multi-lingual: speaking the English left to us in colonial legacy, Urdu – due to the newer arrivals from India – and understanding Sindhi because our parents spoke it.

By the 1970s, Mohajirs faced their fiercest contest for jobs from the two ethnic groups – Punjabis and Pashtuns – who had arrived from other parts of Pakistan to look for work in the industrial port-city of Karachi. Faced with shrinking space, the newer arrivals took shortcuts to get electricity, water, sewerage and paved roads. It became the norm to bribe utility companies and government officials to secure illegal connections and permits. The rule of law went out of the door.

As population pressures grew, corruption took on an entirely new meaning. My father came under pressure from the get-rich-quick businessmen to mix dirt and rubble into the goat hair he exported overseas to make carpets. This was the last straw for my father, who was, in any case, more inclined to humanitarian pursuits. Being a fierce crusader against corruption, he threatened to take customs inspectors to the police – forgetting that they, too, had become part of the rotting social fabric.

From my bedroom, I heard the litany of complaints from the Balochi women workers who cleaned the wool and goat hair in his musty godowns in run-down Lyari. The entreaties of the women laborers floated in the air:

"Sir, raise our pay, we can't support our children with such meager wages."

It was enough to make my father melt. He had the women workers served with tea and biscuits and promised to raise their pay until they went home thoroughly satisfied. My mother despaired that he would never make a successful businessman. Still, with her gentle and humane nature, she too reconciled with caring for people rather than profits.

The poor Sindhi and Balochi workers, who toiled for my father's business in Lyari, were a solid voting bloc for Prime Minister Zulfikar Ali Bhutto and later Benazir Bhutto because of their Pakistan Peoples Party's catchy populist slogans of "*Roti, Kapra aur Makan*" (Food, Clothing and Shelter).

Faced with the maxim, "If you can't beat them, join them," my father bowed out of the rat race. He closed down his business and devoted the rest of his life to running over a dozen charitable institutions in an honorary capacity. At the same time, he became the honorary secretary general of the Karachi Theosophical Society – which upholds the lofty motto: "Brotherhood of Man regardless of Caste, Creed, Color or Sex," and "There is No Religion Higher than Truth."

Come late evenings, I would sit with my father by our hundred-year-old leafy banyan tree and discuss what constituted "Ultimate Reality." These conversations stayed with me and hugely inspired me in my journalistic endeavors.

Political Challenges of the 1970s

The Mohajirs posed the first serious political challenge to Zulfikar Ali Bhutto after he became president and first civilian chief martial law administrator in December 1971. That was shortly after Pakistan's eastern wing seceded and became Bangladesh. In 1972, Bhutto's bill to make Sindhi the official language of Sindh triggered language riots in Karachi. It would force Bhutto to back off and amend the Language Bill to deem both Sindhi and Urdu as the official languages of the province.

In 1973 when Bhutto became prime minister, he rewarded Sindhis from the underserved rural areas of Sindh by appointing them in Karachi's administrative set-up. But simmering ethnic tensions surfaced, as seen in the symbolic shoe thrown at him as he addressed crowds in the predominantly Mohajir settlement of Liaquatabad.

Ethnic and religious opposition to Bhutto fused in the Jamaat-i-Islami to which Mohajirs were largely attracted. The Jamaat argued that millions of Muslims had left India to create Pakistan as an Islamic state. For them, the socially liberal Bhutto – brought up under British rule, educated in Berkely and influenced by the Sindhis' easy-going mystical interpretation of Islam – imbibed all that was wrong about Pakistan. Indeed, Bhutto's lifestyle showed that he really didn't care whether women walked the streets without a veil or whether the hotels served alcohol.

Under pressure, Bhutto began his dance to appease the Islamic fundamentalist lobby. The PPP government stopped hotels in Karachi from serving alcohol, banned discotheques and imposed censorship on movies. In 1974, the Bhutto government passed a parliamentary amendment, which declared Ahmadis to be non-Muslims. Although Bhutto made these moves out of political expediency, it was the beginning of religious intolerance.

The Islamization drive ushered by Bhutto began to change the cosmopolitan nature of Karachi. The government's plans to use a peculiar triangular-shaped building along the Arabian Sea to serve as a Casino, which would attract Arab wealth, were shelved. The evening newspapers stopped publishing photographs of women snapped at diplomatic parties and the blue flashing neon sign of a woman with gyrating hips in the Zardari-owned Bambino cinema went blank.

Growing up as a young woman in Karachi, I felt constraints on my freedom. It was not only the more conservative migrants from India, organized in the Jamaat-i-Islami, who changed the freewheeling atmosphere. The traditional Muslim communities from the rural hinterlands had also brought their notions about a woman's place.

I was in my teens when my family told me that I should stop wearing frocks and skirts and adopt the Muslim *shalwar kameez* (baggy trousers and tunic) with its accompanying veil, called the *dupatta*.

It was a bolt from the blue. In my rebellious heart I knew that no matter what I wore, the newcomers' eyes would follow my movements. The freedom that I had experienced growing up was all of a sudden challenged by a Karachi transformed beyond my imagination.

Karachi was changing but so was I. I found the martial arts a perfect sport to blow off some steam. At 14 years of age, I enrolled in a judo and karate class, where I released my pent-up anger on a punch bag. My friend Salma – who later moved to New York and married an American Jew, Mark Goldstein – arrived daily in her dinky car to pick me up for our training at the National Sports and Coaching Centre.

There, the two of us, wearing our white Karate uniforms, were among a handful of girls who trained to fight with men. I was a wildfire of energy, who trained to execute roundhouse kicks and ferocious punches. We were taught to fight men in sparring matches that mirrored real-life situations.

Four years of Judo and Karate taught me to walk confidently amidst crowds of people. I lost physical fear – a sense that haunts all women. One day, as I walked in the crowded Empress Market in Karachi, I felt someone grab the end of my long, baggy tunic. Each time I looked back, the hand disappeared. It was trying my patience and I could feel my anger rising. When my stalker's hand appeared for the third time, I reached out from the crowd, grabbed him by his collar and executed a swift pseudo-chop taught by my Japanese-trained instructor.

My stalker's cry rent the air. "I didn't do anything." But at that moment, the faceless young man who had tried to blend in with the crowd had no supporters. Instead, the people who gathered around applauded me for doing the "right thing."

Knowing the "Real Pakistan"

My adulthood coincided with a deep interest in politics. Burgeoning population and rising poverty, coupled with my father's decision to devote his time to helping the poor and the disabled, inevitably drove me and my siblings to seek justice for the oppressed.

As a college student in Karachi's Sir Syed Girl's College, I was sufficiently influenced by my older sister to join the left-wing National Students Federation. I led the English Debating Society in debates throughout the city, carrying out ideological exchanges with the Islami Jamiat-i-Talaba – the student wing of the Jamaat-i-Islami.

My experiences with the left did not stop me from being critical of then prime minister, Zulfiqar Ali Bhutto – whose rule was nothing short of paradoxical. On the one hand he invited workers to organize, while on the other he ordered his administration to crack down on trade unions and professional bodies.

In 1973, while I was still in college, thousands of school and college teachers in Karachi held a massive demonstration to demand higher wages. I was part of the rally, where wave after wave of teachers kept marching toward a menacing police cordon. Suddenly, the police – ordered by Bhutto's government – swung into action, lashed at the teachers and cracked tear gas shells in the air.

I felt my eyes stream and my head implode with pain. Blinded by tears, my friend and I jumped over the wall of a house in the neighborhood. Luckily, we found a big pond, where we washed our eyes and freed them from the stinging pain.

It was the first incident of harsh repression that I experienced under the populist Prime Minister Zulfikar Ali Bhutto. It shocked me into realizing that Bhutto's reputation as a firebrand and a rabble-rouser may have been just that: mere rhetoric to attract votes from a people desperate to find a way out of burgeoning poverty.

Fifteen years later, the forces of history would catapult his daughter, Benazir Bhutto into becoming the only female prime minister of the Muslim world. Like millions of people all over the world, I was inspired by the possibility of change. Surely, the Western educated Benazir who spoke convincingly of her determination to change the course of Pakistan's history would make a difference. As a journalist on the front seat, it fell on me to find out.

The End of Populist Rule

I was a college student in Karachi in 1977 when an alliance of political parties, called the Pakistan National Alliance (PNA), mobilized thousands of people to demand Bhutto's removal. The PNA movement was largely led by the Islamic political parties who, in spite of the concessions made by the secular Sindhi prime minister, accused him of straying away from the raison d'etre of Pakistan.

As the PNA movement gathered steam and their wheel jam strikes paralyzed the city for unending weeks, Bhutto challenged the Islamic fundamentalists at a massive rally: "Yes, I drink alcohol, but I don't drink the blood of the people."

But whilst the Jamaat-i-Islami had forced Bhutto toward Islamization, the PNA had now grown into a political movement with a single point agent of removing Bhutto. The crowds kept growing around the Old Exhibition roundabout – near Jinnah's mausoleum. For weeks, we endured "wheel jam strikes" as the masses kept up the pressure for Bhutto's resignation. Driving back home, I would spot increasingly large crowds milling around Jinnah's mausoleum, forcing me to make a detour to reach home.

And then came the moment that people in Pakistan dreaded. On July 5, 1977, the Chief of Army Staff, General Zia ul Haq declared martial law, abrogated the 1973 constitution, suspended fundamental rights and put the elected Prime Minister Zulfikar Ali Bhutto under house arrest.

Six months later, as I flew to Boston to study history at Northeastern University, Bhutto was to be tried for murder. His wife, Nusrat and their daughter, Benazir were put under house arrest. In April 1979, General Zia turned a deaf ear to international calls for clemency and despite a split verdict in the supreme court, hanged the sitting prime minister.

I was in Cambridge, Massachusetts when a retired supreme court judge who delivered the dissenting verdict on Bhutto's execution, Justice Safdar Shah, came to MIT to talk about the case. We heard the Pashtun judge speak in a voice choked with emotion against General Zia's "politically motivated" decision to have Bhutto executed. In a tone full of foreboding, Shah warned about how Bhutto's execution would further divide and destroy Pakistan.

"Go back, go back and serve your country," Justice Shah told us in a tone of voice that I took to heart.

The Only Woman Reporter at *Dawn* Newspaper

In February 1984, I returned to Pakistan to fulfill my childhood dream of being a journalist in my home country. In the six years that I had studied and worked in the US, I kept my eyes on Pakistan. Only days after my return from America, I applied for a reporting position in the nation's premier English language newspaper, *Dawn* in Karachi.

In those days, women journalists worked behind closed doors as sub-editors, columnists and magazine editors and within different sections of the newspaper. My request to become a reporter baffled *Dawn*'s hierarchy. The assistant news editor – Zubeida Mustafa – who knew me as a schoolgirl warned me rather cautiously that there was hardly any precedent for a woman reporter. "Would you like to be a sub-editor?" she asked.

The thought of working behind the desk to edit copy while male reporters traveled, met people and wrote breaking news stories was not particularly appealing. I had returned from the US to fulfill a childhood dream of reporting in the nation's most established newspaper and was reluctant to settle for less. Even as a young girl, I used to thumb through *Dawn*, fancying that I could write better than its reporters. Unwilling to take a back seat because the newspaper had to date not hired any women reporters, I asked: "Can't I be the first?"

My youth, enthusiasm and Western schooling paid off, as the editor of *Dawn* appointed me "staff reporter." I was shown into the bustling city room, which with its old furniture, antique typewriters and older staff, exuded a sense of purpose. Indeed, the staid manner in which *Dawn*'s senior reporters wrote was reflected in the newspaper, which was begun before partition in Dehli, India by Pakistan's founder, Mohammed Ali Jinnah. As the nation's most established English newspaper, *Dawn* carried an image of sobriety and a reputation for credibility.

Although nobody said it, I knew they thought I wouldn't last. They expected that, like other educated women from urban areas, I would get married, have children and stay home, leaving men to do the serious business of covering breaking news.

In fact, I stayed for 16 years, carefully breaking stereotypes of what I, as a woman, was capable of achieving. While the public space for women in Pakistan had shrunk, I had returned from the US with a greater taste for freedom.

My journey as the only woman reporter for *Dawn* coincided with that of Pakistan's first female prime minister. In 1986, while the nation was still under military rule, Benazir returned to Lahore, Pakistan to an historic welcome that demonstrated the deep antipathy to military rule.

As Benazir mobilized millions of people who hungered for democracy, I too jumped into covering politics for my newspaper. It would allow me to witness the machinations of the establishment and become privy to the fragile nature of democracy in Pakistan.

PART I

Politics and Journalism
in Pakistan

Chapter 1

ABOARD THE DEMOCRACY TRAIN

Getting to Know Benazir Bhutto

On August 17, 1988, I was on vacation in Vermont, USA when news came that the C-130 plane carrying Pakistan's military dictator, President Gen. Zia ul Haq, had exploded in mid-air. Also on board were the nation's top military generals and the US ambassador to Pakistan, Arnold Raphael, who had just returned from watching a military parade in southern Pakistan. Everyone was killed.

Stunned, I listened over and over to the news report, which had been taped by one of my engineer friends while I was out of the house. I could not believe that the crafty, self-effacing chief martial law administrator (CMLA), Gen. Zia – who had taken over in a military coup on July 5, 1977 and had been nicknamed "Canceled My Last Announcement" because of his repeated postponements of elections – was actually dead.

In the misty hills of Bennington, Vermont, I found it even more surreal that the strong man, who had come to symbolize harsh military rule for the last 11½ years, could vanish into thin air.

That night I got a phone call from the Pacifica News service, the US based radio for which I reported from Pakistan. They wanted more details on Gen. Zia's plane crash. It turned out that Pacifica had contacted my parents in Karachi, Pakistan and they had forwarded them my US number.

"What are you doing in the US? Why aren't you in Pakistan?" they wanted to know.

Well for one, I told them I had no idea that Gen. Zia ul Haq would be killed while I was taking a break from the hectic reporting assignments from my newspaper, *Dawn*, in Karachi. For the last four years, I had been covering the gory incidents of ethnic violence that had kept erupting despite Gen. Zia's iron-fisted rule.

Those sporadic incidents of bloodshed that had kept me rushing from hospital to hospital in Karachi made Vermont, with its radiant autumnal colors, feel like another planet.

Immediately, I felt the urgency of returning home. The sense of deprivation among different classes and ethnic groups had simmered for the whole of Gen. Zia's rule and in the last four years had reached boiling point.

The Sindhis, who mainly comprise the peasantry from rural Sindh, had never really forgiven Gen. Zia for executing their populist leader, Prime Minister Zulfikar Ali Bhutto in April 1979. Conversely, the better-educated Muslim migrants from India (Mohajirs) who grew into a majority in Karachi had become impatient with Gen. Zia's failure to solve their problems. Given that every ethnic group had engaged in the proliferation of arms and ammunition that flooded the region in those heady Cold War days, there seemed to be no end in sight.

Mostly, as I booked my flight home, my thoughts were filled with what Gen. Zia's death would mean for Benazir Bhutto, daughter of Prime Minister Zulfikar Ali Bhutto. After the military executed her father on April 4, 1979, Benazir and her mother, Nusrat had been put under house arrest. Hundreds of thousands of Sindhis, shocked by the execution, had thronged to the Bhutto residence for condolence.

Thereafter, in a cruel twist, Gen. Zia threw the mother and daughter into prison, where they endured years of harsh confinement. As Benazir developed medical problems, the dictator allowed her to briefly leave the country for treatment.

I had been a reporter in *Dawn* for only two years when Benazir returned from a brief exile in London to an unprecedented welcome in Lahore, Punjab in 1986. She was then the co-chairperson of the Pakistan Peoples Party, a position she shared with her mother.

The turnout of people was unlike anything seen in Pakistan's recent history. Millions of people lined the roads from the Lahore airport; they climbed rooftops and trees to catch a glimpse of Benazir, and afterwards heard her denounce Gen. Zia for the murder of her father. Her meteoric rise would lead journalists to predict that the PPP would come to power and Benazir Bhutto would become the next prime minister of Pakistan.

In 1986, I met Benazir for the first time at a select gathering of judges, lawyers and politicians invited to her late father's ancestral mansion, 70 Clifton in Karachi. After her triumphant return to Pakistan, she had invited us for moral support and consultations on her bid for power. Although her family home was styled on feudal mansions in interior Sindh, it was adorned with the expensive Western furniture and oil paintings that put it a notch above the decor of other elite homes in Karachi.

Inside, my eyes were drawn to a picture of her fiery father Zulfikar Ali Bhutto, a Mao cap on his head and fist clenched as he roared before a vast blur of faces. He had left a lasting impression on millions of Pakistanis as the savior of the oppressed classes and his execution by Gen. Zia in 1979 wounded millions of Sindhis and created a lasting antipathy toward the military.

The Sindhi-speaking servants, who flitted around serving drinks to visitors, tip-toed with their eyes down, demonstrating how privileged they felt to serve the Bhuttos.

The room buzzed with conversation from Western-educated intellectuals. Gen. Zia ul Haq was still in power but he had loosened his grip on the administration, leading to a demand for elections.

Figure 1 Prime Minister Zulfikar Ali Bhutto addresses public meeting in Pishin, Baluchistan on March 1, 1977 (*Dawn* photo).

The pressure from the electorate and Benazir's supporters would build until the military convened elections two years later.

Benazir's guests included the late Supreme Court judge, Justice Dorab Patel – a Parsi who had cast the dissenting vote against executing her father. Justice Patel later became chairman of the Human Rights Commission of Pakistan, of which I was a council member for a decade. Keen to establish rule of law, Justice Patel was initially supportive of her bid to lead the nation.

Benazir, who appeared poised to change the course of Pakistan's history, intrigued me. She exuded a steely determination as we discussed politics in her elegant living room. Tall and stately, she was elegantly dressed in heavy, embroidered fabrics stitched into a traditional *shalwar kameez* and *dupatta*.

Even then, I had misgivings about Benazir's ability to lead. Watching her make small talk, with her manicured nails and matching make-up, I couldn't help but wonder whether she would be no different from the Westernized elites who live in a cocoon in this deeply class-divided country.

From my own experience, I knew that upper class Pakistanis in the cities know more about Western trends and fashions than their own archaic customary laws and traditions. Indeed, these Pakistanis often treat their national language Urdu with studied indifference, embellishing it with large doses of English. Benazir seemed no different. Her familiarity with high-class Western circles was immediately apparent in her conversations and mannerisms.

At home, Benazir dressed in a way befitting a woman who planned to enter politics in a Muslim nation. Early into her political career, she had taken to wearing the *dupatta* over her head and she made sure never to shake hands with men. It was a far cry from other Western-educated women in Pakistan, who rarely cover their heads.

A PPP sympathizer and friend referred to her appearance with good humor: "Benazir has taken to wearing all the veils of women, so they don't have to wear them."

Only occasionally did I see glimpses of the carefree life Benazir apparently led at Oxford University in England. Early in her political career, Benazir criticized her chief political opponent, Nawaz Sharif, for his plans to build a motorway through the Punjab. She had argued at a press conference that an impoverished developing country like Pakistan could not afford such extravagant ventures and instead needed to spend money on health and education.

Carried away by the heat of the moment, Benazir unselfconsciously told our small group of reporters at the Karachi Gymkhana, "I, too, enjoyed driving fast cars on motorways in London."

Pleasantly surprised at her forthright manner and wanting to hear more, I bent forward. But at that point, Benazir had pulled the veil more tightly around her face. Surrounded by male politicians from feudal backgrounds, she looked the part of a Western-educated woman who trained to become the prime minister of a conservative Muslim country. Predictably, her guard came up the next minute.

"But that doesn't mean that we as a poor nation we should build motorways," she added primly.

In speaking to me – obviously a free spirit in the manner I dressed and traveled – Benazir swiftly stomped out any suggestions that she might have had a liberated life-style in the West or, God forbid, have had male friends.

Benazir had adopted her father's demagogic style of speaking to the masses. Often, she was the only woman in the hinterlands who addressed a sea of men. Her voice blared out of the microphones as, fist raised, she challenged the military dictator Gen. Zia ul Haq to stop being afraid of her and hold elections.

At times, her sheer tenacity and courage overrode my misgivings as to whether her sheltered, feudal background would allow her to stomach the complex, chaotic and dangerous world of Pakistani politics.

At one such event in interior Sindh, where the stage had been especially decorated for Benazir, I traveled in a caravan of PPP workers through miles of pitch-black rural wastelands. The cries of the poor, dispossessed Sindhi masses that had traveled from remote areas of Sindh to attend the rally rang in the blackness of the night.

"*Shaheed ki Baitee – Benazir*" (Daughter of the Martyr – Benazir)

"*Ab Aai Aai –Benazir*" (Now She's Coming, Coming – Benazir)

As we reached the rally site, the party workers hoisted me – the only other female on the scene – onto a makeshift stage. To my surprise, I found myself sitting next to Benazir. Evidently astonished to see me in the middle of nowhere, she turned to me and said: "You're very brave, Nafisa."

There was a sheer determination in Benazir as she traveled day in, day out to mobilize humongous crowds. Having lost her illustrious father to Gen. Zia less than a decade ago, she had dried her tears and appeared to be filled with a grim determination to step in her father's shoes. The humiliating way in which Gen. Zia's regime had treated her only hardened her resolve to lead PPP workers who had suffered long years of imprisonment under Zia.

In my interviews with Benazir, she vowed to take the nation out of the dark ages and transform it into a modern industrialized state. Even if this was rhetoric – as I sometimes suspected – it lifted my spirits to think that a modern, educated woman was ready to lead a nation in which women were largely poor, pregnant and powerless.

Moreover, as a woman from a cultured background, Benazir had a gentility that was missing from the seasoned male players who dominated Pakistan's politics. If I had any doubts about her regal airs, these were quieted by thoughts that the nation needed

Figure 2 Benazir Bhutto in her ancestral home town of Larkana, Sindh (Photograph courtesy of Dr Shafqat Soomro).

a woman with the arrogance of the feudal class to cut through the entrenched power of the military and the bureaucracy.

The Democracy Train Takes Off

The mid-air explosion of the C-130 plane which killed Gen. Zia ul Haq and the top military brass in Pakistan was a turning point in my life. It was also the start of a new chapter in the lives of millions of Pakistanis. The military went ahead with its scheduled plan to hold elections, albeit without the old dictator.

For Benazir Bhutto – whose enormous political rallies had become the biggest challenge to Gen. Zia – the moment had arrived.

Evidently, for my editor, it was also a time to make some changes. Like Benazir, I was a young woman newly returned from the West and determined to see a better future for my nation. Sensing my enthusiasm for a woman prime minister, the editor of my newspaper bypassed senior male reporters and nominated me, the only female reporter at *Dawn*, to cover Benazir Bhutto.

In October 1988, I became one of four journalists to ride for a day with Benazir and her PPP entourage aboard the "Democracy Train." It was the start of her party's campaign in interior Sindh to mobilize millions of voters for the national elections announced after Gen. Zia's death. Just one day on the train was enough to suffuse my senses with the enormity of the welcome Benazir received from the dispossessed people of the province.

As we traveled through the dry, hot desert terrain of Sindh – which spreads north of Karachi to India's border – I got a bird's eye view of a region in which nothing has moved for centuries.

The British colonial explorers, who set foot in Sindh in 1843, described the Sindhi peasantry as the "wretched of the earth." The twenty-first century has not brought them relief. Today, peasants still live in mud houses in dry, dusty wastelands, without electricity, clean drinking water or roads. They tend the farm lands of big feudal lords for meager wages and live with archaic social customs and customary laws that degrade women.

As the train draped in red, black and green PPP flags sped through the Sindh desert, I peeked out of the window to see barefoot peasants and children run alongside the tracks.

They mobbed the platforms. Young men and boys fought over each other's heads to catch a glimpse of Benazir's tall silhouette. They had heard that she had come back to fulfill her father's mission of "*Roti, Kapra aur Makaan*" (Food, Clothing and Shelter) for the millions of landless poor.

My male colleagues, all upcoming journalists – Zafar Abbas, Abbas Nasir and Ibrahim Sajid – and I traveled in a glass compartment, especially reserved for the press. We were ambitious and looked for scoops on this turning point in Pakistan's history.

Armed with typewriters and tape-recorders, we were poised to tell the world how Pakistan's first woman candidate for prime minister was received by the masses.

At the platform stops, the Sindhi villagers greeted Benazir Bhutto with unadulterated joy. Welcoming villagers beat large drums strapped across their shoulders to frenzy and spun like *dervishes* on the railway platform. They chanted *"Marvi, Malir Ji – Benazir, Benazir,"* likening Benazir's image to that of a beloved Sindhi heroine whose love for her people is painted in traditional folklore by the Sindhi mystic poet, Shah Latif Bhitai.

The atmosphere rang with joy as PPP activists from Karachi got out from the train to clap and dance to the tune of Urdu slogans:

"Ab Aai, Aai Benazir" (Now she's coming, coming – Benazir)

"Wazir-i-Azam Benazir" (Prime Minister Benazir)

Many of Benazir's PPP workers were Mohajirs who seemed not to mind that they were campaigning for a woman prime minister who drew her strength mainly from interior Sindh. This, notwithstanding that Mohajirs had joined the ethnocentric political party Mohajir Qaumi Movement (MQM) in great numbers.

Inside the moving train, Benazir made her way through the crush of PPP bodies to stand at the doorway. Her party workers created a bubble around her to separate her from her fans.

Standing behind the tall, slender and stately young woman, I saw Benazir's pink complexion turn red with effort as she bellowed into the loudspeaker in the apparently unfamiliar language of Urdu – the lingua franca of Pakistan – and the even more unfamiliar Sindhi – the language of Sindh.

Focusing on the sea of upturned faces on the platform she cried into the loudspeaker: "The dark days of dictatorship are over; we have come to bring you democracy." Although she mixed the past and present tense, no one seemed to care.

Indeed, Benazir's election campaign in the dusty wastelands of Sindh was a far cry from the oratory skills she had polished as president of the Oxford Debating Society. Although a fluent English speaker, she struggled with the indigenous languages – Urdu and Sindhi – in which she had never been formally trained.

But people had come to hear the mood of the message, which, after years of dictatorship under Gen. Zia, fell like rain on parched earth. As the scion of the most politically important feudal family of Sindh and daughter of an executed prime minister, Benazir carried huge symbolic presence.

Benazir wasn't the first politician to be cheered on fare value alone. After all, people had cheered the founder of Pakistan, Mohammed Ali Jinnah as he addressed crowds in impeccable English, without understanding a word of what he said.

As Benazir spoke, thousands of peasants – whose women-folk gathered separately, wearing billowing *chadors* (veils) and clutching their waving children – broke into cheers that reverberated into the hot, arid Sindh desert.

Flushed with the success of her tumultuous reception, Benazir joined us in the press compartment of the "Democracy Train" to unfold her ambitious plans for change. We welcomed her as she made her unscheduled appearance in the journalists' compartment.

"Come and sit next to me, Nafisa," she said, patting the seat next to her. Her hand tugged her *dupatta* more tightly over escaping strands of hair.

I moved gladly and sat next to her. In Pakistan's segregated society, being the only woman journalist to accompany Benazir had given me privileges that my male colleagues could only envy. My admiration and support for the enormous challenges that Benazir faced were written all over my face. It was not lost on her. Her light complexion glowed, reflecting an inner determination to overcome all hurdles to power.

As the "Democracy Train" charged through the hills and plains of the Sindh desert, Benazir unraveled the PPP manifesto to bring Pakistan into the comity of modern states. Her party planned to set up schools and colleges in rural areas to bring literacy and education to the poor of Pakistan and industrialize the primarily agrarian nation to create new jobs and bring women into the fold of daily life.

My sixth sense told me that Pakistan's extraordinarily complex problems demanded special measures for which Benazir's experience might prove to be woefully inadequate. Unlike the nation's seasoned male politicians who could move freely, being a woman was bound to handicap Benazir in Pakistan's masculine society.

And yet, Gen. Zia's sudden plane crash had opened the nation to all sorts of possibilities. Exhilarated by my experience on board the "Democracy Train," I sent back the dispatch on a woman who planned to defeat all odds and change the destiny of the nation.

Not only did Benazir come across as a dynamic leader, she was also the daughter of the prime minister who had introduced sweeping land reforms in 1973 – setting a ceiling for ownership.

Later in my journalistic career, I learnt how the Bhuttos had, themselves, evaded land reform. Big feudal landowners cleverly transferred land in the names of unmarried and widowed sisters and even dead peasants to avoid the ceiling. Apparently, Zulfikar Ali Bhutto had winked at feudals, including his own family members, as they transferred land within the family. Back then, Benazir all too skillfully avoided using the term "reform", even as her party pledged to bring justice to the people.

As evening fell, my three colleagues and I got off the "Democracy Train" at a remote train station in interior Sindh. We had seen enough and wanted to get back to Karachi to file our reports. While we waited for transport to take us back to the city, I pulled out my small typewriter and typed out the report for my newspaper.

Suddenly, we were surrounded by scores of young men. There I was, a young unveiled woman typing in the boondocks. I began to attract crowds of villagers whose circle grew bigger as they watched me with curious eyes.

"What is she doing?" my colleague overheard a young man inquire.

"She's typing a job application," another youth replied in seriousness.

"Why is she here?" another villager was heard asking.

The reply – which made us crack up when my colleague told us later: "Benazir has left her for our welfare."

Rural Sindh is a World Apart

My coverage of Benazir's election campaign took me for the first time into interior Sindh, and opened up a new world.

It was a vivid experience traveling up north from Karachi into miles of dusty terrain where the Indus River irrigates patches of cultivated green. Wearing only thin flowing head covers, peasant women dot the landscape. Driving by, one saw them harvest and drop the produce in satchels tied to their waists. They worked knee-deep in the paddy fields, took animals for grazing and cooked on firewood in front of dark mud huts.

On my travels in interior Sindh, I wore a loose *shalwar kameez* without the enveloping *dupatta*. Even so – and despite traveling unaccompanied to cover the story – I found the common Sindhi folks immensely welcoming.

Their liberal, easygoing Sufi approach was in sharp contrast to the conservative Islamic middle class of Karachi. For the Sindhi peasants – and even landowners – I was not just a woman but also a privileged journalist who could convey the deprivations of a province that lay in darkness.

Once, as I visited interior Sindh in winter – wearing a blue blazer over my *shalwar kameez*, hands in my pocket and looking obviously very urban – a villager asked me in Urdu: "Are you *Angrez?*" – the term used for a European.

I laughed and replied "No" in Urdu.

Like me, who frequently visited the US, many English-speaking urban Pakistanis who lived in Karachi, Lahore and Islamabad were more comfortable wearing Western clothes. But while urban men wore Western clothes, even in some rural parts of the country, women from the city were expected to dress more traditionally.

Still, I wore what made me most comfortable. For me, my own class background – born and raised in Karachi and educated in the West – as well as my profession as a journalist, allowed me the luxury of distancing myself from customary rural traditions and examine village life much as an anthropologist.

In hindsight, I see that this is the manner in which the British explorers acted when they first set foot in Sindh to pave the way for colonization. That there was life in the dusty villages of Sindh north of Karachi had, for me, been no less dramatic than the announcement by the British colonialist, Charles Napier in 1843, that he had conquered the Indian province of Sindh. The British pronounced it Sind.

That was evidently the basis for the Latin pun, telegrammed by Napier to London when he arrived in my province: "*Peccavi* – I have sinned."

Of course, I was no conqueror but rather an urban journalist who had stumbled into the darkness of her own back yard. I had grown passionately involved in explaining rural Sindh to my English-educated, city-based readers.

Benazir's grandfather – endowed by the British with the title, Sir Shahnawaz Bhutto – had amassed land in three districts of Sindh and Balochistan. To top that, Zulfikar Ali Bhutto's farcical land reforms had left the Bhuttos intact as the top landowners in Sindh.

In the absence of land reforms, peasants were born into slavery and their children died repaying their debts. If they were lucky, they fled to the cities to join the ranks of the jobless poor.

Presently, the big feudal lords in the Sindh – only five percent of whom own 22 per cent of the most fertile lands – have entirely shifted their residences from the crumbling villages to the cities. A stroll along Karachi's Defence Society or Lahore's Gulberg area reveals their elite mansions, armed guards, Pajero jeeps and satellite dishes. They have left the rural areas of Pakistan in neglect, without water, electricity, sewerage and roads and a deteriorated law and order situation.

In 1988, as Benazir Bhutto began her election campaign, she pledged a radical transformation of the system. The situation was not without irony. As the "Democracy Train" sped across Sindh, Benazir appealed for votes from downtrodden peasants who worked on her family's ancestral lands. On the other hand,

her privileged background seemed guaranteed to maintain the
status quo.

The Masses Vote for the PPP

In January 1989, as Benazir started the year as the nation's
first woman prime minister, I flew from Karachi to her party
stronghold in Khairpur. Looking between the whirring blades of
the helicopter at the dusty town, dotted with palm trees, I sensed
the excitement down below.

Indeed, Benazir's presence was everywhere. Photographs of her
head – modestly draped – and wide eyes lined with kohl adorned
hand-painted portraits, posters and campaign banners. Although
local tradition keeps Sindhi women invisible in the towns,
thousands of veiled women had queued at the polls to elect their
first woman prime minister.

People in the close-knit community received me warmly,
hoping that I would convey the hopes they pinned on Benazir
and the PPP candidates she had nominated. The names of the
victors were written in bold chalk on cement teahouses while
party flags adorned the mud-brick buildings in a show of joyous
exuberance.

My welcome as a woman reporter appeared to be a sign of
changing times. Apparently guessing that I was a journalist from
Karachi, jubilant crowds, waving PPP flags on pick-up trucks,
cheered as party workers escorted me to the homes of their
leaders.

In silent wonder I walked into the humble, mud-walled *autaq*
(annexe) of Pervaiz Ali Shah, the PPP candidate who had defeated
Pir Pagara – the entrenched feudal lord and spiritual leader of the
district.

With haughty eyes and curling moustache, Pagara looks
every bit the part of a Moghul emperor. His empire consists
of thousands of armed devotees known as *hurs*, ready to
defend him at his beck and call. Pagara is a "king-maker" in
Pakistan's politics and his humiliating defeat at the hands of a

PPP "commoner" like Pervaiz Ali Shah was a dramatic show of "people power."

In 1988, Benazir's strategy had been to allocate tickets to lower-middle-class loyalists who had been jailed by Gen. Zia ul Haq. Avoiding the term "revenge," she had focused on rewarding candidates who had made sacrifices for the party during martial law. In turn, the masses who had suffered under military rule had poured out in their millions to elect Benazir and her party nominees.

So blind was the adulation for Benazir in rural Sindh that we journalists joked that she could have nominated a lamp post on the PPP ticket and got it elected to government.

The mood was even more ecstatic in Benazir Bhutto's hometown, Larkana. There, the stout, bespectacled PPP lawyer, Deedar Hussein Shah had snatched victory from the quintessential feudal lord of Sindh, Mumtaz Ali Bhutto. Mumtaz was Benazir's relative and became the chief minister of Sindh under her father Zulfikar Ali Bhutto. And yet, Mumtaz had contested and *lost* his Larkana seat to the PPP candidate Benazir nominated – Deedar Hussain Shah. Adding insult to injury, Deedar Shah had previously served as the manager for Mumtaz's ancestral lands.

Indeed, all across Sindh, big feudal landlords discovered the bitter taste of being defeated by PPP "commoners," nominated by Benazir. It was an experience they were not likely to forget.

The Face of Sindhi Feudals

Years later, as I flew to Larkana to interview the aristocratic Mumtaz Bhutto at his ancestral home, I found he had also not forgiven the PPP "riff raff" for their challenge to the feudal lords.

With his cool demeanor and long moustache, Mumtaz spoke slow, clipped sentences in British English. It established his credentials as a barrister-at-law from Lincoln's Inn, UK. Well-spoken and comfortable with hosting Western diplomats in his Karachi mansion, Mumtaz was just as at ease in his sprawling estate as in the otherwise poor and underdeveloped Larkana.

The Larkana feudal had stayed away from Benazir's attempts to reorganize the PPP after her father was hanged by the military. Instead, he had watched incredulously as Benazir had worked her way up through the old boy network of entrenched male feudals.

Mumtaz came to receive me at his gates in Larkana after my hosts dropped me off from the airport. We walked back to his magnificent estate. Rows of elderly men touched his feet in reverence all the way back to the house. I felt guilty that grown men prostrated themselves. But the Larkana feudal walked erect, scarcely looking down at the emaciated peasants. This was the traditional welcome for a man who owns land in Larkana, Jacobabad and Shahdadkot and in the adjoining Balochistan province.

Sitting in the shade in Mumtaz Bhutto's brick courtyard where the afternoon sun gently sizzled, we chatted after I finished interviewing him. An avid reader of *Dawn*, he told me he was familiar with my name. It did not surprise me, knowing that Western-educated feudal politicians and bureaucrats alike read the newspaper for which I wrote. At the same time, he complained that politicians shot into prominence – and I knew he hinted at Benazir – because of the media attention they received.

Perhaps the inordinate attention Benazir had received in the press after her exile overseas had seemed excessive to her uncle. In particular, he seemed irked by how green Benazir was for Pakistan's seamy politics.

With a sardonic smile, Mumtaz told me that when Benazir had arrived from London to lead the Pakistani nation of over 100 million, her youth and unfamiliarity in getting the top job as prime minister made her seem like "Alice in Wonderland."

"You know that when Benazir first came to me, she didn't know anyone. Instead, she asked that I introduce her to people," Mumtaz told me.

"Did you?" I asked.

"Yes," he replied in his non-committal way.

But I knew that, as a political rival, Mumtaz was least likely to introduce his ambitious niece to powerbrokers.

Mumtaz was a man who belonged to another era, another system. His style was in sharp contrast to Benazir's father, Zulfikar Ali Bhutto. Bhutto had used his fiery speeches to empower peasants and the working class, who had, for centuries, cringed before the aristocracy. Apart from being a demagogue, Bhutto had left lasting effects. My visit to Larkana – the ancestral home of the Bhuttos – gave me an insight into the contrasting style of the rival politicians from the best-known political family of Sindh.

We sat in the courtyard where the sounds of chirping birds and the fresh country air made me glad to be out of Karachi city. As the servants brought tea, Mumtaz poked fun at Benazir's poor knowledge of her mother tongue, Sindhi. It was an issue I could identify with myself: like Benazir, I was born a Sindhi in Karachi. Being primarily educated in Western institutions, my parents had never encouraged me to learn my own language. But Mumtaz was unforgiving of his niece.

"When Benazir comes to Larkana and I hear her speeches in Sindhi blaring out from the loudspeakers, I want to cover my ears," he laughed sardonically. He saw me smile, in spite of myself.

Mumtaz had reserved his deepest contempt for the commoners who joined the PPP under Benazir. I could see how difficult it had been for him to digest the victory of a PPP candidate of "inferior standing" like Deedar Hussain Shah, who won against him in Larkana.

"You know that fellow [Deedar Shah] used to be my *kumdar* (manager of lands) – who waited outside my office to get my attention," he told me. "And now he has the nerve to stand against me," he added in disgust.

That came as news to me. I knew Deedar Shah as one of the best-read parliamentarians in the Sindh Assembly.

We left the ancestral courtyard after Mumtaz offered to take me on a tour of his ancestral lands in Larkana in his Pajero jeep. It was an unusual move for a feudal to drive a vehicle with an unveiled woman, but there were important things on my host's mind.

As we drove through his constituency, he told me to note the broken roads and a gaping gutter in Naudero, Larkana where a child had fallen a few days ago. He cited them as examples of how his humble PPP rival Deedar Shah had failed to fulfill the needs of the community.

Both Mumtaz Bhutto and his PPP opponent, Deedar Hussein Shah, knew from experience that getting funds from the Punjab was like getting blood out of a stone. Deedar Shah grew hoarse in the Sindh Assembly as he appealed for development funds for interior Sindh. Eventually he quit politics and became a judge.

As a prominent feudal lord, Mumtaz claimed he would have more leverage with the federal government in getting funds for rural Sindh. That, I suspected, was true.

Democracy or Anarchy?

While Benazir's rise to power signified hope for the downtrodden people of Pakistan, the reactions were totally different in Karachi. By 1988, Karachi was a city deeply divided on ethnic lines.

The Mohajirs who formed the majority in Karachi had not voted for Benazir's PPP. Instead, they had almost entirely voted for the ethnic party – the MQM.

The whole-scale victory given by the people of interior Sindh to Benazir became the signal for the MQM to mobilize against her rule on grounds of nepotism, corruption and injustice.

For the 1½ years that Benazir was mostly in Islamabad – about a thousand miles north of Karachi – I reported from my southern home-base about the ethnic violence, rapes and murders that burst open like gaping sores. As the ethnic riots rocked the city, Benazir's fledgling government – which had barely begun to function – was already threatened with collapse.

Prime Minister Benazir Bhutto made brief trips to her newly-constructed Bilawal House residence in Karachi to chair meetings of the low and middle-income PPP men who were newly elected from interior Sindh. Her party men called her *"Mohtarma"* (esteemed lady) – an aristocratic image she carefully cultivated to offset her youth and femininity.

Faced with formidable problems and without the skills learnt by her father in the male-dominated feudal society, Benazir frantically grappled with the best way to lead her party and the nation.

In her first year, Benazir had abdicated some of her responsibilities to the man she had married the year before – Asif Zardari. It was an arranged marriage, the "price" many felt she had to pay in the male-dominated society.

Asif was a cheerful, energetic man from a business family whose influence grew in proportion to the rise in Benazir's political career. His penchant for taking kickbacks from large corporations quickly earned him the nickname of "Mr Ten Per Cent" and gave cannon fodder to Benazir's ethnic foes and to feudal lords, whose opposition mounted with each passing day.

From the start, Benazir faced an impossible task. Starting from day one, people mobbed the newly elected PPP legislators for employment, plots and permits. Years of deprivation had made everyone needier. In the forefront were *jiyalas* – PPP workers who claimed to have performed major sacrifices for the party and now looked for reward.

As Benazir appointed PPP members to government ministries, the more unscrupulous ones began to fill their pockets. Middlemen close to the PPP government took kickbacks for government contracts and "sold" jobs to those who could afford to pay for them.

In Sindh, the feudal lords, whose patronage system had been temporarily disturbed by the PPP "riff raff," watched in amusement as the *jiyalas* fought for a share of the pie.

The hardest hitting jibe came from the feudal politician, Pir Pagara, who had suffered the indignity of being defeated by a commoner. Vindicated by the chaos that had resulted from Benazir's rule, Pagara made comments that were carried by the Sindhi press: "How can those who're hungry give anything to others?"

In Benazir's first tenure, I took a trip back to her hometown in Larkana. Mostly, I wanted to find out how her party members coped in interior Sindh. Traveling through the narrow Larkana Road, with thick leafy trees on both sides, I headed to the "Placement Bureau." This was the office set up by the PPP to help find jobs for the villagers.

Arriving at the party office, I stood quietly by the door and watched. I wanted to take the bureau chief, PPP Secretary General Ahmed Ali Soomro by surprise. He couldn't have seen me anyway – having disappeared behind swarms of energetic Sindhi youth who pushed job applications in his face.

It was a while before Soomro saw me and straightened up from behind the crowd to welcome me inside. He apologized profusely for the chaos that had prevented him from seeing me.

"Please, don't even think about it," I told him.

Indeed, those few minutes in the Placement Bureau had enabled me to witness the tremendous hopes and expectations that the local Sindhis placed in Benazir Bhutto and her party men.

That evening, Soomro and his PPP colleagues came to see me at my hotel in Larkana. After the hot day, we had dinner on the hotel roof where the evening breeze felt welcome. I probed about what ailed the fledgling PPP government.

"Frankly speaking, it's a hopeless situation," Soomro admitted somberly. "There aren't enough jobs and there are too many unemployed people," the young PPP men conceded.

Swamped with day-to-day problems, Benazir's government seemed clueless about encouraging investment and creating new jobs. Instead the prime minister struggled to cope in a culture where jobs were sold rather than earned. It was evident that the young woman led the nation without thinking through the enormous challenges.

In the midst of ethnic tension in Karachi – when ethnic violence and curfews had made life miserable and the MQM's demand for Benazir's removal had reached a crescendo – the young woman was yanked out of power.

The President of Pakistan, Ghulam Ishaq Khan went on television to justify Benazir's ousting for reasons of "corruption" and "failure to maintain law and order."

But Benazir's abrupt dismissal in August 1990 was a slap in the face for the people of Sindh who had, for 11½ years, suffered Gen. Zia ul Haq's military rule before finally getting a chance to vote.

Even though the PPP had failed to deliver food, clothing and shelter to the people, the masses still maintained that Benazir and her PPP were the only ones who could lift them from their state of deprivation.

"Eat from Jatoi, Vote for Benazir"

"Benazir the fighter" refused to give in and prepared her party for a counter-attack. Meanwhile, seeking support from the press, she urged to journalists to cry foul. It began a new round of politicking. As soon as the army dissolved the PPP government, it announced the schedule for elections in October 1990. Once again, Benazir mobilized her party to enter the fray.

Up until now, I had seen Pakistan's politics from the PPP's perspective. Now, as Benazir went into opposition, I took the opportunity to view events from the stand-point of the establishment.

At that time my newspaper received an invitation from the wealthiest landowner of Sindh, the late Ghulam Mustafa Jatoi, to visit his hometown of Nawabshah and observe the government's preparations for the elections. The military had selected Jatoi as interim prime minister while it transitioned between Benazir's chaotic rule to the next civilian set up.

In those days, the Karachi Press Club bustled with journalists who covered Pakistan's rocky road to democracy. Among them was the American academic Henry F. Carey, who came to Karachi to do a comparative survey of emerging democracies. Chip, as he was called, asked dozens of questions about politics from me and my journalist colleague Waris Bilal, jotting our answers in his tense, angular handwriting on reams of papers.

In October 1990, Chip, Bilal and I teamed up and drove to Nawabshah, Sindh to witness the makings of the alternate political set-up that the military proposed to counter Benazir's short-lived "democracy."

I was pleasantly surprised by Nawabshah, which appeared relatively well developed, with good roads and functioning traffic lights. Our hosts told us that Nawabshah's development began in the 1970s, when Zulfikar Ali Bhutto was prime minister and Jatoi was chief minister of Sindh.

Still, little had changed in the surrounding villages where the Jatoi family owns an estimated 50,000 acres of fertile land. Here, the peasantry grows cotton, sugarcane and wheat but live in tiny mud-houses without access to electricity, proper food or any health care.

As one of Jatoi's mansions loomed into sight, I noticed the surprise on Chip's face. In the dusty, brown desert where hot winds blow even in October, the serene palace looked like a mirage. We gladly escaped the heat and dust of the rural areas and entered large, well-furnished, air-conditioned rooms with blue-tiled bathrooms.

Chip peeked inside a bathroom and commented with distinct pleasure: "They look good enough to sleep in."

It dawned on us that we were the only three people in Jatoi's mansion, being waited on by a band of servants. The atmosphere grew more surreal by the minute, as servants kept bringing in trays full of spicy lamb and chicken to our dinner table.

Later that evening, we were summoned by the heavy set, silver-haired feudal lord, interim Prime Minister Ghulam Mustafa Jatoi. He looked larger than life compared with his pictures, splashed on the front pages of the nation's newspapers. This was the man nominated by the military to head the alliance they had cobbled – Islamic Democratic Alliance (IDA) or Islami Jamhoori Ittehad (IJI) – specifically set up to counter Benazir Bhutto and her PPP.

Jatoi stayed unflappable as Chip probed him about the role of the army's top external secret service agency – Inter Services Intelligence (ISI) – in building the IJI opposition to Benazir.

Instead, Jatoi – who was educated in Pakistan's premier British institutions and in London – spoke eloquently about the charges of corruption lodged by the government against Benazir's husband – Asif Zardari. As he spoke, it was clear that the military had picked the wealthy Sindhi feudal lord as interim prime minister to become a key spokesman against Benazir and Asif. Indeed, Asif would remain the main punching bag for the establishment.

Even back then, Jatoi knew that for the Sindhi masses Benazir was the grieving daughter of their beloved prime minister – Zulfikar Ali Bhutto – who had been "martyred" in the service of the people. Attacking her directly was almost impossible.

During our next few days in Nawabshah, we saw how the interim prime minister used government vehicles to stage a comeback. The next day, as we toured Nawabshah, we saw public vehicles clearly marked for civic services that took people to Jatoi's political rallies.

But, by evening, the establishment had mustered a pitiful crowd of only 3,000 people in the densely populated town. From our vantage point on stage, I saw that the chairs at the back were empty.

Jatoi stayed unmoved, as speaker after speaker in his rally condemned the PPP rule and singled out Asif Zardari as corrupt. There was a singular lack of enthusiasm in the audience. Chip told me that he thought the anti-PPP slogans raised by Jatoi's supporters fell flat.

Still, this staged drama was being performed to lead the media into believing that Jatoi was a spokesman for the people. That night, state-controlled Pakistan Television showed the rally on the Urdu nightly news – *Khabarnama* – taken from various angles, giving the impression that Jatoi was hugely popular among the masses.

Jatoi's campaign manager Fazal Ellahi Fazli – energetic and well organized – pressed us to accompany him to witness his boss's election campaign in Narowal, a town in the Punjab.

I was on a free-floating mission from my newspaper, satisfying my own interests in seeing what was really happening at the grass roots instead of filing a report every day. Bilal, on the other hand, had to get back to his daily grind as news editor of an Urdu newspaper. Chip and I left with Fazli for Narowal.

We were driven to a guesthouse where the vegetation was greener and the weather was distinctly cooler than in Sindh. Chip and I received red carpet treatment. Breakfast was served colonial style, with waiters at long tables. We enjoyed the hospitality, even while we wondered how much we'd be allowed to see for ourselves.

Fazli took us to a rally where Chip observed that the Jamaat-i-Islami – a coalition partner of the IJI, cobbled together by the military's Inter Services Intelligence (ISI) – had criticized my presence as the only woman at the event.

Growing wary of official tours, I excused the two of us from our energetic host. We headed to the fields where the peasants tilled the land. They were Punjabi peasants, who are on the whole better fed and clothed than their poor Sindhi counterparts. I had no idea what they would say. Still, I wanted their independent opinion on the mid-term election.

The peasants turned out to be hardcore supporters of the PPP. They were indignant that local Punjabi supporters of the IJI had used vulgar language against the former woman prime minister. They told me rather spiritedly they had turned down Jatoi's offer to ride the tractor trolleys and swell the ranks of his election site. Instead, they shared with us their rather creative slogan: "Eat from Jatoi...vote for Benazir."

Given the outpouring of support that I had witnessed for the PPP in Sindh and the Punjab, I assumed that Benazir would return with a thumping majority. I was naïve to think so.

In 1990, when results were announced on state-controlled television, the Jatoi-led opposition coalition had won over 50 per cent of the seats in the National Assembly. The PPP bagged a mere 21 per cent.

The 1990 elections began a new chapter in Pakistan's decade of democracy. The Sindhi feudal lord, Ghulam Mustafa Jatoi was dropped by the army in favor of a Lahore businessman, Nawaz Sharif. Benazir became the leader of the opposition.

That began a decade of musical chairs for the nation's twice-elected prime ministers, Benazir Bhutto and Nawaz Sharif. The two politicians alternated as sitting heads of government in the decade between 1988 and 1999, while the army played the martial tune.

Elections Were the Tip of the Iceberg

As a guest of the interim Prime Minister Ghulam Mustafa Jatoi, I had witnessed how state funds and propaganda were used to defeat Benazir. But I was still an onlooker, without inside knowledge of what had transpired in the inner circles. Then still an inexperienced reporter, I couldn't guess at how the establishment had defeated the PPP, which, right or wrong, had the support of the masses.

In 1996, some clues emerged. Retired Air Marshal Asghar Khan filed a case in the Supreme Court, alleging that the powerful secret service wing of the army – the ISI – had rigged the 1990 election. Based on Asghar Khan's petition, former ISI chief, Lt. Gen. Asad Durrani took the stand in the Supreme Court and provided an affidavit that the army had indeed distributed PKR 140 million (USD 1.6 million) to anti-PPP candidates, only a few months before the October 1990 election.

The anti-PPP candidates banded in the IJI comprised feudal, Islamic and ethnic parties that resolutely opposed Benazir's populist rule. Subsequently, we learnt that the caretaker, President Ghulam Mustafa Jatoi – who had stayed silent while Chip probed him – had actually taken PKR 5 million (USD 59,000) from the ISI. Meanwhile, Nawaz Sharif – who was ushered in by the military to succeed Benazir as prime minister – was revealed to have received PKR 3.5 million (USD 41,000) from the spy agencies.

Apparently, the army was so scared that Benazir would be elected back into power that their IJI coalition distributed state funds among various interest groups to prevent her return.

As I covered national politics, Asghar Khan talked to me in earnest, as though I was a player rather than a reporter. Then in coalition with the PPP, he told me that Benazir and Nawaz ought to unite to repeal Article 58-2(b). This was the constitutional clause introduced by Gen. Zia ul Haq that allowed presidents like Ghulam Ishaq Khan to dissolve the assembly.

Although I shared Asghar Khan's desire for principled politics, it surprised me that he seemed clueless about Benazir's approach of doing whatever it took to return to power.

Unleashing the Dacoits

In 1991, the new prime minister, Nawaz Sharif received a mandate from the army to contain Benazir, who, despite being ousted, continued to be a clear favorite. That year, the Sindh government – headed by its Machiavellian chief minister, Jam Sadiq Ali – mixed crime with politics by giving a free hand to dacoits to intimidate landowners: the group that formed the bulk of Benazir's supporters.

For a while, I had read in the Sindhi press about the dacoits who hid in the jungles along the major highways in Sindh and emerged with sudden ferocity to ambush vehicles and kidnap passengers. Their influence had begun to seep into Karachi, the industrial hub of the country. Come evening, a silence spread throughout Sindh, where the fear of dacoits forced buses to travel in convoys.

At our weekly meeting at *Dawn*, we talked about the threat of dacoits. The prospect of investigating the bandits got my adrenalin going. I persuaded my editor that we needed to cover the story because of the emerging competition from the newly launched newspaper – *The News*. Our flashy, youth-oriented rival had just launched itself under the daring slogan: "Each *Dawn* will break with the *News*."

That was an open challenge to our credibility as the oldest and most established English-language newspaper in the country. My editor seemed to think so too. Once he had learnt that our competitors planned to cover the dacoit story, he decided to send me too.

My curiosity about the infamous dacoit, Mohib Shidi took me first to his hometown in Matiari – 200 km north of Karachi. This tiny town of baked mud lies in a patch of green along the Indus Highway. It has an eye-catching turquoise shrine in the middle. Drawing closer to the walled town, one saw high brick walls, open sewers and women in black veils that flitted like banshees inside the mud corridors. I felt as though I had been transported back to the medieval ages.

Matiari's landowners were anxious to give me the inside story on dacoits. A short while ago, they had received notes from the infamous dacoit, Mohib Shidi to hand over their income at a specified location. They informed the Rangers – an offshoot of the army – about his presence. There was a shoot-out between the Rangers and the Shidi-led dacoits in Matiari; terrified residents hid indoors, listening to the sound of gunfire.

However, the cultivators – and, by now, the whole town – talked of how the bandit had walked away unruffled. Mohib Shidi had arrived in style at the local mosque on the Muslim festival of Eid and said his prayers with the leaders of the congregation. Afterwards, astonished residents saw him watch the cattle show, attended by big feudals and other dignitaries. There, he mingled with the people and graciously distributed cash and chicken *biryani* (a special rice dish) among them.

What had made the dacoits so powerful? Why was Shidi still free even though everyone recognized him as a dangerous dacoit? Why were the buses, which traveled from Karachi to the localities in interior Sindh, frequently ambushed while the administration appeared helpless?

The trip became an eye-opener into the nexus between crime and politics in Pakistan. As I spoke to locals, they told me of deep connections between powerful landlords and the new Sindh government. In October 1991, Sharif's victory over Benazir had redrawn the political landscape so that Matiari's biggest feudals – the Jamotes – had joined the Pakistan Muslim League (F – "functional") government in coalition with Nawaz Sharif.

The powerful feudal and chief of PML (F), Pir Pagara of Khairpur – who had suffered an ignominious defeat at the hands of the masses in 1988 – had led the move to stamp out the PPP. Big landowners of Matiari and Khairpur – who were dead set against Benazir and her populist PPP – had begun to sponsor the dacoits against the small landowners that formed the grass roots of her party.

As buses headed toward Hala, north of Matiari, passengers were held up at gunpoint, robbed and kidnapped. In dramatic scenes enacted all over interior Sindh, the dacoits forced male passengers to disembark and walk hands up in the air at gun-point toward the marshy jungles along the Indus Highway. They were kept as hostage in the jungles until their families paid ransom.

I took the Indus Highway to the town of Saidabad (near Hala) to meet the small landowners victimized by the dacoits. It was a scary time to be traveling by road. Mohib Shidi and his gang would emerge with sudden ferocity from the jungles to ambush vehicles with Kalashnikov fire. Even my driver appeared anxious as our car sped along the Indus Highway – the only vehicle on the road in broad daylight.

But I was in the grip of a familiar sensation that came from chasing a big story. In Saidabad, I found a small landlord, Haji Waris Rahu and his men in gloomy spirits in the courtyard. The electricity had gone off – a frequent occurrence – and it was too hot to sit indoors. The verandah was bathed in milky moonlight, made even more eerie by the peasants holding Kalashnikovs.

The men were Rahu's relatives, ready to ward off an imminent attack by the bandits. They could have been characters in a novel set in Tsarist Russia. The servant dutifully brought mugs of tea for all of us, while the villagers spoke one by one. I took notes in the moonlight.

Rahu's men blamed the attacks on Mohib Shidi's gang. They dully reeled the names of the dacoits and the big feudals who protected them. The aggrieved landowner told me in a distinctly downcast tone that although he had passed on the names of the dacoits to the administrative head of police – Deputy Inspector General (DIG) of Sindh, Saleem Akhtar Siddiqi – the authorities had failed to respond.

The situation reached epidemic proportions in the small towns along the 70-mile National Highway between Hyderabad and Mirpurkhas, where, according to my sources, the police chief of Sindh had been told by the Chief Minister Jam Sadiq Ali to look the other way while "pet dacoits" acted with impunity.

Small landlords in the farming community of Sultanabad – who had spent years growing mango and banana plantations – found their trees shaved off if they ignored the extortion notes by the dacoits. With no faith left in the government, they had changed their farming practices to growing less lucrative vegetables.

Despite my investigative reports published in *Dawn* about the dacoit menace, I came back to Karachi to find that it was business as usual. Indeed, while Islamabad looked on indifferently, dacoits zeroed in on more wealthy targets in Sindh: Chinese engineers who worked on an electrification project in Dadu were kidnapped, while Japanese tourists who toured Kandhkot in the north of Sindh were taken hostage. Rural Sindh drifted toward anarchy.

Benazir Fights Back

By mid 1991, Benazir came up with a concrete plan to fight the Sindh chief minister. As leader of the PPP opposition, Benazir proposed to pitch a candidate for a parliamentary seat that fell vacant from the town of Jacobabad in interior Sindh.

In normal times, a by-election caused by death or resignation of a parliamentary member is a routine event. But these were not normal times. Benazir planned to throw her weight behind her nominee and get him elected as the chief minister of Sindh.

Benazir's nominee was the seasoned Western-educated lawyer and politician, Abdul Hafeez Pirzada – possessed of a fair complexion with fine, chiseled features and a stubborn jaw. A former federal law minister under Zulfikar Ali Bhutto, he was one of the authors of the 1973 constitution that was suspended by Gen. Zia ul Haq.

But Pirzada was also controversial in that he disappeared from the scene when Prime Minister Zulfikar Ali Bhutto was hanged. Moreover, the ISI listed him as the beneficiary of over PKR 3 million (USD 35,000) in 1991 – money to be used to defeat Benazir's reelection. Despite this, his prestigious background endeared him to Benazir and she decided to bet on him, both as a candidate and a future chief minister for Sindh.

It was an early demonstration of Benazir's tendency to do whatever was needed to attain power. The practice would later be fine-tuned into an art by her life partner, Asif Zardari.

Chip was back in Karachi from his travels. He was joined by an American journalist, Steven Barmazel from the *Far Eastern*

Economic Review. For many in the West, Benazir still represented the best hope for Pakistani democracy. Like me, both Americans sought to see up-close whether the young woman would overcome the obstacles laid out by the military. We left together to get a first hand view of the election in Jacobabad.

Located at the border of Balochistan province, north of Sindh, Jacobabad is named after a British commissioner, Gen. John Jacob. He is remembered in Sindh for his engineering skills – having designed a modern irrigation system – and for his administrative abilities. Indeed, years later, I met villagers in remote areas of Larkana who praised the British administrator's success in maintaining strict law and order in the area. Candles are still lit at Jacob's gravesite by peasants who call him *"Jacum saheb"* (Sir Jacob), giving a native touch to his name.

In June 1991, as I stepped out of a bus in the sizzling 120°F heat of Ghari Khairo, Jacobabad – the hottest town in the sub-continent – I was greeted by a surprised shout from an elderly, white-haired man with furrowed eyebrows. Startled, I looked up at the leading landlord of Sindh, Illahi Baksh Soomro as he called out, "So now journalists are coming from outside to cover the election."

Little did I know that my first encounter in Jacobabad would be with I. B. Soomro. Soomro's relatives are known to be near fixtures in army-backed governments: his nephew, Mian Mohammed Soomro served in the Musharraf government while his brother, Iftikhar Soomro was elevated to the level of minister during various interim administrations. In 1991, the silver-haired federal minister, I. B. Soomro had come back to his hometown to back Jam Sadiq Ali's nominee – Ghulam Ali Buledi.

As Chip, Steve and I went around Jacobabad, some of the local tribal leaders representatives told us that I. B. had forewarned them against letting their people vote for the PPP. Indeed, Jam's administration had ensured that women – who tended to be more pro-Benazir – did not vote at all. In Jacobabad, Jam had slyly connived with Benazir's relative and leading feudal from Larkana, Mumtaz Bhutto. Apparently, Mumtaz had thrown his weight behind tribal leaders to stop their women from coming out to vote.

Benazir and Pirzada held a press conference, widely attended by Sindhi journalists, in which they spoke in English for the benefit of my American companions. Benazir told us that Jam Sadiq Ali brought "some 200 dacoits" to Jacobabad on the eve of the by-election. She spoke of the "long-haired men," armed with machine guns, that had arrested Pirzada's supporters when they arrived from Balochistan border only a few miles away.

At one polling station, I overheard the government's polling agents say that we must be stopped from entering the voting area. We later learnt that the government had provided presiding officers with ballot boxes, which were already "stuffed and sealed."

Every now and then we bumped into Pirzada's vehicle en route to the polling stations. He stood disheveled in the middle of the road, with his angry face red and perspiring, as he talked about the blatant rigging he had witnessed. Pirzada had taken to calling me the "veteran of Jacobabad."

After days of witnessing the electoral charade, my American colleagues and I were not surprised when the Election Commission announced that the government's nominee had won three times the number of votes secured by Pirzada.

An accomplished lawyer, Pirzada refused to give up and instead argued his case vociferously in front of the government's Election Commission in Karachi. The judge nominated by the government, late Justice Naeemuddin, admonished him for his outbursts and threw out his case.

But by then Benazir had already moved on to seek new ways of returning to power. Even while she was in Jacobabad, she had fretted that her stay in the small town might reduce her image to that of a provincial, rather than national, leader. Once again, her eyes were set to rise to the highest office, no matter what it took.

The Road to Islamabad

The tyrannical Chief Minister of Sindh, Jam Sadiq Ali died of natural causes in March 1992. The army lost their strongman and the pressure on Benazir and her PPP eased. By then, however, the free hand given by the establishment to dacoits had cost the nation dearly. The ransoms fetched by the kidnappings of Chinese engineers and Japanese tourists made the dacoits more restive. Like wolves baying for more blood, they advanced to the wealthy industrial city of Karachi.

One morning in June 1992, I woke up to learn that our next-door neighbor – industrialist, Ashiq Ali Hussain – had been ambushed and kidnapped a short distance from his home. Hussain's kidnapping from his chauffer-driven car – which occurred in the presence of his armed guards – sent shockwaves through the top industrialists in Karachi. Even the military establishment realized the dacoits had gone too far.

A few days later, with a heroic flourish, the army launched "Operation Clean-up" in Sindh and began to exterminate dacoits like flies. Although for months, they had ignored our investigative reports on dacoits, the kidnapping of a key industrialist appeared to have been a wake up call. All of a sudden, the forests were cut down across Sindh to prevent dacoits from taking hostages. District administrations, until now allowed to look the other way, were warned against sheltering the bandits. Ranger patrols were stepped up and dacoits were shot on sight.

As the army branched across Sindh for "Operation Clean-up," the poor villagers heaved a sigh of relief. It was also a signal to ordinary Sindhis and the PPP that the time was ripe to reorganize for a return to power.

By 1992, Benazir had learnt that the road to Islamabad did not lie with the electorate but through currying favor with the military rulers. She began hobnobbing with the president who had once dismissed her, Ghulam Ishaq Khan, to convince him to sack Nawaz Sharif's government.

Four years in the knitty gritty world of politics had taught Benazir that securing the support of millions may be good for her populist image, but it would not make her the next prime minister of Pakistan. Eventually, it would be the PPP's recourse to "palace intrigues" – a well-traveled road for politicians seeking power in Pakistan – that did the trick.

Knowing me as the reporter who covered the PPP for the nation's most influential newspaper, the party's top brass began to contact me directly. Each evening, a key aide to Benazir – Nabil Gabol – cleverly timed his phone calls to give me information about Benazir's meetings with the establishment, aimed at securing the dissolution of the assemblies.

The PPP's purpose was served, as I wrote lead stories in *Dawn* about indications that fresh elections were in the offing. It was also a genuine demand by the masses, who argued that Benazir's last tenure had been too short to do any good.

In the meantime, Benazir kept her "train marches" handy in her bid to return to power. One of her party loyalists, remembering the glowing image of Benazir I had presented in my newspaper, playfully asked me if I would be ready to join them again on the "Democracy Train."

By then, however, I had seen far too much anarchy and opportunism in the PPP's policies to make me feel optimistic about their efforts to bring democracy.

I retorted with a metaphor taken from the famous train accident at Sangi railway station in rural Sindh in 1990, when a train careened out of control at the station and killed hundreds of people: "Ah, but remember there's Sangi ahead."

Over two decades later, my mind's eye flashes back to the peasants of Sindh, whose half-shirts flapped in the wind as they ran barefoot along the railroad tracks to hear the PPP – then led by the charismatic Benazir Bhutto – promise them a better future.

It is a promise that still waits to be fulfilled.

Chapter 2

ETHNIC VIOLENCE IN SINDH: THE MQM SAGA

Two Days that Sinned

On September 30, 1988, it was late evening at my newspaper, *Dawn*, in Karachi, when news came that terrorists had started a shooting spree in Hyderabad, a city north of Karachi. Dozens of those killed were Mohajirs – Muslim refugees from India.

Although incidents of ethnic violence had for the last three years escalated across Sindh, the nature of the attacks struck me as extraordinary. It was the first time that the Mohajirs – also called Urdu speakers – were targeted in such large numbers. Even the residents of Karachi, inured by acts of daily violence, had grown anxious and the telephones rang off the hook.

No one had claimed responsibility for the incident but ripples of fear ran through the community that it was an ethnic killing that would become the precursor to unspeakable bloody retaliation.

It was an audacious attack that reeked of conspiracy. Hyderabad had more Sindhis than Mohajirs and the attackers could easily blend into the population. On the other hand, the planners had apparently calculated that there would be a backlash in Karachi where the MQM had, for the last three years, flexed muscles mainly against the ethnic groups – Pashtuns and Punjabis – for control of the city.

The timing of the incident gave us pause. Gen. Zia ul Haq's plane had crashed six weeks before and the military had announced a timeline for elections. Benazir Bhutto – whose father, Zulfikar Ali Bhutto had been executed nine years earlier by Gen. Zia – had received a rapturous welcome home as she prepared to take her "Democracy Train" across Sindh to mobilize supporters for the forthcoming elections.

Quite tellingly, the killings had happened shortly before the two ethnic groups in Sindh – the Sindhis and Mohajirs – were scheduled to vote and make a choice between the MQM, led by its Mohajir chief, Altaf Hussain and the PPP, led by its Sindh-born leader, Benazir Bhutto.

The Islamic Democratic Alliance or IJI, which Pakistan's generals subsequently admitted was created to stop Bhutto's election, had not yet been formed. Instead, Gen. Zia's sudden plane crash appeared to have pushed the intelligence agencies into a hurried plan of action that would foment lines of blood between Sindhis and Mohajirs and give the aspiring woman prime minister a split mandate in Sindh.

The September 30 massacre – or Black September, as it is called – had all the hallmarks of a conspiracy. It was dusk when the masked militants alighted from their vehicles in Hyderabad market place. They had prepared for the operation by shutting off the electricity throughout the market, so that it was dark when they were ready to shoot.

Then, as swarms of people – mainly Mohajirs – jostled unseeingly in the crowded bazaar, the shots rang out at random. Even as people writhed under the bullets, the terrorists kept firing. Apparently satisfied with the large-scale devastation they had caused, they calmly clambered back into their vehicles and melted back into the population.

As news of the terrorist killings came in from Hyderabad, I felt a premonition of the inevitable response that would come from Karachi. Personally, I wasn't worried that the Urdu-speaking militants would retaliate against my family and relatives – among the relatively few Sindhi families left behind in Karachi after partition. But I knew that for other less privileged Sindhis, revenge was coming.

It was brutal and swift. The next day, I woke up to a Karachi where armed assailants had throughout the night ferreted and killed Sindhis in their homes and work places. At the Jinnah Postgraduate Medical Center (JPMC) in Karachi, corpses covered with white sheets lay on stretchers pasted to the floor. Harassed young resident doctors in white coats wheeled victims of gunshot wounds to operation rooms, even as life-saving equipment and blood fell into desperately short supply.

With some trepidation, I asked about the ethnicity of the dead and wounded. They were Sindhis from the low-income suburbs of Karachi. Among the victims sprayed with bullets were Sindhi Hindus who ran a confectionary store in the fashionable Tariq Road shopping area. They were targeted not on account of religion but ethnicity. As masked armed men burst into their store, the Hindu Sindhis tried to duck behind the counters. But seconds later, they lay helpless in pools of their own blood.

Later, I heard stories of how innocent Sindhis had been hunted down by their Urdu-speaking neighbors in homes marked the night before for revenge. Many more were gagged, bound and killed before being stuffed in gunnysacks. Despite the terrifying nature of the incident, they would get only one paragraph in the long list I compiled from the hospitals. There was no space for the human-interest stories; instead I was engaged in a sordid compilation of the dead.

The killings of so many innocent Sindhis touched a raw nerve. My family was Sindhi and my parents – as well as grandparents – had, for generations, lived peacefully in Karachi, alongside Sindhi Hindus. But in 1947, when the British divided India to create Pakistan, our Hindu Sindhi neighbors left Karachi in droves.

Indeed, as the flood of refugees arrived from India, they headed to the cities and towns of Sindh to occupy the evacuated property and jobs left by the fleeing Hindu Sindhis. Although educated Sindhis from small towns of the province would over time migrate to Karachi and Hyderabad, the millions of Muslim migrants from India who poured into these cities outnumbered them.

Still, since childhood my parents had taken every possible measure to help us assimilate in a Karachi where the Mohajirs became the dominant population. We were not even encouraged to speak our native Sindhi language and instead spoke Urdu – the language brought by the refugees from India. It helped me to camouflage my ethnicity.

On September 1, 1988, as I sped from hospital to hospital interviewing families of gunshot victims, no one could figure out whether I was a Sindhi or Mohajir. I was further removed from the fray from having been educated in the schools set up by the British in Karachi. That explained me, a young woman scribbling away in English, even as I interviewed the gunshot victims in Urdu.

On that evening of 1988, as I drove back to report the massacres, I was driven by an urge to let people know what was really going on. Departing from the newspaper's rules against naming the ethnicity of victims, I let readers read between the lines that the massacre had mainly killed Sindhis. It was a bit of a wire act to do so in my conservative newspaper, but I wanted people to know the reality.

My city editor, Akhtar Payami – himself a Mohajir and usually sensitive to my news approach – asked me how I, as a Sindhi, felt about the attacks. I told him that personally, I was not worried that MQM militants would target us. We belonged to a privileged family and were integrated with other ethnic communities. Still, I saw the sense of insecurity among newspaper colleagues who were Sindhis and Balochis – who identify with Sindhis; after the attack, they had gathered in our Reporters Room with a new sense of camaraderie.

My senior Sindhi colleague, the late Ghulam Ali, no longer cracked his usual jokes. A crime reporter, he had taken to jesting that the way to scandalize a rickshaw driver was to ask to be taken to Liaquatabad – the very inferno of Mohajir riots. He always had a collection of jokes at the ready to keep me laughing when times were bad. But that night, as I saw the drawn out faces of my senior colleagues, I wondered what the future would hold for us.

The First Spark

It was no coincidence that ethnic violence first broke out with the creation of the Mohajir Qaumi Movement (MQM) in 1985, shortly after Gen. Zia had held non-partisan elections as part of his plan to usher in controlled democracy.

That year, the Mohajirs, led by a former Karachi university student, Altaf Hussain contested as an independent party and won a landslide victory. Encouraged by Gen. Zia ul Haq to organize on non-political grounds, the refugees from India mobilized in Karachi on the basis of their separate ethnic identity and registered as a political party.

In April 1985, I was tipped off by our crime reporter that gunshot victims had begun to pile up at a hospital in the north of Karachi. Word was that a speeding Pashtun mini-van driver had killed a Mohajir college girl, Bushra Zaidi. The accident itself was not news. Indeed, not a day went by when the newspapers did not report traffic deaths. Terrified of the speeding vehicles, young women often held hands as they ran across this particular intersection. But that day, the young college girl that tried nervously to cross the road was struck down and died.

Bushra's death became a cue for the unemployed Mohajir youth. They banded, in the newly armed MQM, to fan out throughout the city and destroy mini-vans dubbed "yellow devils." They also burnt down rickshaws and taxis, owned and operated by Pashtuns. It was a direct assault on the livelihood of the migrants from the north of Pakistan who bought their vehicles on high interest loans and raced their callously-stuffed passengers at high speeds so that they could repay the loan sharks. The Pashtuns reacted in the only way they knew; they shot back and killed the Mohajir assailants.

Government hospitals were caught unaware by the first major incident of ethnic violence under Gen. Zia. The Abbasi Shaheed Hospital overflowed with victims of gunshot wounds. Medicines and blood were in desperately short supply. Frenzied crowds gathered on the lawns to donate blood and medicines for the victims, rushed in every few minutes by makeshift ambulances that were more suited to carrying vegetables than people.

For the next few days, the riots between Mohajirs and Pashtuns left 65 people dead and 158 injured. It was a vision of things to come. Over the next two decades, tens of thousands of people would lose their lives as the MQM fought with the indigenous ethnic groups – Sindhis, Balochis, Pashtuns and Punjabis – and the military alternately used and killed Mohajir youths in an attempt to wrest back control.

It was an era of the Cold War when the US Republican administration, led by President Ronald Reagan, used Zia's regime as a conduit to fight against the Soviet invasion of Afghanistan. No sooner did the arms, bound for Mujahideen fighters, land at the Karachi Port than they were smuggled out and sold in the black market. The alacrity with which gun licenses were issued to ethnic groups made it appear that Gen. Zia preferred that they fight each other than fight his military rule.

Gen. Zia's patronage of the MQM unfolded before our eyes. His ministers would call on the MQM chief Altaf Hussain at his home in Azizabad – a lower-middle class Mohajir neighborhood in Karachi. High walls cordoned off the MQM's head office – Nine Zero, Azizabad – also known as *Markaz* or the "Center." At the Karachi Press Club, we talked about how Mohajirs had achieved the stuff of dreams: a lower-middle class party that kept key establishment figures waiting to meet their chief.

The MQM chief, Altaf Hussain's personality lent an air of mystery to the party he had created. A dark-skinned man who wore dark glasses at all times, Altaf began the MQM as a movement for the rights of Muslim migrants from India who had arrived to create Pakistan. The MQM talked progressive politics, criticizing the feudals who oppressed Sindhis. But the MQM chief operated in a distinctly feudal style. Altaf Hussain projected himself as *"Pir saheb"* (spiritual leader), whose infatuated followers saw his likeness on the leaves around them.

Years later, MQM stalwart and former Karachi Mayor, Farooq Sattar acknowledged to me in a recorded interview what I had long known – namely, that in 1984, the "intelligence agencies allowed the MQM to come up to counter the PPP." The purpose, he said, in a tone that suggested that it was an open secret, was to prevent the Sindhis from gaining power.

The senior MQM leader referred to the 1983 Movement for Restoration of Democracy, through which tens of thousands of Sindhi villagers – who had protested against Gen. Zia's execution of the elected prime minister, Zulfikar Ali Bhutto – were strafed by helicopter gunships in their own settlements. At the same time, Sindhi intellectuals, writers and journalists who supported the MRD were imprisoned and tortured by the military.

Decades later, the former Chief of Army Staff, Gen. Mirza Aslam Baig too acknowledged on television that the MQM was created by his predecessor, Gen. Zia ul Haq as a political measure to counter the Sindhi insurgency that grew after the murder of PPP founder, Zulfikar Ali Bhutto.

The death of the college girl, Bushra Zaidi led to weeks of rioting between the Mohajirs and Pashtuns, which left 65 people dead and 158 injured. The press was still controlled by the military government but statements poured into *Dawn* from readers that the government ought to nationalize private wagons and buses and confiscate the driving licenses of reckless drivers.

In the forefront were educated Urdu-speaking professionals, bewildered by the sudden upsurge of violence. Their women councilors – many of them newly elected in Gen. Zia's government – appealed for a ban on guns and for dialogue. But such expressions of hand wringing had nothing to do with the insidious workings of the military, which secretly patronized the ethnic party for political purposes.

Moreover, whilst educated Mohajirs were shocked by the violence, the reprisals by Pashtuns convinced many of the need

Figure 3 MQM chief Altaf Hussain addresses election rally in Karachi (undated *Dawn* Photo).

to organize as a political party. Since Pakistan's creation in 1947, many Mohajirs had come to dislike the fact that they did not fit into a native ethnic group – Sindhis, Baloch, Pashtuns and Punjabis. Their feud with the Pashtuns convinced many that the Indian refugees needed a party to guarantee their survival. It would provide a groundswell of support for the MQM.

Pashtuns Take Revenge

After the first ethnic clash between the Mohajirs and Pashtuns, a storm quietly brewed between the two ethnic communities. The Pashtuns united under the Pashtunwali code of honor – a tribal law that calls for the defense of the closest kin. While it is normal practice for Pashtuns to bear arms, the Cold War gave them unprecedented access to the weapons that transited from Karachi to their native Khyber Pakhtunkhwa, which borders Afghanistan.

It was a time when the former Soviet Union's invasion of Afghanistan in 1979 had forced three million Afghans to cross the porous borders into Khyber Pakhtunkhwa, formerly known as the North West Frontier Province. These were Pashtun Afghans who lived on both sides of the border and who followed their relatives in Karachi to look for work. In Karachi, the Afghan refugees had congregated in Sohrab Goth – a tented village erected by the United Nations along the remote dusty wastelands of the city's Super Highway.

In those Cold War days, I reported from the tented village after it became notorious as a drugs and weapons hotspot. The turbaned Afghan Mujahideen, who toured the camps, hunted for young recruits for the US-funded *jihad* against the former Soviet Union. Sohrab Goth was a home for Afghan refugees and a depot for heroin. The army's National Logistics Cell (NLC) trucks, which carried US arms and ammunition to the Mujahideen in the north, were widely rumored to return carrying heroin to be sold in Karachi.

By December 1986, Karachi's Pashtuns – flush with drug money – had stocked a sizeable cache of weapons in a desolate area north of Karachi called Orangi Town. The Pashtuns lived here in brick and stone homes atop the rugged cliffs, much as they did in the hilly tribal regions that border Afghanistan. Their homes jutted menacingly over a sea of Mohajirs – including almost a million Biharis who had settled here after 1971, when Pakistan's eastern wing, "East Pakistan," seceded and became Bangladesh.

My early recollections of Orangi Town go back to 1972, when as a schoolgirl I was brought by my father to work with humanitarian organizations in order to help the Biharis resettle in Karachi. The Bengali nationalists accused the Biharis of collaborating with the Pakistani army during the 1971 war. In fact in 1947 many Muslim Biharis had opted to migrate from India's Bihar state to what was then East Pakistan. They ended up making a double migration in 1971 when they opted to join the Urdu speaking community in Karachi.

Subsequently, 1 million Biharis were resettled in Orangi town by Zulfikar Ali Bhutto's government. As a teenager, I made trips with my father to the deserted area in the north of Karachi to help an exhausted paramedic serve the poor, malnourished Bihari patients. Hundreds of refugees queued outside our makeshift clinics for cough and cold medicines. As the overworked dispenser dished out the medicines that I handed to him, his fantastic claim sparked my imagination: "I'm so busy I don't even have the time to die!"

Fifteen years later, these poor Biharis – who had left war-ravaged Bangladesh to become Karachi's newest Mohajirs – faced the wrath of angry Pashtuns. It was mid-December in 1986 and well past our newspaper deadline when an army of Pashtuns equipped with machine guns charged down the Orangi hills. They made use of the mud walls erected on the hills, shooting and ducking for cover. As the aggressors rained fireballs from their fortresses, the Mohajir areas below them – the Aligarh and Qasbah colonies – went up in flames.

The violence continued into the wee hours as both ethnic groups displayed the worst of human nature. It was reported that Mohajir babies were snatched and thrown into burning oil while Pashtuns were tied up and sliced to pieces in revenge killings. The cycle of violence raged for the next few days and cut off Orangi from the rest of Karachi.

Late at night, as the fires raged in Orangi Town, I got a phone call from a national public radio station in the US asking for the news. I filed my report, thousands of miles from America. It filled me with awe that Orangi Town – which I knew as acres of hilly desert with mud homes and little access to clean drinking water and sewerage – had made international headlines.

It was no less amazing that Orangi had become the scene of clashes between two very different refugee groups – the Biharis from South Asia and the Afghans from Central Asia – separated by thousands of miles of territory. Their peoples had migrated to Karachi to find peace because of the wars that had uprooted them from their respective countries. And now once again their lives were being turned around by bloody ethnic warfare.

The military imposed a curfew in Orangi Town. As the genocide halted, I visited the affected areas in the official van provided by my newspaper. Fear hung in the deserted streets, where broken billboards and hulks of burnt-out vehicles were grim reminders of the killings. The veteran social worker, Abdus Sattar Edhi darted in and out of the unpaved lanes in his rickety ambulances, which carried the dead and the wounded.

Both Mohajirs and Pashtuns had suffered heavy casualties in the incident. Among the devastated Mohajir families, a great number of women had lost their brothers and husbands. An atmosphere of distrust was in the air. People opened the door only after they saw that I was a young woman. The affected family members poured out their woes and lamented the breakdown of trust between Muslims.

The Pashtun-Mohajir riots set back the development work performed by the late Dr Akhter Hameed Khan. Dr Khan had founded the non-profit Orangi Pilot Project to teach residents to build their own houses, construct drainage schemes and help women run their own businesses. Then in his twilight years, Dr Khan proudly told me that his innovative ideas were geared around a related project he had begun in Comilla when it was still East Pakistan. His staff was now challenged by attempts to rebuild the shattered trust between the Pashtun and Urdu-speaking communities.

Pashtuns and Punjabis Ally

After the showdown in Orangi town, the Pashtuns moved closer to the Punjabis, another ethnic group that had come to look for work in the southern port city of Karachi. The Punjabis are the predominant ethnic group within the military and have traditionally been represented at the highest tiers as corps commanders, generals, lieutenants and senior officers. They have a close nexus with the Pashtuns, who enjoy the second best position in the army. The British were known to patronize the Punjabis and Pashtuns on the ground that they were a hardy race, most suited to the martial qualities needed for governance.

In the early Zia years, the MQM threatened both the Punjabis and Pashtuns in Karachi. In comparison to the Sindhis and Baloch, who quietly moved out of Mohajir localities, many of the low-income Pashtuns and Punjabis – who worked mostly as transportation and construction workers – refused to abandon their home territory. Many of them had brought their families to Karachi and they had no intention of leaving.

Those who dared to live in strongholds where MQM militants called the shots paid dearly with their lives. In 1987, a heart-broken Punjabi who lived in the industrial Korangi area called me at my newspaper to describe how his daughter, Iffat Awan, a medical student, was killed point blank as she opened the door to a stranger. It would be incidents like these that would convince a large number of working Punjabis and Pashtuns to relocate back to their home provinces.

On the flip side, the more aggressive Pashtuns and Punjabis united in self-defense. I was assigned by my newspaper to cover their united front – the Punjabi Pashtun Ittehad (PPI). It was a miniscule, shadowy group, mostly limited to press statements. The PPI chief – a hefty, burly man named Ghulam Sarwar Awan – called me late in the evenings at my office to deride the MQM. It was an ineffective gesture of the sort we joked was made by "newspaper tigers."

While the MQM and Pashtun-Punjabi animosity dragged on, urban middle-class Sindhis had begun to speak out against the MQM. In the forefront was the Jeay Sindh Taraqi Pasand Party (or, the Progressive Party of Sindh) that was subsequently charged with the September 30 massacre. Their urban-based organization was however a cry in the wilderness, given that most Sindhis were peasants who lived in widely scattered villages.

Historically, Sindhis have shunned the ethnic bait. Instead, they have been most attracted to the federation politics espoused by the Bhuttos – first Zulfikar Ali and then his daughter, Benazir. Although founded in Sindh, the Pakistan Peoples Party has from its inception been inclusive of all ethnicities, with a single espoused goal of uplifting the lot of the common person.

An Early Karachi Discord

By December 1988, when Benazir Bhutto was first sworn in as prime minister of Pakistan, the ethnic voting blocs were firmly established. Sindhis who generally lived in the rural areas of Sindh voted for the PPP while the more urbane Mohajirs voted for the MQM. It is the pattern that dominates the politics of Sindh and impacts on the whole nation.

Still, as Benazir was sworn in for the first time, the optimism among all ethnic groups helped put the September 30 carnage behind them. A monumental Karachi Accord was signed between the MQM and PPP to form a coalition government in Sindh. It was a rare sight to see Mohajirs and Sindhis embrace each other and distribute sweets in the city. I had spent the last 3½ years counting the victims of ethnic violence in white shrouds but peace had finally arrived.

And yet, there was a surreal quality in the MQM-PPP embrace. On that historic night, as a fellow journalist and I drove around the city, we looked on in wonder as die-hard enemies greeted each other as brothers. My colleague, the more cynical of the two of us, turned to me and said, "How long do you think the honeymoon will last?"

The answer came quickly. The 1988 elections, which launched Benazir Bhutto had also given the MQM a huge mandate from its Urdu-speaking constituencies in Karachi and Hyderabad – making it a formidable force in the parliament and on the streets.

Seated in the opera-like gallery of the Sindh Assembly, we journalists witnessed how legislators from the PPP and the MQM behaved after over a decade of military rule. Barely had a few months elapsed before there were walkouts by MQM legislators, angry at the failure of the Bhutto government to fulfill their promises. The PPP legislators dithered but appeared helpless.

By 1989, the MQM had matured into the nation's third largest political party, with the ability to take on the PPP. The Karachi accord went out of the door. As MQM legislators resigned, the city plunged into its worst state of mayhem yet. Every day the MQM leadership called for strikes, which were followed by looting, arson and murder. A pall of thick black smoke hung over most parts of the city as Mohajir militants exchanged fire with the police.

Each time the MQM gave a call for "wheel jam" strikes, Karachi shivered. Public vehicles stopped running, their drivers afraid of getting torched. Since most people relied on public transportation, the strike turned Karachi into a ghost town. Keeping the "PRESS" sign boldly displayed, I drove through a city under curfew. Karachi looked as it might have looked at partition: empty of people and overwhelmed by dangerously heavy and chaotic traffic.

On strike day, violence flared up in most parts of Karachi as the police fought running battles with the MQM workers. The MQM loyalists lay in wait for the police and ambushed them as soon as they entered their localities. Come evening and people telephoned to ask about the "score." They did not mean the cricket score. It was short for how many people had been killed that day.

As the city plunged into ethnic turmoil, Benazir Bhutto summoned a small group of us journalists to Bilawal House, named after her first-born son. We sat around a wooden oval table, where the youthful prime minister looked more somber than usual. Benazir had barely been in office for a year when her government had begun to totter.

Apparently, the ethnic violence that had engulfed Karachi was only the tip of the iceberg. Benazir had offended the military by replacing the ISI chief, Lt. Gen. Hameed Gul with a retired officer who was close to her father: Shamsur Rahman Kallue.

That mistake would cost her dearly. Hameed Gul had emerged as a powerful player of the Cold War, when the US used his office to funnel billions of dollars worth of weapons to oust the Soviet Union from Afghanistan.

With ethnic unrest all around in Karachi, Benazir told us frankly she suspected that the state was trying to destabilize her government. "How can I control the intelligence agencies?" she asked us, her "inner group" of journalists.

The meeting was an eye-opener. Up until now, I had believed that the elected head of Pakistan was all-powerful. I had also witnessed the overwhelming popular support for Benazir across the country. But now, the elected prime minister was telling us she did not have control over the army's intelligence agencies.

That early encounter became a road map to my understanding of why Pakistan had been unable to develop into a stable democracy. The over-indulged state had, since the creation of the nation, taught political leaders one simple lesson: where they fell out with the military, they could be shaken down like dates from a palm tree.

September 30 Accused Go on Trial

Benazir's first shaky government was overthrown in August 1990 and Nawaz Sharif replaced her as prime minister. A year later, the state agencies brought to trial the men accused in the September 30 massacre. Some of these leaders of the Jeay Sindh Taraqi Pasand Party (JSTPP) had already been arrested under Benazir's government, while others who fled underground were declared absconders.

In 1991, I began to visit the Karachi Central Jail to cover the daily trial of the JSTPP, led by its stocky, pugnacious chief of Baloch origin, Dr Qadir Magsi. The nationalist group was vocal in its opposition to the MQM. Their leaders came to the Karachi Press Club, armed guards in tow, to raise a red flag about how Sindhis suffered unreported indignities at the hands of the militant MQM.

It was a sensitive subject in a city increasingly controlled by the MQM and one that needed to be reported gingerly.

The party's leadership had ferreted out my Sindhi roots and telephoned me from their headquarters in Hyderabad to get me to write considerately on behalf of oppressed Sindhis. I listened and reported, without losing perspective. With my front line view, I had seen Gen. Zia ul Haq's military play off one ethnic group against another to foment violence and avoid becoming the target. The Sindhi militants could not convince me that violence was the answer.

In 1991, it intrigued me that the accused of the 30 September massacre arrived with a "devil may care" attitude that suggested that they were political prisoners rather than criminals. Their treatment by the state authorities implied otherwise. They were herded into a big cage, handcuffed and restrained through bars, which separated them from the judge, lawyers and journalists. We had been told they were "dangerous." Certainly, the accusation

Figure 4 JSTPP chief Qadir Magsi addresses a rally in Larkana, June 12, 2009 (*Dawn* photo).

that they had mowed down over a hundred people made me scrutinize them carefully.

Once the iron gates of the prison clanged behind us, we were in a separate world. My daily presence in the prisoners' court made me part of the world that I had begun to cover. As the trial proceeded, some of the accused smiled and gesticulated to me in a rather friendly manner. They had read my daily coverage of the 30 September massacre in *Dawn* and wanted me to understand that it was their ideological motivation that drove them to "defend" the people of Sindh.

The lawyer for the accused, Qurban Ali Chohan traveled regularly from Hyderabad for the trial. He quickly introduced himself to me – letting on that he believed my coverage would make a difference to its outcome. After the hearings, the lawyer pulled out two chocolate cakes – bought from Hyderabad's premier Bombay Bakery – and give one to the judge and the other to me. I took the cakes, all the while amused that the lawyer could imagine that it would affect my coverage.

What really made the difference in the case was that no witnesses turned up to testify. It was dusk when killers went on the shooting spree. The accused knew that mowing down a hundred or so people in cold blood would terrorize eyewitnesses – who were, in any case, unprotected by the weak judicial system. Indeed, the JSTPP leaders exuded the type of confidence that indicated an assurance by the higher-ups that they would not be touched after the "job."

What was even more scandalous was that there were no arrests and no public trial for the mass murders, which had taken place in Karachi on October 1, 1988, when over a hundred Sindhis were killed. Nor would anyone be touched for the ethnic murders that had occurred on a mass scale under Gen. Zia. The legal system was in shambles and terrorists ruled. It was this loss of confidence in the government that forced Sindhi families to leave Karachi in droves.

In the course of the trial for Qadir Magsi and his party men, I met so called Sindhi nationalists who had resorted to theft, dacoity, murders, kidnappings for ransom and other criminal activities. Among them, a rather debonair felon from Jeay Sindh, Sattar Morio, came up to me after a hearing. My glance fell on his expensive watch and a thin gold chain flashing around his neck. He had flashing green eyes and wore a starched white *shalwar kameez* (baggy trousers and tunic).

"You are Sindhi – right?" he addressed me in Sindhi in a tone that said he knew the answer.

I nodded.

With feigned hurt, he continued in Sindhi, "Then why do you treat us like this?"

It was an old trick. But it did not work on a person who has always condemned terrorism. Nor would the intimacy sought by Sindhi nationalists who spoke to me in my native tongue, change my perceptions of them. Moreover, those who used Sindhi nationalism as a guise to engage in criminal activity had failed to win the hearts and minds of the people of Sindh.

Operation Clean-up Splits the MQM

The dismissal of Benazir Bhutto's first government in August 1990 was mourned by her supporters, many of whom considered it to be part of a larger conspiracy against Sindhis. On the other hand the largely urban MQM celebrated her downfall, hoping for a better deal under Nawaz Sharif's government.

Under Sharif, the MQM took a life of its own, strengthening its economic base through crimes including extortion, theft, car jacking and kidnappings.

The Citizens Police Liaison Committee (CPLC) set up in Karachi in 1989 by Sindh Governor Fakhruddin G. Ebrahim to beat crime, found that MQM workers routinely took extortion money from shopkeepers and tax collection agencies. Even ordinary Mohajirs were victimized by the extortionist culture.

Despite being a coalition partner of Prime Minister Nawaz Sharif, the MQM created problems for his government. There was no let up in ethnic riots, killings and damage to property. Matters reached a head when Sharif began to issue statements in the press that the MQM was bad for the investor climate in

Karachi. That was the first indication that the military had a plan up their sleeve.

In January 1992 – whilst Nawaz Sharif was still in power – the army issued a host of criminal charges against the MQM. In a move called "Operation Clean-up" – also used to tackle dacoits in the rural areas – the army arrested hundreds of MQM militants on criminal charges. It had a chilling effect on the apparently indestructible MQM and caused the party's demigod, Altaf Hussein to flee to London, where he has since taken asylum.

Inside the Sindh Assembly, my ears began to hear the unthinkable. For the first time, MQM party leaders had begun to criticize Altaf Hussain from the floor of the assembly. Their newfound ability to do so filled me with wonder. To publicly criticize Hussain was for MQM loyalists akin to blasphemy and punishable by death.

By June 1992, we discovered that the military had secretly patronized a group of dissident legislators, elected on the MQM ticket, to downsize the party led by Altaf Hussain. Pakistan Television showed the dissidents – called MQM Haqiqi – perched atop army trucks to uncover Altaf Hussain's "torture camps." In Karachi, journalists were shown blood-spattered walls and ropes that hung like nooses. The Haqiqi leaders, Afaq and Aamir – whose party later renamed itself the Mohajir Qaumi Movement in contradistinction to Altaf's Mutehidda Qaumi Movement – told state media that their rivals tortured opponents, drilled holes in them and stuffed their decapitated bodies into gunnysacks.

In Sindh, the state propaganda against the MQM did nothing to change people's minds. Those who disliked the MQM were convinced that the party was a terrorist organization. Among them were the Pashtuns and Punjabis, many of whom had been forced to leave Karachi after the ethnic murders. They returned to their provinces to spread negative reports about the MQM.

On the other hand, Mohajirs in the MQM grew even more disillusioned with the Pakistan, where they had arrived in their millions since India was partitioned in 1947. Having long blamed the state for their suffering and deprivation, they grew even more convinced that the military was out to get them.

As the MQM plunged into a deeper state of alienation and paranoia, Karachi became a battle ground between Altaf Hussain's followers and the dissidents. The city was divided into "no-go areas" where rival MQM factions could not enter. Intra-ethnic warfare began to kill more Mohajirs than any other ethnic group. In the 1990s, Karachi acquired the reputation of being one of the most violent cities in the world.

In June 1992, I was invited to a South Asian journalists' conference in Kathmandu, Nepal to explain Karachi's violence. When delegates from India and Bangladesh heard me narrate the MQM saga, they were bewildered. The Mohajirs had been their countrymen – who migrated from India in 1947 to create the Muslim homeland of Pakistan. And now the Pakistani army portrayed them as "terrorists."

It was difficult to explain to the South Asian journalists the complex, mafia-ridden world of Pakistani politics. True, the refugees who came to Sindh from different parts of India at partition failed to find a sense of identity and fought a battle for survival of the fittest. Still, it was rather paradoxical that the military, which helped to build the MQM tiger, resorted to false techniques to rein it in.

Benazir Issues Shoot to Kill Orders

When Benazir Bhutto returned to power for a second time in 1993, she was given a free hand by the military to defang the MQM. She appointed a retired general as the minister of interior – Naseerullah Babar – and gave him the authority to "flush out the terrorists." A hefty Pashtun with a broad forehead and a pendulous nose, Babar instructed the police in Sindh to shoot MQM militants rather than bring them to trial.

But although Benazir's bid to cut down the MQM was backed by the establishment, she miscalculated that the ethnic party had roots among the people. The MQM activists were frequently lower-middle-class urban dwellers who simply wanted a better life for their community. Benazir's blanket policy of ordering that MQM militants be shot at sight not only intensified her unpopularity with Mohajirs but also drew sharp criticism from human rights groups, who had previously been her foremost supporters.

As police and MQM casualties mounted in Karachi, the Human Rights Commission of Pakistan invited Benazir to discuss the cold-blooded killings at a public meeting in the city. I saw an older and more determined Benazir calmly tell the meeting that while she sympathized with the families of Mohajir youth killed, she had a duty to the people of Karachi to keep them safe from "terrorists."

This argument did not hold up in a predominantly Mohajir city. Inside parliament, MQM members cried "genocide." Outside, an armed cadre backed their legislators' anti-government tirades with violent strikes. In the Mohajir-dominated localities, buses were torched and public property destroyed and looted. By the end of 1994, some eight hundred people had been killed in police clashes and intra-factional rivalry.

As Karachi bled throughout the 1990s, hawkers brandished Urdu newspapers with photographs of bloodied Mohajir youth on the streets. The front-page pictures depicted dead young men in handcuffs, who had been shot at close range. With the court system in disarray, extrajudicial killings became the order of the day. Apparently, these were the new rules set by the army with which Benazir showed her willingness to play along.

The MQM retaliated against the PPP government's police force – ambushing and killing those found alone. One Sindhi police officer I knew went into a hotel in the center of his city to wear his uniform and then changed back into civilian clothes to go home. Wearing police uniform in a Mohajir-dominated area like Liaquatabad would have invited attacks by armed militants, who lay in wait for unguarded police, ready to take revenge.

Karachi's Killing Fields

In 1995, Karachi's reputation as a "killing field" spread to Europe. In December that year, Amnesty International invited me to visit ten cities in Germany and speak about the extrajudicial killings in Karachi. Five of us "human rights defenders" from conflict areas were dispatched across Germany to discuss our respective situations.

As we grouped on a railway platform in Germany and then split off to visit different cities, I knew how the early Jesuits must have felt when they traveled to spread the message of peace. Interestingly, some Germans compared the experiences of Mohajirs under Benazir to those of Jews in Nazi Germany. I worked to dispel this illusion. It took some explanation to convey that the MQM problem was complex and rooted in the creation of Pakistan.

When the German public asked what they could do to help, I urged them to lobby against greedy arms manufacturers. Years of reporting had convinced me that the easy access to guns – dumped by the US and Western countries in Pakistan – had allowed the establishment to manipulate ethnic and Islamic groups for their ends, resulting in needless bloodshed.

Back in Pakistan, a PPP advisor told me with disapproval that I had been unfair to blame Benazir's government for cracking down on the MQM; he believed the MQM were terrorists who would likely be let off by the courts for lack of evidence and hold society hostage if they were not tackled at the source.

The trouble with this position, I told him, was that for every "terrorist" killed, there were five others willing to take his place.

The MQM Saga Lives On

After 1999, when Gen. Musharraf – himself a Mohajir – came to power, the army looked to the MQM as the wild card in maneuvering the political set up in Sindh. Like Gen. Zia ul Haq, Gen. Musharraf patronized the MQM in a quid pro quo relationship that guaranteed his military-backed rule. After the 2002 elections, ISI officials negotiated with the MQM and facilitated their key positions in government. The purpose was a familiar one: to block the populist PPP – and its charismatic leader Benazir Bhutto, then living abroad – against forming the government in Sindh.

Under Gen. Musharraf, MQM members, including those facing criminal charges were rewarded with ministerial portfolios. Among them was MQM activist, Ishrat ul Ibad, who had fled to London during "Operation Clean-up" in 1992 but, under Musharraf, returned to become the Sindh governor. MQM loyalist, Rauf Siddiqi was made the minister of interior. With senior administrative positions in Sindh filled by the MQM, the ethnic party was reportedly able to settle scores against the extrajudicial killings of Mohajirs in previously PPP eras.

But decades of murders by law enforcement agencies, political groups and infighting had left the MQM isolated. Despite reaching out to other ethnic communities, including those living in other provinces of Pakistan, its membership remained exclusively Mohajir. MQM chief Altaf Hussain – who had taken British citizenship – was unable to return to Pakistan not only because of the criminal charges against him but also fears that he would be assassinated.

In September 2010, the murder of MQM leader Dr Imran Farooq in London – where he had taken exile after Musharraf's military coup – created fresh shock waves for the party. Altaf Hussain, who had recently parted ways with Dr Farooq, was depicted sobbing on *YouTube*, apparently mourning the loss of his "close companion." Conspiracy theories aside, the murder would fuel fresh paranoia in the MQM that the mafia had reached foreign shores.

In the post-Benazir era, her widower, Asif Zardari, taking a leaf from history, began with a charm offensive on the MQM's headquarters – Nine Zero Azizabad – to "seek forgiveness," for the murders of MQM activists in the PPP era. The MQM chief, Altaf Hussain reciprocated. In a quid pro quo scenario, the PPP government rewarded the MQM with ministerial positions, whilst the latter voted for a PPP prime minister and for Zardari to become president.

All of this has come at a price for the vast majority of Sindhi villagers. In the words of middle-class Sindhis, the PPP submits to the MQM's urban "blackmail," by diverting funds from the rural and Sindhi-populated areas. The PPP Prime Minister, Yusuf Raza Gilani has unsuccessfully attempted to rectify the situation. However, in 2010, he was forced to retract his statement that Hyderabad would be restored as a single administrative unit "to enable just distribution of funds," after the MQM threatened to break the coalition.

On the other hand, the Pashtun-based Awami National Party, also in coalition with the PPP government, has engaged in violent clashes with the MQM. This has led to spasmodic fighting between Pashtuns and Mohajirs in Karachi, in scenes that eerily resemble the bloody 1980s.

In 2010, the Pashtun-Mohajir conflict claimed so many lives that the MQM chief, Altaf Hussain called for the army's intervention, only to back down under political criticism. The MQM has frequently threatened to break off its coalition with the PPP government, only to withdraw the threat after getting more concessions.

For the time being, the PPP and MQM have managed to ward off September 30 style conspiracies that threaten violence between the two major ethnic groups of Sindh. Still, it is a fragile coalition that is constantly strained by the separate interests of the Sindhis – who lived in the province before it was Pakistan – and the Mohajirs – who left India to create it.

At the end of the day, it is Sindh's ethnic divide that keeps its two main ethnic groups – Sindhis and Mohajirs – loyal to their respective political parties and gives the establishment room to manipulate from the center.

Chapter 3
NEWS IS WHAT THE RULERS WANT TO HIDE

"What are you Writing? You're Writing too Much"

September 24, 1991: It was almost 10.00 pm when I turned my car into the dimly lit road that led to our family house in Garden East. Over the years, it had become normal practice for me to alight, turn the key of the small gate and push the large gates open to drive my car inside.

But that evening, driving back alone as usual to my colonial style, fortress-like home, I had an uneasy premonition that I might have become a target because of my investigative reporting.

That year, Sindh Chief Minister Jam Sadiq Ali had cracked the whip on scores of journalists for exposing his underhanded tactics to rein in the PPP opposition. Benazir Bhutto was dismissed after a short, chaotic tenure as prime minister almost a year prior, after which the army had ushered in a new prime minister, Nawaz

Sharif, and accorded him a free hand to ensure that the PPP power base was subdued.

1991, the year that the former Soviet Union collapsed, was also a time when Pakistan's military – newly strengthened by its Cold War alliance with the US in Afghanistan – turned its attention toward strict domestic surveillance. As the chief of the ISI, Lt. Gen. Asad Durrani was served in Sindh by the Intelligence Bureau (IB), headed by the notorious Brig. Imtiaz Ahmed. The ISI and IB, which are legally authorized to bug telephones, spied on "domestic enemies," – i.e. PPP members of parliament and independent journalists.

That was also the year that the Chief of Army Staff, Asif Nawaz – who was unusual in the fact that he resisted the army's interference in political affairs – headed a Military Intelligence (MI), which collected evidence of the manner in which the ISI and the IB hamstrung Benazir Bhutto and her PPP from returning to power.

This is when I inadvertently stepped into the picture.

Almost 24 hours before, Kamran Khan – then a reporter for *The News* and a correspondent for the *Washington Post* – had been stabbed and taken bleeding to hospital. The assailants were young men who attacked him as he stepped outside his office on the busy I. I. Chundrigar Road and were overheard saying in Urdu, "What are you writing? You're writing too much."

That afternoon, when a colleague narrated the incident, chills went down my spine. Instantly, I became aware that my reporting on the chief minister's corrupt tactics could make me the next target of attack.

Within an hour, the Karachi Union of Journalists had mobilized a protest meeting at the Karachi Press Club – a British-built gray stone building in the center of the city. I saw the intense expressions on my colleagues; men and women journalists determined to protest the attack against one of our own. Knowing that our future as independent print journalists was at stake, we hurriedly spilled out into the street with banners and placards in English and Urdu that called for an end to the attacks on journalists.

As we marched, one of my colleagues pointed out that the Deputy Inspector General of the Crime Investigation Agency (CIA), Samiullah Marwat, who took orders from the Sindh Government, drove leisurely in step with our procession. Marwat was known to haul up PPP supporters for brutal interrogation and was suspected to have ordered the stabbing of my injured colleague.

Still, trying to ignore his presence, we kept marching toward the Sindh Chief Minister's House. Our spirited rally of editors, senior journalists and reporters camped in front of the locked gate with banners and placards, aware of the pressure needed to keep the media free.

In 1991, the English, Urdu and Sindhi print media were in the front lines of independent journalism in Pakistan. Television and radio was state controlled and this was a decade before private electronic media was due to explode onto the scene.

Late evening, driving back home from work, my mind was still preoccupied with our protest. Turning the corner to my house, I slowed down my car in the dark pathway, transfixed by what I saw from my windscreen. There were two shadowy figures that lurked beneath the milky tube-light outside our family home.

As I drew nearer, they advanced toward my car and I saw them more clearly. They were two young men who looked like they had been deputed for the job. In the deserted and faintly lighted street, they stood on either side of my approaching car. I saw a small knife flash as one of the youths made the first move.

Forewarned by the day's events, I pressed the accelerator and sped past them, driving at break neck speed. Instincts told me to drive toward the nearest police station. Then better sense prevailed and, looking at the rear view mirror to see if the assailants were in hot pursuit, I kept speeding toward my newspaper office.

As I ran up the steps, my colleagues took one look at me and knew. My city editor, Akhtar Payami got that serious preoccupied look he got when any major incident occurred. Instantly, he was on the phone with my editor, even as he assigned two reporters from my newspaper – the late Aleemuddin Pathan and Ali Kabir – to jot down the details.

Aleem, my light-skinned Pashtun colleague – who foreign journalists often mistook for Italian – heard my narration with his usual aplomb. He began typing for the Pakistan Press International wire services in his slow, deliberate style with cigarette in mouth.

Ali Kabir – my senior colleague with a curling moustache and a sardonic air who had tried to give me a hard time for being a free spirit – soberly pounded the story on a manual typewriter.

"It is the first ever attempt on a woman journalist in the history of Pakistan," he wrote in a news report that appeared the next morning with the headline: "*Dawn* woman reporter escapes attack."

While my colleagues typed, I waited for my eldest sister, Naseem to take me to her home in Defense Housing Society. It was too dangerous for me to go back home that night. Instead, I told my parents about the incident on the telephone. They listened to me as though they had been half expecting it. My aging parents were no strangers to a daughter who did dangerous, investigative reports and now even they had been dragged into the fray.

A week earlier, my father, then in his seventies, had pulled his car out of the driveway, parked it by the front door and walked back to close the gates when a thug followed him. He pressed a gun to my father's waist, asked him to be quiet and took away his car keys.

A short while later my mother opened the front door to see a heavy-set man in the driver's seat. The man stared unblinkingly at her. It did not even cross my mother's mind that the car in which he silently sat was ours, or that it had been stolen at gunpoint from my father. That was the last time we saw the car, carrying the files of the charity agencies for which my father worked voluntarily.

At my sister's house, I grappled with the events of the day. Living as I did in the inextricable world of politics and journalism, it became palpably clear to me that I had become one more victim of the political situation that had developed in the province of Sindh.

Coming after Gen. Zia ul Haq's long military rule, Prime Minister Benazir Bhutto's short and unceremonious dismissal had caused much anguish to her die-hard supporters. On the other hand, the nation's feudal, religious and ethnic political parties had formally bonded in the ISI-funded IJI coalition, with a mandate to prevent the PPP from returning to power.

ISI chief Asad Durrani's affadavit to the Supreme Court in 1996 revealed that Nawaz Sharif's appointed chief minister Jam Sadiq Ali had received PKR 5 million (USD 59,000) from the spy agency. As chief minister, Jam would repay the army for every penny they spent on him, wasting no opportunity to vilify Benazir and her husband Asif Zardari – even while the latter was holed up in prison on charges of corruption.

In that highly polarized atmosphere, my independence as a journalist had been cast aside to bracket me with the PPP and I had been dealt with accordingly.

In the grip of a nightmarish night of being chased by knife-wielding thugs, I became bitterly angry at the realization that the government wanted to intimidate us journalists into silence. With the knife threat fresh in my memory, I couldn't be absolutely certain that they would stop here. Perhaps they would follow through their plan to make sure I was killed.

The sound of the telephone bell ringing early morning made me almost fall out of my bed. I feared the worst. But it was only my brother Pervez, who taught at a university in Islamabad. He had read the report titled "Another Journalist Attacked," in *The News* – our rival newspaper – and discovered that the journalist was his sister. Furious, he suggested – and my family agreed – that I should fly to Islamabad, situated a thousand miles from Karachi, and lay low until the storm blew over.

The news item about the attack had appeared in all the newspapers across the country, giving me exposure that I had never imagined that I'd experience. The next morning, when my sister booked my ticket from Karachi to Islamabad on Pakistan International Airlines (PIA), the booking clerk told me that he had read about the attack in the newspapers – and that he knew why I was leaving!

That afternoon, on my way to the airport, a ragged hawker thrust an Urdu newspaper – *Qaumi Akhbar* – into the car my sister was driving. On the front page was my face, wearing an intense expression, and a slug in Urdu: "Murder attack on Nafisa."

Figure 5 Newspaper article of author after attack on September 23, 1991 (Photo by Asghar Bhatti).

Apparently, a creative reporter from the *Qaumi* newspaper had discovered that they had my photograph from the previous day's rally and called up my parents the night before to get the information for the report.

On the plane to Islamabad, I found myself sitting next to a European woman from a non-governmental organization. She had a copy of *Dawn* newspaper neatly folded her lap with the news item of the attacks on the press prominently displayed on the side. As we struck up a conversation, she told me with concern that she'd read that journalists were being attacked in Pakistan.

I turned the half folded newspaper over, and pointed to the news item entitled "*Dawn* woman reporter escapes attack," with the words, "That's me."

The look of surprise on my newfound acquaintance's face was unforgettable. Bolting upright in her seat, she drew sideways and looked at me closely. We talked about what it was like to undertake investigative reporting in Pakistan until the plane landed in Islamabad two-and-a-half hours later.

"It was the Best of Times, it was the Worst of Times"

As I recuperated from the shock of the knife attack in Islamabad – Pakistan's capital city, framed by the Margalla hills – I gained a fresh perspective on the political situation in the country.

With its quiet, well-planned roads and foreign embassies sprawling amidst lush greenery, Islamabad was a far cry from the volatile city of Karachi. It was here that the parliament had tightened the screws on the Sindh administration – a move that had contributed to the attack on my person.

To borrow a phrase from English novelist Charles Dickens, "It was the best of times, it was the worst of times." Although Benazir had not even begun any land reforms, the prospect of her unleashing the power of the people had led the establishment to intimidate independent journalists.

The chief minister of Sindh, Jam Sadiq Ali began to exert his influence over the press, offering incentives to journalists for being sympathetic to the administration whilst punishing those who did not comply with the government's policy of vilifying Benazir Bhutto, her husband, Asif Zardari, and other PPP loyalists. He began with the carrot approach.

Even as a provincial minister under Prime Minister Zulfikar Ali Bhutto in the 1970s, Jam was reputed to be generous with state funds. It was rumored that, at one time – when Bhutto and Jam drove around the mausoleum of Pakistan's founder, Mohammed Ali Jinnah – the prime minister had leaned over and whispered, "Jam – at least don't sell off land around the mausoleum."

So, when journalists received an invitation from the chief minister to have lunch with him at the CM House, we joked half-seriously that the administration might try to buy our loyalties with plots of government land.

I had never seen Jam at close range. As he walked by unsteadily, I felt an odd repulsion. Perhaps it was the way he eyed the women dressed in flowery *shalwar kameez*, dyed with bright splashes of summer color. As his gaze rested on me, I saw him flinch. He saw my skeptical expression as he sized me up.

The chief minister's aides stood by dutifully as Jam handed me a beautifully wrapped package. I took the gift in the spirit of Sindhi hospitality. Of course, they were not the papers for a government plot of land we had joked about. Instead, afterwards we found we'd received expensive fabric woven with brilliant rainbow threads – likely to be used as a sofa cover or bedspread.

There was nothing unusual about Jam Sadiq Ali offering the carrot to journalists. This is how political parties and organized groups in Pakistan interact with the media. Those who host lunches or give presents obviously mean to tilt the news in their favor. Indeed, in the open and hospitable Pakistani culture, there is a fine line between being gracious and offering bribes. Mentally, I made the distinction. Although I accepted these gifts, they never stopped me from being critical.

Benazir Bhutto relied much more on the carrot than did Nawaz Sharif. She had left her gregarious husband, Asif Zardari – well built with a moustache, flashing white teeth and a vibrant, hearty laugh – to ooze charm on journalists.

I first met Asif Zardari in early 1992 when he was brought as an accused to the Special Courts in Karachi. As my colleague – journalist, Mazhar Abbas – introduced me, I was struck by the grin that Zardari wore, even under such difficult circumstances. He told me that whilst in prison, he had followed the uproar about the attack on me in the newspapers.

Accustomed to Benazir's formal personality, I was thrown off guard as he gushed: "Where have you been all this time? How come it's taken you all this time to discover my good looks?"

I had heard stories about Zardari's ways with women and took it in good humor. He exuded an energy and affability that had earned him the title "a friend of friends." Even when I visited him in prison, where he showed me marks of torture on his tongue, he seemed in control and able to manipulate the situation in his favor.

But while Zardari's hobnobbing with journalists may have wiped some of the sting, he could not stop the criticism he faced in the open press. His penchant for taking kick backs from business entrepreneurs had earned him the nick name, "Mr Ten Per cent," a reputation that stuck as hard as his last name. The English language press cleverly used Asif Zardari's first and last initials to coin the inimitable term "A to Z is corrupt" – meaning that everyone is corrupt in Pakistan.

Even while Benazir was alive, she couldn't defend Asif from media criticism. Then, as I wrote critical reports about the PPP in *Dawn*, her spokespersons – and at times even Benazir personally – defended her party.

On the other hand, Prime Minister Nawaz Sharif ensured good publicity through his "helicopter group" of pet photographers and embedded journalists. In 1992, when floods hit Sindh, Sharif was provided photo opportunities of him wading knee-deep in waters to publicize his "love" for the affected villagers.

It was under Sharif that the term "envelope journalism" was coined with reference to the wads of rupee notes that his party, the Pakistan Muslim League (N – "Nawaz") reportedly doled out to journalists at their press conferences. My contacts in Lahore told me this was a Punjab-based strategy, from whence Sharif drew his power.

1991: A Year of Living Dangerously

Unfortunately for the military and their protégé, Nawaz Sharif, 1991 was a period of glasnost for the press. Gen. Zia ul Haq's plane crash had ended the era of flogging and imprisonment of journalists and left them in a combative mood. As the media restrictions eased, a glut of cheap Urdu, Sindhi and English newspapers flooded the market and their circulation stabilized according to the forces of supply and demand.

In this back drop, Chief Minister Jam Sadiq Ali rode against the current when he used the parliament to abuse the former woman prime minister, her husband and their party. Asif Zardari – who rose to become Pakistan's president – was Jam's favorite whipping boy during the 1990s. The chief minister also used colorful language against Benazir's party men, painting them as twits and minions and slandering them by name to make them lose face before the public.

For me, it became an art form to recreate the drama enacted in the Sindh Assembly between the Jam government and the PPP opposition leaders. My coverage of the PPP leader of the opposition in the Sindh Assembly, Nisar Ahmed Khuhro – with his darting eyes and quick wit – appeared each morning on the front pages of *Dawn*. Being a faithful narration of parliamentary proceedings, the Sindh Press Information Department could hardly refute my reports. Unfortunately for Jam, his vitriolic rambling and Khuhro's eloquence would only raise the PPP's esteem nationwide.

At the same time, I used my position as an independent journalist to go behind the scenes and investigate the reign of terror that the Jam government had unleashed in interior Sindh.

My colleagues in the Urdu and Sindhi newspapers envied the fact that we in the English language newspapers enjoyed an uncensored freedom that was unimaginable in the vernacular press. English education is confined to the well-educated, mostly privileged class and it was this elite readership that was permitted to follow the nuances. That enabled English language editors and publishers to perform a dance with the government to get newsprint and advertising without sacrificing too much news coverage.

A newspaper colleague from an Urdu newspaper told me, by way of a backhanded compliment: "If what you write in English is translated into Urdu, it will drive people mad."

Taking advantage of my freedom, I zeroed in on the activities of the son-in-law of the President of Pakistan, Ghulam Ishaq Khan who then served as advisor to the chief minister. He was Irfanullah Marwat, the burly muscle man responsible for the knitty gritty directives issued to the Crime Investigation Agency (CIA) to kidnap Benazir's party men and force them to change their loyalties.

In early 1991, I was inside the Sindh Assembly covering the feisty PML (N)-PPP exchanges, when I heard that Marwat had smuggled a PPP member of parliament into his chamber. It raised a red flag among us journalists: We suspected that Benazir's party man was about to be "broken" and forced to switch his loyalties to support Jam's PML (N) government. A colleague had already noted the number plate on Marwat's vehicle from whence the PPP member had emerged.

Together with my male journalist colleagues from the emerging rival newspaper, *The News* and Sindhi newspapers, we sped to the advisor's office – hoping to catch him red-handed. I took the lead and knocked on Marwat's office in the grand assembly quarters. The tall, hefty Pashtun came out and glared at us, arms akimbo.

I stood my ground: a young woman, surrounded by her male colleagues, confronting the suspected mastermind of criminal activities in Sindh. The president's son-in-law had been named by my sources as organizing the kidnapping of political opponents. Still, the backing from my influential newspaper and my journalist friends gave me courage. "We've heard that you've brought a PPP member to your chamber and want to check if he's inside," I told the advisor to the chief minister.

His look turned icy. Then, speaking to me directly, he took a step back and half closed the door of his chamber with the words, "You may not come in."

With my press colleagues around me, I responded with aplomb, "We will write that you stopped us from checking for ourselves."

"Don't threaten me *Bibi* [young woman]," Marwat snapped.

When Marwat confronted me, he didn't realize that my fellow journalists were listening. One of my colleagues from the rival *The News*, Abbas Nasir – who decades later became the editor of *Dawn* – had taken mental notes of my spirited exchange with the chief minister's advisor and ran with the story.

We became increasingly creative in exposing the shady activities of the Sindh government. The *Herald*, a slick English language monthly magazine and part of the *Dawn* group of newspapers – then led by a woman editor, Sherry Rehman – splashed an investigative report on the front cover on how the Criminal Investigation Agency (CIA) had kidnapped PPP loyalists to force them to change their loyalties.

As the *Herald* hit the newsstands and the educated elite began to buy the magazine, the Sindh government panicked. They signaled to the intelligence agencies to act. Suddenly, plainclothes police descended on the pavements of Karachi's main bazaar – Saddar – and began to remove the magazines. They also threatened hawkers, who furtively sold the magazine – with its daring, glossy front cover – to curious motorists.

I took even bigger risks whilst reporting. In those days, I visited the white, fortress-style Karachi Central Jail, which held Sindhi nationalist prisoners with secrets. In September 1991, some of these political prisoners, who were readers of *Dawn*, acknowledged me as a potential newspaper ally in fighting the Jam government.

On one such visit, the prisoners told me that Jam's advisor on home affairs, Irfanullah Marwat had offered to reduce their jail sentences if they agreed to become approvers in criminal cases against Benazir's husband, Asif Zardari. Zardari was already being prosecuted in the Special Court for Suppression of Terrorist Activities, set up under Nawaz Sharif. However, these sorts of political cases were routinely dismissed due to lack of evidence and the army-backed Sharif government sought new and more creative ways to convict him.

Once I had the story, with the names of the prisoners who had offered the information, the desire to expose the officials got into my blood. I convinced my city editor, Akhtar Payami to run with the story.

In September 1991, *Dawn* ran my investigative report with a single column headline on the back page: "Prisoners offered remissions to become approvers against Zardari."

As my mother read the by-line on the news report, she murmured with her usual maternal concern, "I hope they don't hurt you."

By then, I was already too deeply involved in investigating the Sindh government to worry about the consequences. In those heady days – stopping for lunch at the Karachi Press Club – I heard stories from my journalist colleagues about reporters and photographers from interior Sindh who had been threatened, roughed and their newspaper offices ransacked for reporting the Sharif government's excesses against the PPP. It only raised my adrenalin and made me determined to fight back.

Only days after *Dawn* published my report on the prisoners, knife-wielding thugs were sent to jolt me into realizing my mortality and the price of keeping the press free.

The Press Fights Back

1991 will go down as the year that the Pakistani press united to stop further attacks on journalists. Several had been attacked before us, but the assaults on me and Kamran started a fire.

There was a reason for it. Kamran worked for the *Jang* group of newspapers, while I was reporter for the *Dawn* group of newspapers – the two biggest publishing houses, which combined owned about half the effective print publications in the country at the time. Their tycoon owner-publishers, the Mir Shakilur Rehman and Haroon families were represented in the highest newspaper bodies – All Pakistan Newspaper Society (APNS) and the Council of Newspaper Editors and Publishers (CPNE) – which wield a huge influence on Pakistan's governments.

The week after I was threatened with knives, the Pakistan Federal Union of Journalists (PFUJ) and the All Pakistan

Newspaper Employees Confederation (APNEC) energized journalist protests in rallies and demonstrations held across Pakistan. PFUJ and APNEC serve as the backbone of the journalist industry and their activism under the harsh dictatorship of Gen. Zia ul Haq yielded dividends in keeping the media free.

The military-backed Nawaz Sharif's government refused to accept responsibility for the attacks on journalists. Between April 26 and October 24, 1991, the US-based Committee to Protect Journalists (CPJ) sent four letters to Sharif, protesting against the mounting attacks on the press. They were met with stony silence.

It was left to my journalist colleagues to fight for press freedom. In the aftermath of the attacks on me and Kamran, journalists walked out of the assembly in the four provinces of Pakistan – Sindh, Punjab, Balochistan and Northwest Frontier Province – and forced the assemblies to condemn the attacks on the press. Each day, the newspapers appeared chock-full of statements by politicians, human rights groups, labor leaders, women and civil society to condemn the Sindh government and demand the arrest of our attackers.

From my sanctuary in Islamabad, my mother told me the phone at our Karachi home rang off the hook. Government officials, politicians, journalists and, of course, friends called to ask about my welfare. Embarrassed by the negative publicity they received, officials in Jam Sadiq Ali's cabinet offered to appoint police officials to a security post they proposed to build across from my house. It was like asking the fox to guard the chicken coop. I rejected their offer.

Knives Were Used to Send a Message

As I lay low in Islamabad, Benazir Bhutto issued a statement from overseas which squarely blamed the federal and Sindh government for the attacks on me and Kamran that read:

"Both journalists have a distinguished record of investigative journalism, which includes an expose of the MQM and the criminal activities being conducted at the CIA headquarters. There is no doubt that these attacks have been coordinated by the Jam Government on the instructions of Nawaz Sharif and Ghulam Ishaq Khan."

It was a fair indictment of the perpetrators, except that it cast doubt on the MQM's role in the attacks. Although the ethnic party used to dictate news coverage, threaten hawkers and burn newspapers considered to be unfriendly, by the fall of 1991 they were themselves victims of the army's "Operation Clean-up." As such, they were not in a position to conduct the attacks.

The MQM chief, Altaf Hussein – who had fled to London earlier that year after the army tried to divide his party – attempted to clarify the perception that his party was involved. In his press statement of September 27, 1991, Altaf said:

"We too differ with some of the media contents, but we go to the people and ask them to stop reading a particular paper. The MQM has never attacked any newspaper office or resorted to such things."

I took the MQM statement with a handful of salt. At that moment, however, I recognized that I had grown entangled in the war between the intelligence agencies.

Back then, the MI – which is the political wing of the military and which also provided me and Kamran with information – was apparently at odds with the techniques used by the ISI and the IB in arm-twisting the PPP's political opponents. The IB's chief, Brig Imtiaz Ahmed – whose agency snooped around to guess which journalists could expose their tactics – had put us on its "hit list," with a directive to the local Crime Investigation Agency to ensure that we did not interfere in their mafia operations.

An Historic Protest

Five days had passed and I watched the national outcry against the knife attacks from my brother, Pervez's place in Islamabad. That weekend, Pervez's colleague at the Quaid-i-Azam

University, Dr A. H. Nayyar arrived, carrying heavy editions of the newspapers. Dr Nayyar – a nuclear physicist, like my brother – was hugely invested in the political situation inside Pakistan and had a wry sense of humor.

Apparently tired from the weight of the weekend editions of the English and Urdu newspapers he had been carrying, Nayyar plunked them on the table in front of us and flopped down himself.

"What's the news?" my brother Pervez asked.

"Nothing," Nayyar replied wearily. "They're full of statements on Nafisa."

I went through the newspapers. Statements were splashed across every newspaper by political parties, journalist unions, women's organizations, minority groups and human rights groups. In several instances, they named the influential culprits and demanded punishment for the attacks on me and my colleague.

Even while the federal government assured our employers and the journalist unions that our attackers would be caught and punished, we knew that nothing of the sort would happen. The matter of free press was inextricably linked with the polarized politics in Sindh and could not be resolved short of dismissing the Sindh government. The newspaper bodies correctly surmised that the media would suffer unless we demonstrated a collective show of strength.

And so newspapers, magazines and periodicals announced they planned to suspend publication on September 29, 1991. It was an unprecedented event, designed to halt 25 million copies for one day in order to protest against the attacks on journalists. The journalist community declared that, as a mark of protest, no reporter would attend or cover the government functions on that day – a Sunday.

On the day of the press shutdown, my journalist colleagues from *The News* took me to the home of their editor, Maleeha Lodhi. Lodhi would later serve as Pakistan's ambassador to the US under Benazir Bhutto and then Pervaiz Musharraf. Maleeha looked at me searchingly and said, "You know, Kamran is associated with the intelligence agencies. But with you we know there is no such association."

A journalist friend of mine, Ayoub Shaikh had once asked me, eyes twinkling, "I sometimes wonder, who does Nafisa work for?"

"No one," I had said, "I work for myself."

"I know," he had said, smiling.

On the day of the strike, the Rawalpindi Union of Journalists organized a national event in Rawalpindi – Islamabad's twin city – which was addressed by media stalwarts such as the president of the All Pakistan Newspaper Society, Farhad Zaidi, veteran journalist turned politician, Mushahid Hussain, *The News* editor, Maleeha Lodhi, senior editors and representatives of journalist unions.

I spoke in a highly charged manner, fired up by my close encounter. Mostly, I told journalists in Islamabad about the incredibly polarized political situation in my southern home province of Sindh. "If we do not stand together, I am afraid that a journalist may be killed any day now," I said. It was a speech

Figure 6 Karachi journalists protest attack against press on September 30, 1991 (*Dawn* photo).

made from the heart and it appeared in the press on October 1, when the newspapers went back into circulation.

A Pakistan Television team was on hand to film the rally at Rawalpindi Press Club. I was surprised to see them, wondering how the government had allowed them to film the protest. Later, watching the video footage of the nationwide protests in the districts, towns and cities – and an impressive march in Karachi from whence the attacks had emanated – it was evident that Prime Minister Nawaz Sharif was not entirely in charge.

What Price for a Free Press?

I came back to Karachi, energized by the uproar in the newspapers. The ripple effects continued as column writers marveled at how the entire journalistic community had put aside its differences and united for a common cause. The newspaper industry had successfully communicated its message to the government. The attacks on journalists ended, giving me renewed courage to return to reporting.

I discovered a strange notoriety in the furor that had been caused by the attacks. Soon after the incident, as my father drove home he was confronted by the police. A traffic light was changing from orange to red when my father had passed through and the constable signaled my father to stop.

Traffic violations are extremely common in Karachi but when a police officer finally catches up with a motorist, the music begins. As my father stopped his car the policeman sauntered over, opened the side door and slid into the back. That, everyone in Pakistan knows, is the prelude to taking a bribe.

My father mischievously exploited the situation.

"Do you know who I am?" he asked the policeman.

"No" the cop replied with some trepidation.

"I am Hoodbhoy, father of Nafisa… you know the reporter from *Dawn* who was attacked recently."

The policeman was impressed but decided to check out the facts. I was at home for lunch during my reporting assignments when I got a phone call from the police official, who had decided to check out my identity. When I confirmed who I was, he named the person with him, saying, "He claims he's your father. Should I let him go?"

I could just see my father, with his sense of fun, testing out the policeman. Embarrassed, I demanded he be released at once. A short while later my father walked in chuckling, saying the policeman had apologized profusely for the inconvenience!

Exchanging Places With Daniel Pearl

A decade after my knife attack, *Wall Street Journal* reporter, Daniel Pearl went missing in Karachi. He was on perhaps the world's most dangerous assignment. The wounds from US retaliation against 9/11 plotters – who had been traced to Afghanistan – were raw when Pearl arrived in Pakistan to investigate Al Qaeda militants' links to the military and multiple affiliated intelligence agencies.

I felt like I had traded places with Pearl. In 2002, I taught in Western Massachusetts, where Pearl had worked as a reporter in the 1980s. While I lived in his neck of the woods, the *WSJ* reporter arrived in Karachi to probe the Al Qaeda network, talking to some of my contacts in the city about how militants had regrouped to escape US bombardment in Afghanistan.

In a nation where the sentiment is (at best) moderately anti-US, Pearl's timing couldn't have been worse. In a Karachi, fast evacuated by foreigners, he stood out as an American and a Jew. Whilst the military ostensibly sided with the US, journalists who sought to reveal its covert ties with militants were treated like spies. It did not surprise me, therefore, when Pearl's kidnapping provoked former President Gen. Pervaiz Musharraf to express irritation at the "undue interference" in the nation's internal affairs.

Local reporters too watched Pearl's brief foray into Pakistan with skepticism. My colleagues in Karachi knew he had gone missing but did not leap into action. Just as Pearl went missing, a former newspaper colleague of mine was picked up as he investigated the shady links of a mafia don linked to the December 2001 attack on the Indian parliament in New Dehli. As journalists built up pressure, he was released but remained uncharacteristically silent.

Although the Bush administration's invasion of Afghanistan in October 2001 brought thousands of journalists to Pakistan's border areas, Pearl paid the ultimate price for leaving the pack. After Pearl was revealed to have been killed, I met the last person he had contacted in Karachi prior to his disappearance: former chief of the Citizens Police Liaison Committee (CPLC), Jameel Yusuf.

The CPLC chief, who often gave me scoops on political crime, told me that he had briefed Pearl about Al Qaeda's affiliations with terrorist networks in Pakistan. However, Yusuf says that Pearl did not divulge anything about his mission in Pakistan. With his Sherlock Holmes instincts, the CPLC chief noticed that Pearl's cell phone rang twice while he was in his office. But the intrepid reporter did not mention who called and left, saying he had an appointment.

The CPLC's recovery of Pearl's cell phone and perusal of his phone bills would enable them to trace his kidnapping to a British-born militant of Pakistani origin, Ahmed Omar Saeed Sheikh. Sheikh was allegedly partnered with the sectarian Sipah Sahaba Pakistan and the Lashkar-i-Jhangvi – franchise groups linked to Al Qaeda, which had recently been forced out of Afghanistan.

Under Western pressure, Pearl's alleged kidnapper, Omar Sheikh was arrested as he took refuge with a former Musharraf associate and former ISI official, Brig. Ejaz Shah, who then worked as Punjab Home Secretary. As the highly-connected Sheikh's case came up for trial, the CPLC chief was threatened against testifying. Yusuf told me that Pearl's case had forced him to adopt extra security.

"For the first time, I have been going around with an armed back-up," he said in a voice that typically grew low when he became fierce and resolute.

Pearl Becomes a Player in Media Politics

In this environment where Western journalists could ill afford to take risks, Pakistan's print journalists bravely dug in murky waters. Kamran Khan – who had escaped a knife attack along with me in 1991 – wrote an article in *The News* which linked the prime suspect behind Pearl's kidnapping, Omar Shaikh with the Islamic militants who had attacked the Indian parliament in New Dehli in December 2001.

The Musharraf government reacted angrily to the article – which hinted at the ISI's involvement in Pearl's kidnapping – and stopped all advertisement of the newspaper. *The News'* editor, Shaheen Sehbai was asked by the government to fire four journalists who were suspected as "trouble makers." When Sehbai asked the publisher of the paper, Mir Shakil ur Rehman, *who* wanted to fire him, he was told to see ISI officials.

The international uproar that followed Pearl's murder led Musharraf's administration to pass the "Defamation Ordinance" which imposed a fine of PKR 50,000 (almost USD 900) and a three-month prison sentence for "libel." For journalists who earned a pittance and had no security from their newspaper bodies, the amount was a powerful deterrent against investigative reporting in areas where the military ostensibly carried on its anti-terror operations.

While Musharraf ruled within the US sphere of influence, my forays into the border areas of Afghanistan led me to discover how journalists were alternately threatened and abducted and had their homes bombed and families harmed as they attempted to sift fact from fiction in Pakistan's ostensible "War on Terror." That post-9/11 period would be the most trying for journalists – caught between Taliban militants and security agencies.

In December 2005, when the eighth reporter, Hayatullah Khan went missing from the Waziristan tribal area, alarm bells sounded throughout the journalist community. The Taliban denied they had abducted him. Musharraf's media spokespersons, too, claimed ignorance about his whereabouts. Still, the pains they took to convince me that the disappeared journalist was a "terrorist," and the level of detail they possessed about the missing journalist struck me as highly suspicious.

Six months later, Hayatullah's family got a telephone call from a Major Kamal, who tersely informed them that the missing journalist's body had been dumped in Miranshah, North Waziristan. The family discovered Hayatullah had been shot at close range, with his hands still tied in military handcuffs.

Although the 2001 US invasion of Afghanistan called for credible reporting, the Musharraf government strongly discouraged journalists from their professional activities. Foreign journalists found at the Afghan-Pakistani border were shipped back to their host countries while their fixers were taken aside, interrogated and imprisoned. Journalists caught near US air bases were charged under the "Official Secrecy Act" and produced in court only after their disappearances were challenged by the professional media organizations.

Pakistan's Minister for Information and Broadcasting, Shaikh Rasheed – known for his crude, plain speaking – told me that journalists were stopped from investigating the border areas between Pakistan and Afghanistan "because their findings are often at variance with the government."

With the military left as the sole spokesman for Pakistan, the foreign media got contradictory reports about the effect of US missile attacks. A classic case occurred in January 2006 when the military claimed that a missile attack in Bajaur had killed the son-in-law of Al Qaeda's spokesman, Ayman Zawahiri. This was contradicted by then Prime Minister Shaukat Aziz, who was in turn contradicted by President Musharraf.

Even as the foreign media relied on military spokespersons for their news stories, Peshawar based journalist and well-known expert on the Taliban, Rahimullah Yusufzai told me that the *New York Times* report that Zawahiri's son-in-law was killed was floated by Pakistan's intelligence agencies without conducting the necessary DNA tests.

In an attempt to give his side of events, Musharraf's media team used the Pakistan Electronic Media Regulatory Authority or PEMRA (enacted through an ordinance in 2002), to block the media's coverage of public opposition to his rule. Cable operators were warned against beaming channels which covered anti-Musharraf rallies, failing which, their licenses could be revoked. Predictably, the axe fell on channels that depicted the humongous crowds that galvanized around the Supreme Court chief justice he had ousted, Iftikhar Chaudhry.

President Musharraf met his Waterloo as the feisty broadcast media joined civil society to battle the emergency he imposed in Nov 3, 2007. It was an all-out battle by the media and one with high economic stakes, as television channels, *GEO*, *Aaj TV* and *ARY* lost millions in advertising revenue. Thereafter, the Pakistan Broadcasters Association, the Association of Television Journalists and its parent organization, Pakistan Federal Union of Journalists mounted a successful campaign to restore censored programs and show hosts who had been banned, all of which helped to end the emergency

A Brave New Media

Almost two decades after the attack on my person, the media landscape in Pakistan has transformed. Not only has the rocky path toward democracy taught politicians and journalists a few lessons, but also the nation embraces a vibrant electronic media.

Today, as Pakistan's experienced print journalists take over the reins of private television and radio channels, the public is exposed to riveting news and current affairs. International television and radio, beamed in by satellite, have added their voices to the medley. It has transformed Pakistan's media into a major revenue-generating industry where the electronic media dominates the marketplace discourse.

For the most part, the PPP government has left the media free. That has also opened it up for criticism, as commercialism drives raucous programming. The print and electronic media has engaged in mudslinging and personal attacks – including poking fun at President Zardari. They join the global networks – the Internet, *YouTube*, blogging and texting – that provide unprecedented freedom for Zardari's opponents.

In his early days, President Zardari walked in the shoes of his military predecessor as he barred television channels from filming crowds clamoring for the reinstatement of the chief justice. The move did not sit well with the PPP's liberal leadership. PPP's Federal Information Minister Sherry Rehman had as the editor of *Herald* in 1991 resisted the crackdown on the media. She was the first to register her dissent by resigning from her official position.

Overall, PPP Prime Minister Yusuf Raza Gilani has resisted invoking the PEMRA ordinance against news channels, which thrive on sensationalism and unbalanced reporting. Instead, the government has suggested the media monitor itself through a "Code of Ethics" – meaning that it should avoid images or material that may "endanger national security or offend viewer sensitivities."

Although the numbers of journalists detained and interrogated by the security agencies have dropped, a growing number of these incidents now occur in the volatile Balochistan province. In such instances, the PPP government becomes a bystander. The task of protecting these journalists falls to Pakistan's thriving journalist federations, which receive support from international groups working for the freedom of the media.

With Pakistan's border areas in the grip of an insurgency, reporting from the tribal Pak-Afghan border is among the most dangerous professions in the world. Taliban militants do not hesitate to kill journalists perceived as pro-government or leaning toward a rival faction. In these border areas, where cell phones are barred and traveling is dangerous, there is little access to information. That has effectively ended independent reporting and instead led to the concept of "embedded journalists," – whether they embed with the army or the Taliban.

It is in this brave new world that journalists are engaged in a new dance with the three forces that control Pakistan's destiny – the US, Pakistan's army and its elected government. The PPP government – itself in the US orbit of influence – desperately needs better coverage, but also knows the consequences of taking on a combative media.

Decades of experience under dictatorship and civilian rule has taught Pakistan's journalists to preserve the freedom that makes them among the better-informed and more powerful media organizations in the region.

PART II

Human Rights

Chapter 4

WHERE HAVE ALL THE WOMEN GONE?

"Cry Rape to Get a Visa to Canada"

> You must understand the environment in Pakistan. This [Rape] has become a moneymaking concern. A lot of people say if you want to go abroad and get a visa for Canada or citizenship and be a millionaire, get yourself raped.
> (President Gen. Pervez Musharraf in an interview with *The Washington Post*, September 13, 2005)

The Pakistan's military ruler's off-color remarks, uttered during his official visit to the United States in September 2005, infuriated many women and men around the world. Their response appeared to puzzle the President. The point, he told a gathering of women who came to hear him at the Roosevelt Hotel in New York, was that Pakistan was being unfairly singled out, even though rapes occurred all over the globe.

Brandishing a copy of an Indian newspaper, he said there were examples of several rapes in India in its pages, adding – in the same breath and without a trace of irony – that this was not a time for "point scoring."

To Pakistan's general, who faced the onerous task of leading the nation after his military coup of October 1999, the prosecution of rapists appeared to have little bearing on women's rights and everything to do with politics. Indeed, the "Zina Ordinances (Enforcement of Hudood)" – which were passed by Gen. Zia ul Haq in 1979 – had, over the years, grown politicized after Islamic parties discounted women's testimony in rape and instead required evidence from "four Muslim male adult eye-witnesses of pious character" to award a conviction.

The Hudood Ordinances were passed by Gen. Zia, only two years after he rode on the crest of the Pakistan National Alliance movement, led by Islamic parties, and ousted Prime Minister Zulfikar Ali Bhutto in a military coup on July 5, 1977.

Under the Hudood laws, punishment was meted out like amputations for theft and flogging for drinking. The uproar from civil society forced these to fizzle out. Women became the most affected by the implementation of the Zina Ordinances, which imprisoned hundreds of them after the courts refused to accept their testimony in rape.

Although late Prime Minister Benazir Bhutto – who rode a wave of populist support in 1988 – referred to Nawaz Sharif as a "remnant of the Zia regime," she too was loath to touch an issue that divided the Islamists from the secular lobby.

In the post 9/11 period when Pakistan was back in the orbit of US influence, the State Department had faulted the Zina Ordinance in its 2005 Human Rights Report. Just before his US visit, Musharraf tried to win American approval by moving a Women's Protection Bill in the National Assembly that rape be punished under secular rather than Islamic law. Pressure from the Islamic opposition in the National Assembly led him to further water down the amendment.

A number of women's groups, which demanded the outright repeal of the Hudood Ordinances, cite the Women's Protection

Act passed under Gen. Musharraf as a hotchpotch of laws. The Act retains the standards for evidence laid down by the Zina law, even though it allows for verification of rape by DNA tests and other secular standards.

In September 2005, as an audience of disillusioned women took Musharraf on for his comments on rape victims in the *Washington Post*, he backtracked. "These were just side remarks, which are not to be taken seriously," he told the Pakistani audience and their US allies. But as the crowd kept hooting, the general shifted gears and began shadow boxing the perceived enemies of Pakistan: "If you can shout, I can shout louder."

The Nurses Rape Case

In 1989, I came face to face with the impact of the Zina Ordinance on women. On a routine visit to the hospital, I learnt that two nurses were raped inside the paying ward of the hospital. One of the paramedics, who sometimes tipped me off with inside stories, came to my newspaper with the seamy details.

The story fairly sizzled: two nurses had been raped at gunpoint as they left the elite ward. A senior medical student from the affiliated Dow Medical College and his male colleagues had grabbed them, clapped a hand over their mouths and raped them at gunpoint on the empty hospital beds.

It was the type of issue I had waited to sink my teeth into. I was in my twenties when I returned from the US, filled with indignation at the way women were treated in Pakistan. That would let me see the story rather differently from my male colleagues, who had an average age of 50 years and whose hands were full covering daily news outbreaks.

The case grew in the media because the senior nurse, Farhat Sadiq – a dark, plump Christian woman from a community of sweepers – took heart from women's support and spoke out against her rapist. Although her younger nursing colleague avoided the press, Farhat seemed to think it would help her case to have it publicized.

Barely whispering, she told me how the armed young men had forced the two nurses on the beds as they held guns to their heads. "First one and then the other did it with me," she told me, eyes downcast and in a voice that trembled with shame.

It was a bold move, given that the odds were heavily stacked against women. Even worse – in a hierarchical society like Pakistan, with its separate laws for women and non-Muslims – the victim was a Christian woman from the poorest community.

Fleshing out the drama in my staid, black and white newspaper, *Dawn*, I found myself in the eye of the storm. I wrote boldly in a society where the news was both male-dominated and rigidly controlled. The Zina Ordinance passed under Gen. Zia had manifested macabre results; with a woman's own testimony inadmissible in rape cases, judges equated rape with adultery and punished the rape victims instead. It naturally prevented women from reporting rape.

Even then, there were some encouraging trends. The Women's Action Forum was created by urban, professional women to protest against the outrageous punishments meted out to women victims. The War against Rape, comprised of women and men, followed suit, campaigning to break the silence on rape.

As a woman reporter, I took a different track from the one traditionally used by the male-dominated press. Instead of falling back on sensationalist media practice of publishing the names and details of women victims of rape, I turned the spotlight on the accused. Witnesses told me that the accused, Khalid Rehman and his gang came from a relatively privileged background; as such, I knew they could easily buy their way out of punishment.

The Women's Action Forum invited me to accompany them as they took the rape victim to a police station to file a First Information Report (FIR). It was dusk when we arrived at the rather dingy police quarters near Civil Hospital. Surrounded by women the nurse Farhat Sadiq, her head covered, looked ashamed but still comforted by the presence of supporters. The policemen looked incredulously at the women from privileged backgrounds spread out in their quarters, who insisted that police register a crime report against a well-off medical student.

The scene would have been comic but for the circumstances. Sitting at his wooden desk, under a dim light bulb, the sub-inspector shuffled his papers, sighed and looked from one charged activist to the other. He was trying to discourage the women from filing a police report. He knew that the accused was well connected and could get him in trouble with a simple phone call to his superior officer.

But there I was: a journalist turned witness. Given my background from an influential newspaper, the women had brought me along to ensure that the police filed the FIR. If the policeman failed to file the crime report and I reported the fact in my newspaper, it could have cost the officer his job. The sub-inspector looked up at us, licked his finger and reluctantly began to pen down the charges.

In Pakistan, an FIR is the first step toward bringing an accused to trial. It would help me to formally build up the case against the alleged rapist and give me the first real taste of the media's power to influence society. I began to report every day on the nurse's rape. The effect of daily reporting had a snowball effect. Every day I got stacks of press releases from women and human rights groups, demanding that the accused be arrested.

It is the familiar recourse that civil society has taken in the violent and unjust environment in Pakistan. Given the absence of rule of law and a weak judiciary, civil society increasingly relies on the press to make itself heard. Indeed, if statements alone could bring change then – judging by the weight of the press releases that pour into newspaper offices – the nation should have transformed by now.

Aware that press statements alone could not change society, the Women's Action Forum mobilized a demonstration to protest the rapes and build pressure to arrest the accused. They invited women from an Islamic fundamentalist party, the Jamaat-i-Islami to join. It was a bold step given that it was the Jamaat that had pressured Gen. Zia to pass the Islamic laws, which in 1985 were indemnified to the constitution as the Eighth Amendment.

I went to cover the demonstration feeling elevated that the protests had spilled out of my staid black and white newspaper into the public arena. Police had cordoned off traffic on the congested M. A. Jinnah Road as women from different organizations, dressed in traditional *shalwar kameez* and *dupatta* (loose trousers with tunic and scarf), fanned out in the hot sun. Although privileged women shied away from the noisy overcrowded public places, they were out for a cause. With a dramatic flourish, they unfurled their banners in the sunlight that lighted up the dark exhaust fumes from passing vehicles.

Marching side-by-side with the elite Western-educated women were women from the Jamaat-i-Islami, dressed in black billowing veils with only their eyes peeping from underneath. Rape had united all women on a one-point agenda – arrest of the rapists. Like their secular compatriots, the Islamic women held banners and placards calling for the arrests of the rapists. For a while, all the women appeared to be united.

Suddenly, the secular Western educated women from Women's Action Forum pulled out placards and banners that called for the repeal of the Zina Ordinances. There were a few seconds of confused silence as the Jamaat-i-Islami women saw the posters

Figure 7 Women protest against religious fundamentalism on February 12, 2009 in Lahore (*Dawn* photo).

and then a cacophony of high-pitched female voices rose in protest. Banners and placards were folded by the veiled women, with a shrill protest that they were leaving. "We joined to demand punishment for the rapists, *not* for the repeal of the Islamic laws," the women said as they left in a huff.

It is the conflicting ideologies between secular and Islamic groups that have dogged the women's movement. The Islamic groups, which pushed for Islamization under Gen. Zia ul Haq's military rule in 1977, keep their distance from liberal, Western-educated women in Pakistan. They term such women "*maghrebzadah*" (westernized), believing that they have failed to grasp that Islam *liberates* women and treat secular women's organizations as fringe groups who do not grasp that Islam is the raison d'etre for Pakistan.

I had covered the press conferences of the Islamist women ideologues, where they appeared dressed in enveloping veils – revealing only their eyes or spectacles. My own *shalwar kameez*, without the enveloping *dupatta*, did not deter these Islamic women from approaching me. More than once they tried to persuade me, the unveiled "Westernized" woman reporter, to join their *jihad* to change society.

But despite shared goals of seeking a better society, I could not reconcile myself with these laws in a day and age when women's roles had changed globally. The Jamaat encompassed a "divine" ideology that ordained women's role predominantly as wife and homemaker. Indeed the Jamaat had been part of Gen. Zia's Majlis-i-Shoora (Consultative Council), which formulated a spate of women-related laws that were incorporated in the secular constitution framed under Prime Minister Zulfikar Ali Bhutto in 1973.

Apart from the Hudood Ordinances, the Zia government passed the "Laws of Evidence," under which two women's testimony is equal to one man in financial matters. This was coupled with "*Qisas* and *Diyat*" (Retribution and Blood Money), which fixed the "blood money" (compensation) for female victims of violence at half that of men. Sections of the *Qisas* laws deny women the right to abortion under any circumstances.

Back then, the departure of the *Jamaat* women from the demonstration convened by the Women's Action Forum left a shrinking number of women's organizations to keep up their lonely march for the repeal of the Hudood Ordinances.

A Young Man Flees the Moral Jury

In 1989, the nurses' rape case became an example of how hard women had to work in order to get a semblance of justice. As non-governmental organizations sent press releases to demand the arrest of the culprits, I painted a sketch of the kind of people who normally got away with crimes – simply because they were rich or powerful.

The incident resonated among members of civil society who sought justice for the most unprivileged. As women contacted human rights lawyers, the latter joined in the demand for the arrest of the accused. Under pressure, the police issued summons to the accused, Khalid Rehman, to appear in court and respond to the rape charges.

The hearing in the bail application of the alleged rapist took place in the District and Sessions Court in Karachi – an impressive British colonial-style stone building on Mohammed Ali Jinnah Road. Many of those who had arrived for the rape hearings had read about the case in newspapers. The courtroom quickly filled up with lawyers, women's rights activists and the press. Outside the court, the police stood waiting in full force.

The senior nurse, Farhat Sadiq arrived – her head covered and looking crestfallen. Accompanying her was her poor father, a Christian who worked as a low-paid sweeper. The Women's Action Forum, which agitated on various levels against Pakistan's controversial rape laws, had reached out to other non-governmental organizations to mobilize them for the case. Women occupied the front rows of the court and listened intently as the state prosecutor read the statement against the accused.

The accused, Khalid Rehman, stood nervously facing the judge, his back to the women. Their presence was akin to a moral jury. But just as the judge looked up from his pince-nez spectacles to speak, the accused dashed out of the courtroom. I was seated in the same row as the women's rights activists and this sudden flight by the accused startled all of us. Without thinking, we spontaneously ran out of the room after the young man, wondering if this was the end. And then, the tension turned to laughter.

The police, who waited in the dazzling sunlight outside, had caught the young man by the scruff of his neck. As newspaper photographers clicked away, the accused was dragged ignominiously before the judge, handcuffed and thrown into a van full of gleeful policemen. He was driven away in a police van and locked up.

Next day, there was pizzazz in the newspaper reports that a young man accused of rape had run away from a courtroom full of women. It had turned the tables for women, who, despite being rape victims, were the first to receive unwanted publicity.

But Rehman had spent only a few days in police lock-up before he was released on bail. Women rights activists racked their brains for ways to get him convicted. They consulted with prominent Islamic lawyers to secure punishment for him and his gang. To their dismay, they had come to a dead end.

The Zina Ordinances mandated that there should be "four Muslim, male adult eyewitnesses of pious character" to obtain a conviction. Being a woman and a non-Muslim, the nurse's evidence was inadmissible in court. Although the nurse's lawyer told the court that medical examination of the nurse showed a broken hymen, the judge said he had no way of knowing that it was not due to consensual sex.

The nurse's lawyer – an elderly man, hard of hearing – argued before the stony faced judge till he was blue in the face. He was being asked to do the impossible – defend a woman and non-Muslim under a law that did not hear them out. The situation took an absurd turn: the lawyer warned the rape victim that unless she claimed that the incident never happened, she would be imprisoned for having sex outside of marriage.

Alternately aghast and furious, the Women's Action Forum raced through the alternatives. But as the case dragged on, the nurse found herself in a quagmire. She finally took the advice of her lawyer and pleaded that the incident never happened.

After 2½ years, the case was quashed with the effort ultimately unsuccessful.

Breaking Out of the Veil and Four Walls

Gen. Zia ul Haq took power on July 5, 1977 with a series of pronouncements that were meant to satisfy the clamor of the Islamic lobby. Barely a few weeks after his take-over, the law enforcement agencies had begun to segregate men and women.

Pakistan was then only a young country of 30 years, when the official ideology that the nation was created as a separate homeland for Muslims was exploited by vested groups. The meagerly paid policemen too found purported Islamization to be a good way to embellish their earnings.

Shortly after Gen. Zia's military take-over, uniformed police descended on the sandy shores of Clifton beach and scoured it for unmarried couples. They swooped down on unsuspecting couples; took the sheepish male aside and threatened to lodge a case against him for abducting the girl under the Zina Ordinances. The couple would be let go after the police had pocketed a good-sized bribe.

In 1983, whilst still in the US, I read that a women's demonstration in Lahore had been baton-charged for protesting against the proposed "Laws of Evidence." Under Pakistan's current Laws of Evidence, two women are required to testify in financial matters in place of the testimony of one man. Muslim clerics have supported the law with their interpretation of a Quranic verse taken to mean that if one woman forgets, the other should be there to remind her.

With great indignation that I read that the women who protested against the law were mercilessly beaten by police and dragged away to the police stations. Thereafter, *fatwas* (Islamic pronouncements) were issued against these women "infidels" and their marriages were declared null and void.

Incidents like these made my heart race. I longed to jump into the fray and use my writing to make a difference. Unlike Pakistan's intellectual elites who had studied in British schools and to some extent integrated in the prosperous West, I wasn't particularly interested in walking on a well-trodden path. Then still in my twenties I saw myself as an actor in the wild uncharted course of politics in Pakistan, with which I felt organically connected. And so I took the less traveled road and returned home.

In February 1984, I applied for and was accepted as a reporter at *Dawn* newspaper. The "Reporter's Room", as the City Desk was then called, had no ventilation and the fans threw off stale air, leaving us dripping in sweat during the hot summer days. I was assigned a wooden desk with an antique typewriter that bordered the desks of senior male writers.

Being the only woman to report on city events was especially unique in an environment where Pakistan's rape laws had forced women out of public places. Gen. Zia's military government had already been in power for seven years and, with the help of Islamic fundamentalists, had worked to instill the fear of Allah in those who dared violate the rules. The state owned media had begun to equate women's mere presence outside the home with licentiousness and pornography. It had emboldened ordinary people to comment loudly on women who did not wear the *dupatta* over already modest clothing.

In this backdrop, my city editor, I. H. Burney took a special delight at sending me to all-male events. Looking at me – banging away at my rusty typewriter – he once thundered in his typically witty fashion: "Just as there is one God and one Prophet, there will always be only one woman reporter."

Often, when I arrived at a function where the speakers and reporter were male, it raised awkward questions. In the event that I occupied the press gallery, this resulted in a row full of empty seats next to me. The glances of my male colleagues told me that they were afraid that sitting next to a young woman in a period of strict Islamic military rule might get them into trouble for "dishonorable conduct."

Once at a Rotary Club function, I found myself the only female sitting across a table of men bunched together. As was the custom, a male guest speaker had delivered his keynote address in English. The speakers at the event were supposedly liberal and enlightened; I found myself wondering why there were no women in the audience. Then, a man – comfortably ensconced between his male buddies – leaned over and asked the inevitable question: "How do you feel being the only woman here?"

How did I feel? I turned it into a joke. It was a question that occasionally infuriated me. I knew the men waited for me to go home but I had no intention of quitting. I loved traveling, meeting new people, writing and trying to influence public opinion. People knew me as the woman reporter from *Dawn* who accepted dangerous assignments with zest – ethnic and sectarian riots, terrorist incidents, bomb blasts and shoot-outs between drug mafias.

Indeed, I had developed such a reputation for covering risky events that once, when my colleagues covered a bomb blast in a crowded marketplace in Karachi and my name was not among the joint by-lines on the front page, my colleague jested that he had been worried that I was killed in the blasts.

The more conservative men couldn't handle it, uncomfortably pretending that I didn't exist. I saw the frustration mount in a male colleague who supported an Islamic party. Time and again, he saw me, a young woman, drive up in my car to cover the shoot-outs, bomb blasts and ethnic riots that rocked Karachi. He just couldn't get over the fact that I seemed to be everywhere. Apparently, one day he just couldn't take it anymore. To my amusement, he bellowed right in my face: "Doesn't *Dawn* have any *men* left?"

Poorest Women are the Victims

Under Gen. Zia, the double standards ran deeper. Westernized elites paid lip service to Islam while retaining their privileged and often decadent lifestyles, drinking alcohol and attending wife-swapping clubs behind closed doors. That left the newly promulgated Islamic laws to reinforce customary practices that paralyze the weakest segments of society – namely poor, illiterate women.

Among the conservative rural communities, the customary laws were harsh enough to kill women for having sex outside marriage. Adding insult to injury, the Islamic law introduced in 1984 by Gen. Zia namely the "*Qisas* and *Diyat*" (Retribution and Blood Money) mandated that compensation for women victims of violence be fixed at half that of men. While honor killings trivialized the murders of women, *Qisas* and *Diyat* laws devalued their murders.

In 1992, a colleague tipped me, through police sources, about a harrowing story of a woman's infidelity that she paid for with her life. Traveling to the outskirts of Karachi, I alighted at a typical Pashtun home in Pakhtoonabad, Mangophir, built atop hard barren rocks, where the wind blew dust for miles around. These were the kinds of homes that the Pashtun tribes – many of them fresh arrivals from Afghanistan – had built at barren hilly elevations in Karachi.

Inside the humble home, an elderly light-skinned Afghan, Sattar Mandokhel sat with bowed head on his *charpai* (a knotted bed) – his remorseful blue eyes, lost in thought. The 70-year-old Mandokhel had just killed his 16-year-old wife for sneaking off in the middle of the night to meet his son from a previous wife. His son had given her away and actually helped Mandokhel kill her.

The police had registered a murder case against the two men. Still, the old man seemed indifferent to the prospect of punishment. Instead, his blue eyes had a faraway look in them – perhaps lamenting the loss of the young woman he had acquired. Maybe he loved her and had killed her in a fit of jealousy. Already, the fact that the men were at home instead of in prison spoke volumes about the level of punishment that they would receive. Family members comforted Mandokhel, telling him that he had done the right thing.

"This is the treatment that a woman gets if she is disloyal to her husband. These are our customs," an older woman in the household told me rather sternly. They saw me – a young woman scribbling on her notebook, suppressing her horror at the human tragedy that had unfolded.

There were hundreds of Pashtun-Afghan families like Mandokhel's. They had migrated from Afghanistan to the contiguous Khyber Pakhtunkhwa province in Pakistan and practiced customary laws like honor killings, even when they lived in urban settings. These murders are not unique to Pashtuns but rather, it is a practice under which thousands of women have been killed in Pakistan's tribal provinces for "dishonoring" the family.

In the wake of Islamization under Gen. Zia, society would become the larger prison for women. At family planning clinics, doctors told me that abortion was illegal under all circumstances. A clause in Gen. Zia's infamous *Qisas* and *Diyat* Ordinance further deemed that women could be imprisoned for seven years for having an abortion. This came to a nation with an already rapidly growing population – one in which the average woman bears six children and has one of the highest fertility rates in the world.

With abortion illegal, poor women either resorted to infanticide or simply disappeared after the child was born. Pakistan's veteran social worker, Abdus Sattar Edhi tried to clear the fallout from the anti-abortion laws by appealing against female infanticide. Edhi and his wife, Bilquis placed cribs in public hospitals where women victims of rape or those unable to get an abortion left their infants and disappeared. The veteran social worker placed the babies in orphanages, where if they were lucky they were adopted.

What Hope for Women?

In this darkness, the only star that glimmered on the horizon appeared to be the young, politically ambitious Benazir Bhutto. It was a time when Gen. Zia had leaned heavily on clerics to issue *fatwas* (Islamic pronouncements) against women's ability to rule. An Islamic advisor, Maulana Ansari suggested that Zia pass a law that no woman below 50 years of age could run for prime minister – and even then would need her husband's permission. Women's outcry stopped the proposal from reaching fruition but Benazir and her mother, Nusrat Bhutto were clearly on everyone's minds.

I first met Benazir Bhutto in 1986 at the Karachi Press Club (KPC) – where she had come to meet members of the press. A bevy of journalists surrounded her as she was taken to the upper floor of the building. The former president of KPC, the late Mahmood Ali Asad thrust me through the crowd to introduce me as the "active lady reporter from *Dawn*." Poised and dignified – a white silk *dupatta* around her hair – Benazir smiled graciously and made room next to her with the words: "Oh, I thought you were a school girl."

I was seated next to her and I worked to take advantage of it. I asked Benazir if she would give me an interview for *Dawn* on the Islamic fundamentalist laws relating to women. The Zina Ordinances had by then forced women to disappear from public spaces. As a woman who campaigned for the public post of prime minister, Benazir's position on the Islamist laws had not been publicized and I hoped to be able to do just that.

Benazir looked hard at me, indicating that she was weighing up the benefit of giving me an interview that would strike against the ruling Gen. Zia. In characteristic fashion, she threw me a counter question: "Can you write a paper detailing the laws that have been passed under Gen. Zia and their implications for women?"

The counter-offer took me by surprise. And yet, living with the effects of the discriminatory laws every day, I was happy to further her understanding of them. We parted with a common understanding that I would write a paper on the situation and she would give me an exclusive interview on the subject.

For the next several weeks I researched the Islamist laws at a little library in Karachi, set up by an academically-oriented women's organization called Shirkat Gah. It was the forerunner to the activist Women's Action Forum and War Against Rape – civil society organizations from a privileged class, which took enormous risks to protect the most vulnerable sections of society.

I had the document delivered to Benazir and received word from her party members that it was a "well researched piece." Still, three months went by and there was no word from the woman who went on to become prime minister.

Finally, out of the blue I got a phone call from 70 Clifton, Benazir's ancestral mansion in Karachi, saying that she wanted to see me. Armed with a tape recorder, I sped to her residence, ready to interview her. To my surprise, a handful of women activists were already there. Benazir had invited them to consult whether she should give me the interview.

It was 1986 and Benazir was still unmarried. That was apparently the stumbling block for the 33-year-old woman, who – notwithstanding her Western education – had roots in Larkana's feudal culture. "What will the Mullahs think about me, a single woman...talking about issues such as rape?" she quizzed us frankly.

I was perplexed. As privileged women, we knew that the Islamist laws were implemented in the harshest possible way on poor women. But I wondered if Benazir had thought about the irony of becoming the prime minister of a country where discriminatory laws would still treat her as a second-class citizen.

The Western-educated women – mostly from the Women's Action Forum – had long waited for the opportunity to turn around the situation for women. Knowing that Benazir stood a good chance of becoming Pakistan's first woman prime minister, they convinced her that the time was right for her to pledge her support for women's rights.

Apparently, our presence prevailed on Benazir. The next day, I got an urgent message from 70 Clifton that Benazir wanted to see me right away. Once again, I sped in my purple, soap-shaped car to her ancestral home. Benazir didn't need to be asked any questions. Instead, in an unstoppable monologue, she regurgitated the points I had provided in my paper.

The following day, July 11, 1986, *Dawn* published my 45-minute interview with the headline, "Benazir Decries Laws and Attitudes that Degrade Women." Benazir had praised her late father, Prime Minister Zulfikar Ali Bhutto for his role in the advancement of women's rights. Most importantly, she made a commitment that if elected as prime minister she would repeal the discriminatory laws passed by Gen. Zia ul Haq.

A Powerless Woman Prime Minister

My forays into interior Sindh – where nothing has moved for centuries – made me increasingly pessimistic that Benazir could effect change for women. Westerners can best understand the slow pace of life in traditional, rural Sindh as a throwback to thirteenth-century Christian Byzantine Europe, where women were veiled, house-bound and essentially considered as the property of men.

Living in the West, I was often asked how a woman from the traditional Muslim society could rise to become prime minister. The simple answer is that to the masses Benazir was the daughter of the populist Prime Minister Zulfikar Ali Bhutto, whose execution had transformed her into an "avenging angel." Also, as a woman from a privileged background, she skillfully used her connections inside and overseas to maneuver her place to the top.

Otherwise, the dark realities for rural women are even hidden from the nation's elite. In 1991, a male colleague and I headed to a small town in interior Sindh, where the peasants and low-income traders were spiritual disciples of feudals in Benazir's cabinet. We were escorted by guards through a magnificent fortress with high walls and cemented pathways, which wove into a labyrinth. My male colleague and I were taken into a grand drawing room with fine carpets and engraved tables.

The feudal lord greeted me pleasantly – the "honorary male" from a prominent newspaper. Afterwards, when we finished a frank, at times "off the record" type of conversation, he suggested I visit the women's quarters. Politely, I rose and was escorted by the servant to the women folk. My colleague stayed back; he was after all a *Na Mehram* – a man unrelated by blood to the women.

I walked through a maze that led up to the women's quarters. Wearing loosely draped *chador* (a type of veil), the women here lived in an age reminiscent of sixteenth-century Moghul India. Never exposed to the outside world, they did not have a lot to talk about. We exchanged pleasantries; I explained that I had come from Karachi to do a story. They did not know what it meant to be a journalist, nor did career prospects seem interesting to them.

When these women from feudal families went outdoors, they donned black veils with tiny holes for their eyes. Even so, it was the feudal lord who determined the liberties that the women of his family could avail; they were required to travel in chauffer-driven cars with black drapes, dress modestly at all times and under no circumstances speak to men outside the family.

I spent a night at this *haveli* (feudal home) living as the women did, with days and nights of solitude. At night, uniformed guards patrolled their ancient fortress. My ears picked up the changing of guards in the dead silence of the night. *"Allah Sain Khair"* (by God's grace), *"Maula Sain Khair"* (all is safe).

I left the fortress and continued traveling across interior Sindh. My freedom was in stark contrast to the lives of these women – creatures starved even of simple sensory impulses. The time I spent reporting in Sindh would inform me of the importance of the veil. By a process of osmosis, girls grew up to believe that their path to fulfillment lay in marriage and children.

In 1993, I attended a wedding in a small town in interior Sindh. It was a private event but my journalist's eye took mental snapshots. Women arrived in carefully designed, expensive *shalwar kameez* and *dupattas*, with matching jewelry and make-up – all designed to show their standing in the feudal hierarchy. Chaperoned by male relatives and wearing black veils, the women showed their faces only after they were exclusively surrounded by their own sex. Outside, volunteers stood guard to stop any peeping toms.

The carefully made-up women exposed adaptations of risqué dresses worn by foreign models that one saw on *CNN* and the Indian *ZEE* television channels. Captivated by the glamorous images of women, their female viewers copied the fashions in the privacy of their homes and exposed them to other women.

Apparently, the spread of cable television in the remote areas of rural Sindh had created all sorts of unfulfilled desires among the cloistered women. On one occasion, I sat with the young wife of a feudal lord as she watched cable television in a remote town of Sindh. Turning away momentarily from watching a Western film, she sighed wistfully: "It's very hard to be locked indoors after living in Karachi." Still, sensitive to small town gossip about who was a "good woman," she had never left the house alone.

In the rare case where a young woman from a small town joined a university or medical college, she would likely join the urban women's movement. Still, societal pressures on women to marry and have children were overwhelming. It left the women blissfully unaware that the military government had passed Islamic legislation that gave them an inferior status before the law.

Brides of the Quran

Journeying through interior Sindh, I stumbled upon large numbers of unmarried, graying women who lived in ancestral homes located in Hyderabad, Thatta, Matiari and Hala. Time hung heavy on their hands. Equipped with little education and no exposure to the outside world, these women had never been exposed to men in their lives.

In 1992, during a journalistic jaunt, I discovered a horrendous custom that kept these women housebound. Under Islamic law, women inherit property when they marry. But in the absence of male relatives, feudals in Sindh refuse to give daughters their inheritance. Instead, big feudals of Sindh and southern Punjab, who derive their power base from the land, prefer to keep their daughters unmarried.

In a more elaborate example of how feudals manipulate women's lives for financial gain, the Syed communities – who trace direct ancestry to Prophet Mohammed – have their daughters married off to the Muslim holy book, the Quran. That literally seals their prospects of marriage. Under this practice – called "*haq bakshna*" (waiver of rights), women place their hand on the Quran and waive the Islamic right to marry and inherit property. Even more ingeniously, they are told that their virginity gives them a spiritual status and a duty to dispense talismans to sick children.

The paradoxes were stunning. Feudal politicians took orders from a woman prime minister, Benazir Bhutto even as they kept their own women locked up or "married to the Quran." Some of them were superiors in her party and took orders from the woman prime minister to wield power in their own fiefdoms. The big feudals, who form the backbone of autocratic governments, have kept their control of women well-hidden from public view.

Women are Broken to Break Benazir

Benazir Bhutto's first year and a half in power flew without her taking on the issue of women. But what was truly shocking was that after she was ousted in August 1990, opponents exploited her vulnerability as a woman and used rape to humiliate her female supporters.

Early one morning in November 1991, I received word that a friend of Benazir Bhutto, Veena Hayat – the daughter of a feudal politician and one of the founders of Pakistan, Sardar Shaukat Hayat – had undergone a traumatic experience.

Driving up to Veena's home in Defense Society, I found her lying in bed, numb with shock and anger. Upper class and Western educated, Veena had lived alone – a rather rare occurrence in Pakistan's society. Surrounded by friends, she told me in a voice shaking with anger that five armed men had barged into her residence late at night. They had cut off her telephone connections and proceeded to torment and rape her all night, asking about her connections with Benazir Bhutto, Asif Zardari and other key PPP figures.

Veena's allegations made the headlines sizzle: she had blamed an advisor to the Sindh chief minister, Irfanullah Marwat who was also the son-in-law of Pakistan's president, Ghulam Ishaq Khan. Although a poor washerwoman with PPP affiliations, Khursheed Begum had also been raped at gunpoint by armed thugs at around the same time, the response to her rape had been relatively muted.

In a third incident aimed at demoralizing the Benazir camp, her opponents had tortured a woman office-bearer of the PPP's student wing, Rahila Tiwana. With Benazir seeking a return to power, her women supporters were now being singled out for rape.

In the aftermath of Veena's rape, press statements poured in calling for the arrest of the influential culprits. Veena's father, Sardar Shaukat Hayat made headlines as he stepped into the fray. A former associate of the founder of Pakistan, Mohammed Ali Jinnah – the victim's father – headed a *jirga* (a consultative assembly of male tribal elders) that demanded Marwat be punished. Upper-class women rallied around the Hayat family to demand an end to the use of rape as a political weapon.

Still, as in so many incidents, the well-connected accused were never brought to trial. Instead, coming after the attacks on journalists, the outrage at Veena Hayat's rape would become one more incident which eroded confidence in the Nawaz Sharif government and helped pave the way for Benazir Bhutto to return to power for a second term.

The Beijing Conference on Women

In 1993, women cheered as Benazir returned to power. For urban, professional educated women it was one more opportunity to win women's rights and repeal discriminatory laws. The more established women's organizations like All Pakistan Women's Association and the Federation of Business and Professional Women held city-wide events to express pride that Benazir had risen to the unique position of becoming the twice-elected woman prime minister of a Muslim country.

This time, Benazir tried to fulfill some promises by appointing women in top governmental positions. The move did not sit well with members of the civil service, who suddenly found themselves yanked aside by the PPP's political appointees. They complained that the positions had been doled out by Benazir to gain loyalty for her party rather than on the basis of merit.

The PPP's opportunity to bring change for women arose around the 1995 Fourth World Women Conference in Beijing. By then, my reputation as a reporter espousing women's rights was firmly established. Despite my critical reporting on the PPP government, I was invited to Islamabad to help prepare a National Report to recommend a Platform for Action in 13 key areas ear-marked by the United Nations.

The NATREP, as it was called, was to be presented to international delegates at Beijing. As the head of the "Women and Media" group, I spent weeks in Islamabad writing a chapter for NATREP with wide-ranging recommendations for women. Shortly thereafter, the PPP government nominated a few of us from the non-governmental sector to form part of their government delegation to Beijing.

At a personal level, it was wonderful to be in China – part of the 30,000 women who had arrived from all over the world to work for the advancement of women around the world. We were bused from our grandiose hotel to the splendid, towering site of the UN meeting.

As representatives of respective governments, we partook in the proceedings in a grand hall with microphones attached to our desks. These were lengthy legal agreements on which governments from different continents deliberated and which took into consideration the religions and cultures of participating nations.

Privately, the male leader of our delegation, Masood Khan – then a UN representative in New York – had forewarned us against making interventions, saying he would do most of the talking. Still, as the global body debated on the plight of poor women, my companion, Tahira Mazhar Ali Khan – a senior women's rights activist from Pakistan – took the microphone and spoke passionately on how the world needed to reduce defense spending to better serve women.

It was nothing I could disagree with. But the outburst scandalized one of the more loyal members of our delegation; to my amusement, she flew out of the room to complain to the male head of the delegation about the digression.

Like the Nigerian delegation, which ranked as the most corrupt in the world, our government delegates dressed fastidiously. The head of our delegation, Salma Waheed – tall, imposing and elegantly dressed – was approached by someone and asked if she was a princess. Prime Minister Benazir Bhutto – who wore an exquisitely tailored *shalwar kameez* and arrived with glowing complexion – cut a glamorous figure. World leaders who had packed the hall, strained in their seats to hear the woman Prime Minister of Pakistan speak.

I had no doubt that Benazir would take the global community by storm, speaking articulately as she did about the measures taken by the PPP government on behalf of the women of Pakistan. The PPP's National Report (NATREP), which recommended actions for women in Pakistan, was so slick that we ran out of the copies for other delegates.

Personally, I had less reason to be impressed by Benazir's eloquence, knowing of the bitter realities for women back home. Indeed, nothing had changed from the report compiled in 1985 by the Commission on the Status of Women. The commission, headed by Begum Zari Sarfaraz, had made a bold report under Gen. Zia. Having traveled the length and breadth of Pakistan, she conveyed the reality that rings true even today: "The average rural woman of Pakistan is born in near slavery, leads a life of drudgery and dies invariably in oblivion."

As a government delegate from a poor developing country like Pakistan, I was uneasy with the luxurious scale of our accommodations in Beijing. The lobby was spectacular, complete with a cascading waterfall reflected on moving glass escalators. Each one of us had a spacious room that overlooked the starry lights of Beijing.

And yet, on my query to an emissary of Pakistan's ambassador to China as to why they had not arranged for a more economical hotel, the answer was: "Why do you bother...it's only the government's money?"

At the end of the day, our delegation had minimal impact on the "Outcomes Document" adopted at Beijing. While the PPP government agreed in principle to implement the far-reaching recommendations at the Fourth World Women's Conference, my time in Beijing had convinced me that the government was making speeches merely for diplomatic consumption.

Still, every weekend, I flew to Islamabad on government expense to join women's groups to make good on the promises made at the Fourth World Women's Conference. Indeed, Benazir' government had promised a Platform of Action that would incorporate sweeping changes to uplift women's lot in the government's national Five-Year Plan. The weeks rolled by and I found myself in an endless web of planning.

By 1996, I wondered whether the recommendations we had submitted in the NATREP would ever take effect. The government had signed the Convention to Eliminate All Forms of Discrimination against Women (CEDAW) in March 1995. Still, all discriminatory laws passed by General Zia ul Haq remained unchanged. Moreover, there was no relief in sight for the millions of women trapped by illiteracy and poverty.

Apparently, the establishment also took stock of the money drained from the national exchequer. In August 1996, as I worked in Islamabad on the Five-Year Plan for Women, a panic rumor did the rounds that Benazir's government was about to be sacked. As a journalist who knew that the military called the shots, I sensed that Benazir's time had come.

That evening, I flew back to Karachi to learn that the rumor was true. Benazir and her elected government had been sacked for the second time – once again on familiar charges of corruption and failure to control the deteriorating law and order situation.

Whither Women?

At the festive Fourth World Women Conference there had been little to suggest that twelve years later, Benazir Bhutto would be assassinated and her husband, Asif Zardari would lead a nation that would slip to hit almost rock bottom in the World Economic Forum's rankings of nations with a global gender gap.

With image being everything, the Zardari government moved quickly to show it was serious about women's rights. In 2009, its preparations for International Women's Day's were kicked off with a government emissary's phone call to a founder member of the Women's Action Forum, Anis Haroon, that she had been nominated to head the Pakistan Commission on the Status of Women. As someone who takes the issue of women's rights quite seriously, Anis told the concerned quarters she would think about the proposition and get back to them.

"But by the evening, I received congratulations from my friends. Prime Minister Yusuf Raza Gilani had already announced my name on television," she shared with me.

In March 2010, Anis headed a government delegation to the Beijing Plus 15 conference in New York. Afterwards, she talked about her government's success in passing a bill against the harassment of women in the work place. President Asif Zardari had signed the parliamentary bill even though his own party members had opposed it. The bill became law after it was assisted by a women's parliamentary caucus that cuts across party lines.

Although it was a good gesture, its passage just a few days before International Women's Day 2010 appeared largely symbolic. Prime Minister Yusuf Raza Gilani, while strengthening the Commission on the Status of Women had also appointed a dozen, mostly conservative, members to the Council of Islamic Ideology (CII). This "balancing act" of the PPP government would annul progressive measures for women.

In August 2009, for example, the CII shot down a bill against domestic violence introduced by women parliamentarians in the National Assembly, arguing it would "fan unending family feuds and push up divorce rates." Similarly, there are measures that the Women's Commission would like to take on behalf of women, but are likely to be vetoed by the CII.

In May 2010, the women's parliamentary caucus held a largely symbolic regional convention of women parliamentarians in Islamabad to search for ways of empowering women and bring peace to the strife-ridden region. While the convention came up with good recommendations to end violence against women, a woman parliamentarian told me what they really needed was "implementation."

While the Zardari government has increased women's quota seats in parliament to 21 per cent – up from 17 per cent under

Musharraf – and appointed a woman, Dr Fehmida Mirza, as speaker of the National Assembly, change is slow to follow. Pakistan's women parliamentarians are the wives, sisters, daughters and nieces of feudal and tribal politicians whose traditions often keep them from speaking up on issues of national importance.

Even the constitutional reforms package passed by the Zardari government has avoided repealing the discriminatory laws passed by Gen. Zia ul Haq. Gen. Zia had initially passed the laws as ordinances before they were indemnified to the constitution. That has left the discriminatory laws against women, Laws of Evidence and *Qisas* and *Diyat* intact.

On the other hand, decades of hue and cry from Pakistani women have transformed the Zina Ordinances. While the Musharraf government converted it into the Women's Protection Act, the Zardari government took it a step further and brought rape within the ambit of the secular Pakistan Penal Code.

As anywhere in the Muslim world, the veil has come back to Pakistan in almost a knee jerk response to US presence in the region. In a male-dominated set up, the different forms of the veil in Pakistan not only defy Western influence but are the preferred traditional form of escape from sexual harassment. Still, women are free to wear Western dress without any fear of retribution.

Indeed, the relatively liberal personal life styles of President Musharraf and President Zardari and inevitable globalization have left Pakistan with a dusting of modernity. Nightclubs have gradually opened while private parties serve alcohol more openly. Most of the superficial changes contribute to a liberal atmosphere in cities like Karachi, Lahore and Islamabad but don't necessarily empower its women.

Today, in a fragile democracy, the PPP's government has abdicated its writ over large parts of the country. There, women suffer from galloping population, domestic violence, rapes, honor killings and "marriage to the Quran." In this backdrop, the civilian government teeters forth – unable to take bold steps that could unlock women's potential and draw Pakistan out of centuries of backwardness.

Chapter 5
UNCOVERING
A MURDER

A Young Woman Disappears

When people ask me how I met my husband, I sometimes say "Through the newspaper." That could give the impression that we met through matrimonial ads in Pakistan's newspapers with the kind of captions that read, "Young bride wanted from good Sunni Muslim family, devoted to the home and children."

The truth is, I found my husband while hunting for his sister's killer.

In January 1990, I was the health beat reporter for *Dawn* and, as such, covered the public hospitals. Three government hospitals in Karachi cater to the poor and needy and it was well known that their corrupt administrations siphoned off even the meager funds they were allocated.

My sources were doctors who contacted me confidentially with grievances that they wanted me to bring to light. Through my write-ups, they hoped to force the hospital administrations to take action.

By that time, I had gained a reputation as a sympathetic reporter. Women, religious minorities, doctors, consumer interest groups, politicians and trade union leaders who felt discriminated against came to me hoping to find recourse through the newspaper.

My senior journalist colleagues watched through the corners of their eyes. At times, I saw their curiosity and touch of envy as clusters of people congregated around my wobbly wooden desk. The room I worked in had no ventilation and no air-conditioning and we sweated in the hot stale air circulated by ceiling fans. However, in the heat of conversations, no one seemed to mind.

Among my sources, one doctor frequently contacted me with bits of information about the malfeasance in hospitals. I had grown to trust him over the years, because his complaints weren't personal and his tips often proved fruitful.

He was a short, earnest looking young man with glasses. Normally, he spoke so fast in Urdu that he would stumble over his words. Apparently, that stemmed from his desire to communicate "inside information" on sensitive stories that other reporters wouldn't want to touch. Over time, he had developed a trust in me that allowed him to confide the most troubling problems he witnessed first hand in the system.

Late one evening in January 1990, while I worked at the city desk at *Dawn*, the earnest young doctor came to visit me. This time, he was whispering.

"She's disappeared," he said.

"Who has disappeared?" I said a bit exasperated since I was immersed in juggling other news stories.

"Fauzia, remember the woman doctor I was telling you about?"

I remembered he had telephoned me weeks ago to tell me about a fellow woman doctor who felt she was being discriminated against after she was abruptly ejected from her government housing. The government provided housing for medical interns near the hospitals where they worked. However, there were few rooms to go around and these had to be obtained at a premium.

Shortly thereafter, the earnest doctor's colleague had called me, fuming. I guessed that he had got her to telephone me as well. Her indignation startled me. She was talking so fast that I heard myself saying, "Wait, wait and slow down." But her words spilled out fast and furious: "I came back to my room one day to find my furniture and possessions strewn all over the hallway," she was saying.

Her fury had been directed at Fauzia, who was now missing. Apparently, Fauzia had acted like an upstart and thrown belongings out of the room originally allotted to this woman doctor.

For a few seconds I wondered what the issue – which was prima facie so personal – had to do with a forum as public as my staid newspaper. But there was more to the story. Apparently the woman, Fauzia Bhutto – who had displaced my contact's colleague – was rumored to be having an affair with a senior member of parliament. Indeed, many had seen the newly-elected member of the Sindh assembly come frequently to pick up the young woman from her room near the hospital.

For me, the fact that a government official had found housing for a young woman was enough to raise a red flag. I knew full well that in a sex-segregated society like Pakistan, men don't do favors for women without expecting something in return.

Moreover, the incident reeked of existing ethnic tensions. The official in question, Rahim Baksh Jamali was a Sindhi-speaking Member of the Provincial Assembly (MPA) from Benazir Bhutto's Pakistan Peoples Party. The woman – Fauzia, now missing, too – was a Sindhi speaker from Shikarpur in interior Sindh. As Benazir mania swept the rural areas, Fauzia had campaigned to get Jamali elected on the PPP ticket allotted to him from his hometown of Nawabshah.

It was a time when the Sindhi majority, who lived in the underprivileged rural areas, looked toward Benazir's rule as an opportunity to lift themselves out of centuries of deprivation. On the other hand the Mohajirs (Muslim migrants from India), who were the majority population in Karachi, looked at the Sindhi-supported PPP rule with suspicion.

Both of the doctors who approached me were Mohajirs and felt the particular sting of being displaced by a Sindhi parliamentarian and the woman he had brought from interior Sindh.

At that time, Karachi had fallen into its worst bout of ethnic violence between the ruling PPP and the MQM. Benazir's government had been in power for only a year but already the initial and fragile peace accord between the two political parties had given way to kidnappings, torture and murders of rival party members. The city burned when it was not under curfew.

As urban Mohajirs, my sources resented that incumbent PPP officials had brought their own people – Sindhis – into coveted jobs and positions in Karachi.

Twenty six year old Fauzia Bhutto, a former student of Nawabshah Medical College, was part of the Bhutto tribe – one of several prominent tribes among the larger ethnic group of Sindhis. Like most Sindhis she supported Benazir's leadership of the country.

Tall and lean with shoulder-length hair, the high-spirited extroverted Fauzia was an active social worker. And yet like many young idealistic students in the small town of Nawabshah, Fauzia never had much exposure to men. She quickly became enamored of the well-connected landowner from Nawabshah, Rahim Baksh Jamali, for whom she campaigned in the 1988 election.

A year later as the older balding Jamali was elected MPA in Benazir's cabinet, he lobbied to bring the pretty young woman to Karachi. Here, he found her a job as a medical intern and got her government housing.

Fauzia became known for her generosity among colleagues, nurses and patients, with her warm, sociable nature quickly winning her close friends. But in a traditional Muslim society like Pakistan, where unrelated men and women do not meet openly, she hid her relationship with Jamali. Only a few select friends knew about it.

Jamali had been known to visit her frequently. Now, her sudden disappearance – without any efforts on his part to find her – had my earnest doctor contact deeply concerned.

Barely whispering, with his body language saying more than his actual words, my contact told me that he suspected foul play. Indeed, by the time he had finished whispering his story,

I grew just as concerned that a young professional woman had disappeared and her patron had made no effort to find her.

My source wanted me to mention Fauzia's disappearance in my newspaper reports – hoping that by publicizing her case, we would succeed in finding her.

I waited for the right time to show a connection between the missing Fauzia and the man I knew to be visiting her. On January 12, 1990, I inserted an innocuous paragraph in a larger news report I was doing on a nurse's strike in the hospital where she worked. I wrote that a PPP member of parliament elected from Nawabshah, Rahim Baksh Jamali had placed his "girl friend" in Room 104 of JPMC doctor's hostel. This was the room that Jamali had obtained for Fauzia from the hospital administration.

While on the surface this seemed harmless, I had publicly linked Jamali to Fauzia. Unbeknownst to me, Jamali already had a wife and children in his hometown in Nawabshah. By using the term "girl friend," I had inadvertently stepped on the toes of a man from a tribal background – where extramarital relationships are punishable by "honor killings."

The next day my report was out in *Dawn* and I saw its impact. My editor, who oversaw the city desk – Akhtar Payami – signaled to me to come quickly to his adjoining chamber. Glimpsing the urgent expression on his face in the conjoint room with sliding glass windows, I practically skipped inside.

A quiet, unassuming man who looked like he harbored many secrets, Payami told me in hushed tones that Jamali had just telephoned him. Apparently, the MPA had protested at the "objectionable" language used in a reputable newspaper like *Dawn*. He had been offended, not just by being associated with the missing Fauzia, but by my choice of the term "girl friend."

"She is not my 'girl friend', she's my wife," he told my editor belligerently.

I was thrilled. It was the first public admission that Jamali had made about his alleged connection to the missing girl. His surprising claim that Fauzia was his wife, while hardly believable, had become necessary. While a Muslim man could have four wives, having extramarital relations is punishable by death. He couldn't refute the relationship since he had got Fauzia a job and room near the hospital.

Still, when Jamali called, he did not mention that his "wife" was missing or whether he had filed a missing report with police. Despite his influential position, he had made no move to find her. Instead, the man, driven by tribal instincts – as I later found him to be – had only expressed pompous annoyance that I had "soiled" his reputation by my choice of words. The timing of his phone call would be his first mistake.

Missing Girl was Murdered

On the morning of January 9, 1990, shepherds tending their flocks in the dusty wastelands along Karachi's Super Highway stumbled upon the body of a young woman. They turned around the body, wrapped in an *ajrak* (a multi-purpose red Sindhi cloth), and saw that her eyes were shut. Her long tresses covered part of a bloodstained tunic, which she wore over a *shalwar kameez* and *dupatta* (baggy trousers and a scarf).

The shepherds informed police, who in turn contacted Pakistan's veteran social worker, Abdus Sattar Edhi. Edhi picked up the unclaimed body as a routine service to the city and buried her as an "unidentified girl." The police lodged a routine First Information Report (FIR) of the murder against "unknown persons." As was standard practice among local tabloids, a little-read Urdu newspaper then published a photograph of a dead girl with the caption, "unidentified young woman."

None of us knew about the body that was found, nor had we seen the photograph in the newspaper. The photograph documented what we knew later – that Fauzia had been murdered between the nights of January 8 and 9. It definitively established that Fauzia was already dead when my paragraph connecting Jamali with the missing girl appeared in *Dawn* four days later.

Throughout January, Fauzia's family had kept up hopes of finding the missing girl alive. Although her immediate family lived in Shikarpur – a good eight hours by road from Karachi – they became increasingly worried when a week went by and she failed to contact them. Fauzia's father had passed away four years before, so the eldest son, Javed Bhutto came to Karachi to look for his sister.

Javed, who was eight years older than Fauzia, had recently returned to Pakistan with a master's degree in philosophy from Sophia, Bulgaria. A slender, reflective man with a thick crop of hair, he was possessed with finding her. He searched for her at familiar haunts in Karachi, Hyderabad and Nawabshah, where she had worked or studied and asked friends and acquaintances where and with whom they had last seen her.

Apparently, the intense search for Fauzia by the Bhutto family and their supporters put pressure on Jamali to account for his whereabouts and his relationship with her. Being a lawyer, he did so with exacting detail.

In late January, desperate to find any trace of his missing sister, Javed broke the flimsy lock in his sister's hostel room. Here, he discovered a hand-written note slipped under her door from Jamali. In it, he had written to Fauzia: "I met you on 8 January but had to go away on 9 and 10." The note went on to explicitly mention the dates when he was out of town: 11, 12 and the 13 of that month.

Even then, although Fauzia was still counted as missing, Jamali's mention of specific dates in what was a "casual" note made Javed even more suspicious. Having by then gathered sufficient evidence to tie Jamali with Fauzia's disappearance, Javed named him in a First Information Report filed with police.

Javed also requested that his friend – the heavy built, amiable landowner from Shikarpur, Junaid Soomro – telephone Jamali and ask whether he had seen Fauzia. Junaid was a former-MPA from Shikarpur and his political connections made it easier for him to question the sitting member of Benazir's government. Still, in a society where men and women do not associate freely, it was bold of Soomro to confront Jamali. There was an awkward pause as Soomro phoned Benazir's party man to ask:

"So where is she?"

"No really, is she missing?" – Jamali feigned concern. Then in a reassuring tone, he told Soomro, "I'll be coming to Karachi soon. We'll look for her together."

The two met at Soomro's friend's home in Karachi. Both men were accompanied by their political supporters. There, Jamali showed Soomro a *nikah nama* (marriage contract) in order to prove that Fauzia was his "wife." Although it was a planned move, it failed to convince the audience. Instead, astonished at the marriage document, Soomro instinctively told Jamali, "That's a fake piece of paper."

There were others in the room that witnessed Jamali recoil and fall silent. Tactfully, Soomro brought the conversation back to the central issue and said emphatically: "What is important is to find out is where she is right now."

Javed continued to look for his sister, still believing her to be alive. All of his questions elicited answers that pointed toward Jamali. Weeks flew by. Then one late evening a close friend of Javed's, Agha Rafiq – who had helped him hunt for Fauzia – showed him an old crumpled Urdu newspaper. It was the local tabloid with the blurred picture of a dead girl, which, until now, had gone unnoticed.

Rafiq had received the tabloid from Fauzia's colleague, a young woman named Munnawar Sultana. She seemed scared and hesitant as she told him that Jamali had asked that the newspaper, dated January 9, be shown to her family. Apparently, Jamali figured that the family's hunt for Fauzia – which was now all over the newspapers in Pakistan – must end. Javed stared at the dim photograph and knew it was his missing sister.

With a sickening feeling Javed felt the world come crashing down around him. The bitter reality sank in. He knew he would never see his sister again. A silence descended in the room as his men friends saw him struggle with the news. They comforted him as best as they could.

As morning broke, the victim's brother collected himself. With his close friends by his side, he went to meet the veteran social worker Abdus Sattar Edhi, who had buried Fauzia as an "unidentified girl."

I knew Edhi from the mid '80s as the white bearded man dressed simply in long tunic and baggy trousers, who arrived at every emergency in his rickety ambulance. He tended victims with compassion, regardless of race, religion and ethnicity. At times, we were the only two people at a conflict zone. I caught his surprised expression as he looked at me – the only the woman reporter on the scene. Without saying a word, he would lift the dead and wounded and drive them off to hospital.

Today, Edhi is a household name in Pakistan, with a host of international offices. Over time, he has built a network of social services through public donations that surpass the level of government assistance to the poor, sick and wounded.

At the Edhi center, the man with the flowing white beard greeted Javed with a heavy heart. Taking him back to his desk, he laid out the photographs of Fauzia that were taken shortly before her burial. It confirmed the young man's worst fears. The post-mortem report obtained by Javed from the government-run Abbasi Shaheed Hospital in Karachi revealed bullet wounds. Fauzia Bhutto's disappearance was confirmed as a homicide.

Javed was taken to the graveyard where Fauzia had been buried anonymously by the veteran social worker. The body was later exhumed and buried in the family's hometown of Shikarpur.

There was no doubt in Javed's mind as to who had killed his sister. He now turned his complete efforts to bringing the killer to justice. Within 24 hours, he had lodged a police report that named MPA Rahim Baksh Jamali as the suspect.

Fauzia's Murder Makes Waves

The young woman's murder made headlines in national newspapers and reverberated through society. Fauzia was unusual in that she came from a provincial town in Sindh, but had developed an independent career. With her vibrant and lively nature, she was hugely popular in her social circles. Even though newspaper readers in Karachi were hardened by reports of daily violence, many were shocked by her brutal murder.

Fauzia's murder affected me more than I cared to express. It angered me that a well-connected, influential man had ruthlessly cut down a young woman in the prime of her life and then summarily discarded her body. Without even knowing her, I felt emotionally linked to this woman seven years younger than me.

There was a stigma attached to women working in a society that presumes that their place is at home. But it was also symbolic of the manner in which the feudal society treats women: as sexual objects and disposable commodities.

I argued endlessly with my parents about the injustice of the murder. My father prudishly maintained that a young woman had no business having an affair with a married man. He always warned us about the cruelty of Sindhi feudals and shuddered at the thought of his daughters getting involved. My mother put herself in the shoes of the deceased girl's mother and grieved for the family.

Being a reporter in an influential newspaper gave me an outlet to fight injustice. It was an opportunity that other women did not have. I had just emerged from writing a series of articles, seeking justice for two nurses raped at gunpoint in a government hospital. Now, I felt that my readers – especially women – again looked toward me. We knew full well that the administration would never act unless pressured.

Meanwhile, rumors cropped up that the murder was ethnically based; that it was the ethnic group, MQM, which had killed the Sindhi girl. Indeed, I had received a phone call from my early contact – the Urdu-speaking woman doctor whose room was taken over by Fauzia. Almost in tears, she told me that Jamali had accused her in front of the hospital director of conniving with the MQM to get rid of Fauzia.

"That scoundrel is behind her disappearance, but he's trying to throw off the blame and convert this to an ethnic issue," she told me.

The PPP government, which struggled with a poor media image, initially resisted the attempt to interrogate a high profile member of their party. As is normal in Pakistan, an influential person like Jamali was exempted from police questioning because of his status as a member of the Sindh assembly.

Instead, the Sindh police hauled up Jamali's driver, Mohammed Ishaq – a poor, thin straggly son of a peasant, who normally kept his eyes glued to the ground. As his driver was hauled up in police custody for questioning, Jamali grew increasingly desperate. I saw the effect.

One day, with the matter of Fauzia's murder still red hot, the door to the reporter's room creaked. I looked up to see a beak-nosed man with shifty eyes make a beeline for my desk. Without waiting for an invitation, he pulled up a chair by my desk and introduced himself as Dr Abdul Karim Jamali, a resident doctor at JPMC. His manner indicated he knew my role in reporting Fauzia's murder and he began trying to convince me that Jamali was innocent and the ethnic group, MQM was to blame.

I was intrigued to hear the younger Jamali defend his tribesman and blame the MQM instead. My expression stayed skeptical. I knew that Dr Karim had managed to gather a handful of supporters to publicly implicate the MQM and plant rumors – even organize a demonstration against the ethnic party at the affiliated Sindh Medical College. Their demands chalked on the college walls had read, "Arrest the real killers of Fauzia."

I took this impromptu meeting as an opportunity to ask the younger Jamali point blank: "What proof do you have that the MQM is behind Fauzia's murder?" The younger Jamali's expression became even more sphinx-like. Despite my Sindhi background, he knew there was no way I would support him on ethnic grounds. He was now spinning a yarn, telling me that everyone knew that the MQM was behind every violent incident in Karachi. And yet, his failure to give a single name or motive made him unconvincing. I could see that he had no evidence.

The accused next turned to the press for his defense. Even as the police interrogated his driver, a report appeared on the front page of the influential Sindhi newspaper – *Hilal-i-Pakistan* – that it was the MQM who had raped and killed Fauzia.

The article by a "staff reporter" cited Fauzia's murder as only one in a chain of atrocities that the MQM had committed against Sindhi women. Appearing at a time when Sindhis and Mohajirs were already at each other's throats, the widely circulated newspaper effectively incited Sindhis to rise up and avenge Fauzia's murder.

The news item threatened to foment rivers of blood between Mohajirs and Sindhis. It even embarrassed the PPP government. The soft-spoken chief minister of Sindh from Shikarpur Aftab Shahban Mirani, who struggled to keep order amidst violent ethnic disturbances, investigated its origin. He found it had emanated, not unsurprisingly from the panicked Jamali himself.

But before Jamali could escape under the cover of ethnic riots, Javed Bhutto empathically quashed the inflammatory report that the MQM was responsible for Fauzia's murder. Javed's statement – which appeared in the English, Urdu and Sindhi press – claimed that the murder was the handiwork of a suspect whose name would shortly be released by police.

I saw Javed for the first time when he walked into my office to contradict the Sindhi newspaper's report. Looking up from my desk, my gaze was drawn by the slender, lanky unselfconscious youth. He seemed driven by a sense of purpose. The young man, with male friends in tow, did not turn around to look at us – or at me, the only female reporter. Instead, as he walked straight to the city editor's room, his sober intent struck a chord in me. I was impressed that the young man was focused on achieving justice.

Accused Member of Parliament Runs Away

At this critical juncture, the Inspector General of Sindh Police, Afzal Shigri called reporters to announce the findings, based on a confession by Jamali's driver. Police told the press conference that the driver had confessed in front of a magistrate that on

January 8, he and Jamali picked up Fauzia from the hospital and took her to an apartment complex in Clifton – Al Habib arcade. The apartment belonged to a male relative of Jamali.

According to the driver's testimony, shortly after arriving with Fauzia, Jamali left the house to meet his relative. Fauzia went to the kitchen where she boiled eggs.

Jamali returned about an hour later. Inside the apartment, the driver heard arguments between the two from an adjoining room. Moments later, he was startled by the sound of gunfire. He looked into the bedroom, where he saw Jamali holding a gun while Fauzia lay bleeding on the carpet. Jamali turned the gun and threatened to kill the driver if he told anyone he had witnessed the scene.

In this gruesome testimony, the driver said he helped Jamali drape the dead girl in an *ajrak*, loaded the body in the trunk of his vehicle and drove to the fastest get-away for criminals – the deserted super highway. Some 12 years later, police discovered American journalist Daniel Pearl's body in a shallow grave along the same highway.

Back in the 1990s, when ethnic disturbances were a daily occurrence in Karachi, vehicles were stopped at police check-posts. However, Jamali's government license plate allowed his car to pass without detection. Drawing up to the highway near Gadap, the driver confessed that he and Jamali threw the young woman's body into the desert wastelands before they sped off to Nawabshah in interior Sindh.

The Sindh police chief privately disclosed to Javed that he was resisting intense pressure from some members of the ruling PPP government against arresting one of their own. That was predictable. In Pakistan, legislators routinely use their clout to bend the arm of the law. A phone call from an influential politician to a police officer often frees accused persons from custody.

But as newspapers reported the evidence against the PPP parliamentary member, women, doctors and political and human rights groups mounted intense pressure for his arrest. The small but determined women's groups in Karachi were enraged at the manner in which a male politician – who had roots in tribalism and feudal arrogance – could treat life with so little respect and expect to get away with it.

And yet, in a lawless society like Pakistan – where politicians, police, judiciary and the press are tarred with corruption – that is exactly what Jamali tried to do. He ran away.

Seemingly overnight, taking a few possessions, Jamali disappeared. We suspected that high-ranking officials within the PPP had tipped him off about his imminent arrest. And so he chose to flee when he could.

In Jamali's absence, police took over his apartment in Clifton, Al-Habib Arcade. They discovered the carpet and the mattress where Fauzia was murdered. Although the blood-stained mattress had been meticulously scrubbed, stains were visible on the underside. Forensic experts confirmed the stains matched the blood found on Fauzia's clothes during the autopsy.

A police team was dispatched to Jamali's hometown in Nawabshah to recover his licensed gun and the car used for the murder. These items would never be found. Jamali was later found to have sold his car to a dealer in the tribal areas, where no one could trace it. It was clear to us that the PPP MPA could not have acted without the help of his "friends" in government. Over a month had passed since Fauzia's murder and the sole accused from Benazir's party was nowhere to be found.

While covering the Sindh Assembly on my regular beat, I seized on the opportunity to confront PPP Sindh Chief Minister Syed Qaim Ali Shah as he addressed a regular press briefing on the law and order situation in Sindh.

The short, thin and balding party loyalist had won a landslide victory in Khairpur, which I had visited a year ago. Now, I asked him, in his capacity as chief minister, how long his party man and fellow parliamentarian could remain absconding for murder. Pen in hand, my fellow journalists sat poised to note his response. Shah pursed his lips and frowned, as he did whenever he grew thought hard. Looking at me in the eye, he said that police had been directed to arrest Jamali wherever he was hiding.

As Karachi burnt in ethnic riots, Shah was replaced by Sindh Chief Minister Aftab Shahban Mirani. The gentle, heavy-set

Mirani with salt and pepper hair visited the bereaved Bhutto household in Shikarpur to offer prayers for the murder victim. He came from the same town as Javed's family, but Mirani was mostly compelled to visit them because of the national attention the case had received. State television drew mileage from the visit and cameras trailed him as he personally condoled with Fauzia's grief-stricken family.

What national television did not show was that the victim's brother, Javed told the chief minister that he knew that influential members of the PPP government were "hiding the murderer."

Murder's Impact on Society

Fauzia's murder exploded a bombshell into society and revealed wide-ranging strata of opinions. Tongues wagged as soon as the accused was identified. Fauzia's family thought that she had most likely pressured the already married Jamali to legalize his relationship and marry her. Apparently enraged by her persistence, they speculated, he pulled the trigger on her.

I saw that Fauzia's murder was likely to have a negative effect on middle-class parents. Pakistan is a segregated society where marriages are mostly arranged; this incident would not help. More than once, I heard parents express disapproval how the girl had had a relationship with a man to whom she was not married.

Non-governmental organizations saw the murder as closely linked to women's low status in society. They used it to agitate for reform. The Women's Action Forum, comprising urban, young, professional women, took on the issue as symbolic of the rights of working women. WAF was joined by another newly-created group – War Against Rape (WAR) – that mobilized men and women of all ethnic groups on the case.

Overall, working women looked to the woman prime minister to improve their situation. Benazir Bhutto had come to power pledging "to take a firm stand against the ill-treatment and exploitation of women." Now, delegations of human rights activists met the woman prime minister to demand that her MPA be arrested and unseated from office.

But the PPP did not unseat their member, saying they would not do so until the court reached a verdict. It was an ingenious argument – murder cases dragged on for decades without a resolution.

Every evening, the press material on the Fauzia Bhutto murder case landed with a thud on my desk. Women and human rights groups were growing frustrated at the government's inability to catch Jamali. It weighed on me as well. With a government official accused of murder and protected by those authorized to prosecute him, there appeared to be no recourse to the law.

We Hunt Together for the Killer

Within two weeks of finding the body, the chief investigator in the Fauzia Bhutto murder case, Deputy Superintendent Police Sattar Shaikh had built a solid case against Jamali. I heard the smile in his voice when he told me that no sooner did he give a piece of information to the victim's brother, Javed, than it appeared in the next morning's newspaper.

Javed had finally come to trust me with sensitive information. Come late evening and I would get a phone call from him, updating me on the latest find by the investigating authorities.

Call it destiny or chance: I had begun walking on the same path as the victim's brother. In the process, I gained respect for Javed, the man who sought justice, not revenge. His decision to bring the accused before a court of law seemed especially remarkable in a society crumbling under anarchy. I was struck by his handsome presence – gentle, polite and well-spoken.

And yet, we were a study in contrasts. In comparison to his laid-back introspective style, I was restless for action. As we began our separate investigations into the young woman's murder, he came to know me as an aggressive reporter who barraged him with questions in order to meet a newspaper's deadline.

At an early stage of the murder investigation, Javed had come to speak with a reporter in the adjoining newspaper office to convince him to do an investigative piece on Fauzia. I called him a couple of times on that telephone extension but despite assenting politeness, he failed to come around to my office to talk to me.

So, I walked into the other paper's office and asked the questions in person. I found him reticent to speak. He knew that I worked for a daily newspaper and he knew me too little to divulge the latest information. Without being rude, he had tried to brush me aside. Clearly, this was a man who did not trust easily.

We were both fired up for the same mission but remained complete strangers. I knew though that if we did not move quickly on Fauzia's case, her murderer would vanish and she would be among the thousands of nameless, faceless victims of crime.

I decided to undertake my own investigation into the murder case. The opportunity came when my newspaper sent me to report on another issue in Nawabshah. It provided me the perfect opportunity to call upon Jamali's driver, Mohammed Ishaq – who, after being released on bail, had returned to his village near Nawabshah city.

Once I had located his address, I took the office van to the driver's mud dwelling. The driver went inside and called Ishaq. A few minutes later Ishaq emerged nervous and disheveled. He was aware that the fact that I had traveled from Karachi meant that I was on important business.

The two of us sat upright, opposite one another in the spacious van and Ishaq narrated the story of that fateful night. He spoke in a resigned tone, in Sindhi-accented Urdu. It was the same account he had given to the police.

"Yes, he killed her," he told me nervously. His matter-of-fact tone made me angry. Ishaq had driven off with Jamali to Nawabshah after the murder and would never have confessed had the police not arrested him. Knowing that I was staring at him, Ishaq dared not look up. Instead, eyes down, he muttered, "What could I do? He threatened to kill me if I told anyone."

Fear had crippled this poor man of peasant origin. For the lowly driver to have testified against his master – a wealthy landowner, well-connected lawyer and an MPA – would have meant devastation for his entire family.

Although Sindhi feudal landlords are represented in the country's two major political parties, they have kept their peasants ignorant and fearful. As a cynical Urdu-speaking friend of mine was fond of saying, "When one landlord wants to take revenge against another, he opens a school in the other's locality".

To Ishaq, I was a powerful figure from the city that belonged to the same social class as the landlords. When he described the entire murder scene, he never once looked up. Not just because I was a woman – people of lower status are not supposed to look into the eyes of the higher class.

As I left, I knew that although he had confessed to me privately and testified in front of a magistrate, he would never have the courage to testify against his master in a court of law.

Women Surprise Government Legislators

The city was abuzz with news about Fauzia's murder. In the forefront were women activists, resolute on building pressure to catch the murderer. I attended their meeting at the Karachi Press Club where Javed was also present. His face was alive with expectation. He had come to depend on civil society to bring his sister's killer to justice.

We discussed the possibility of my smuggling a group of women inside the Sindh Assembly building – banners and placards in tow – to demonstrate inside the premises and demand that the run-away Jamali be brought back to face murder charges. It was a novel idea proposed by WAF and WAR and I shared the excitement of what this could do to publicize the case.

The next morning, the handful of women activists piled in my car and we drove to the imposing Sindh Assembly. We planned that the bulk of protestors would unfurl their banners outside, once our "inside group" got in. They would then join a much larger group of activists on the street outside the parliament building.

As I drove to the majestic assembly gates, the guards peered in. They took one look at my assembly pass and then waved us in...just a harmless group of women. I parked inside the

Figure 8 PPP parliamentary leader Nisar Ahmed Khuhro addresses Sindh Assembly (*Dawn* photo).

prepossessing Sindh Assembly building – its grandeur masking the unruly sessions between government and opposition. My women friends waited in the assembly's cafeteria room and I went to the opera house style press gallery.

The press gallery affords a bird's eye view of the legislators under a large canopy of the British built parliament building. From here, I frequently watched the vitriolic exchanges between the government and opposition members.

Over a month had passed since Jamali had fled. I looked down to his seat to see if the assembly session had coaxed him back to his seat. Not surprisingly, his seat was empty.

As the session ended, the unsuspecting legislators walked out of the front door, smack into the middle of the women's demonstration. The women had lined up for the protest in their modest *shalwar kameez* in vibrant spring colors, with *dupattas* strung across their necks. They dramatically unfurled banners and placards with slogans that read "Arrest PPP MPA Rahim Baksh

Jamali" and "Arrest Jamali – Fauzia Bhutto's murderer." Female voices rent the air: "Arrest the killer of Fauzia Bhutto."

Traditionally, the Sindh Assembly is a male enclave of feudal and urban parliamentarians, reporters and security personnel. But that day the legislators were taken aback by the sudden appearance of upper-middle class women demonstrating for women's rights.

I saw the discomfort on the faces of the PPP legislators as they tried to avoid the demonstrators and instead walked briskly, mobile phones in hand, toward their Pajeros, the huge vehicles that symbolize feudal prosperity.

But before the parliamentarians could escape, the journalists who normally cover the Sindh Assembly went into action. As reporters took notes, newspaper's photographers bent out of shape to snap legislators fleeing the bad publicity. It was not that easy for the PPP parliamentarians to escape. Outside the Sindh Assembly building there was a larger demonstration of women with banners and placards, demanding Jamali's arrest.

Our inner group came out of the assembly gates and joined these daughters, sisters and wives of the crème de la crème. The assembly reporters had their work cut out for them. Even while many members of parliament had already revved up their high-powered vehicles and fled, the story of their runaway colleague would follow them the next day.

That night as I drove home after work, I knew the satisfaction of a day well spent. And yet, as I drove through the dark, silent streets of Karachi, I felt as though I was being followed. It was a familiar feeling. Years of driving home alone at night had taught me to shake off pursuers.

But that night something was different. I had glimpsed a man in my car mirror, who trailed me in a pick-up truck. Trying to shake off the eerie feeling, I looked behind and saw the street was empty. Gathering courage, I disembarked to open the gates of my house. Cautiously, I drove in and closed the gates behind me. This was my daily ritual.

Just as I walked up the three short steps to my house, I sensed a figure had crept up from behind. Instinctively, I called out, "Ma."

It was just as well. At that moment, a hefty man had jumped over the boundary wall and pulled my tunic from behind. My karate reflexes came into play – I wrenched free and hit him with my bag.

In that split second, my mother had opened the door and the assailant vanished. My mother told me it had been the note of urgency in my voice that had made her run to open the door. My father turned on the balcony light and ran out into the courtyard to see if he could spot anyone. But the attacker had vanished.

History is Made

Three weeks after Jamali's disappearance, as I dropped off a routine news report for my city editor Akhtar Payami, he quietly drew my attention to a news item from the wire services.

After many weeks, Jamali had surfaced before a court in Lahore, Punjab, where he had obtained a conditional bail-before-arrest. The Punjab court had ruled however that he needed to reconfirm bail from a Karachi court a week later.

We correctly surmised that since the body had been found in District East, this meant the runaway assembly member was required to appear in front of the District and Sessions Judge from Karachi East. I wrote a news item in my newspaper, giving the date and place where the accused was scheduled to appear.

The British had built the district courts in Karachi with the kind of imposing architecture meant to inspire respect for rule of law. That lofty ideal has fallen by the way side. Located on the chaotic M. A. Jinnah Road, the tall granite buildings of these lower courts – complete with ornately carved balconies – are today besmirched with air and noise pollution. The inmates arrive packed like sardines in police vans…their chains clanking as they shuffle behind policemen. The court's grandeur has given way to a bazaar scene.

Seated in the courtroom during hearings, with tattered window screens and pigeons hopping in and out, I used to wonder how the judges could remain independent and dignified. Court clerks would step in the hallway and bellow the names of the parties involved – drawing out their names into lengthy syllables: "Ra – HEEM – Baksh Ja – MA – Lee".

The scene was reminiscent of a crowded railway station in South Asia, where vendors peddle their wares. Even the black-robed lawyers who argued before the district judges were poorly qualified and often spoke the court language – English – with comical results.

But that day, when the educated elite of Karachi thronged the court to hear the case entitled "State vs Rahim Baksh Jamali," the atmosphere was different. Many observers had read the case's intimate details in the press. Late Fauzia's brother, Javed was there. As our eyes met, I saw his wonder that so many people had come out to hear his sister's murder case.

All eyes turned to the dark, balding Jamali as he slunk into the courtroom. He looked visibly dismayed at the sight of so many spectators crammed inside.

The courtroom drama was completed as Khawaja Naveed, the self-appointed lawyer for the victim's family, bounced into the court and began reading the confession of the Jamali driver, Mohammed Ishaq, in a loud voice to give the gory details of the murder. Naveed was a famously flamboyant lawyer, youthful looking, with a curly lock of hair on his forehead and a ready laughter.

I understood his need to capture the limelight after a subsequent visit to his office. There on his table was a prominently displayed photograph of him where he appeared standing next to a cardboard image of US President Ronald Reagan – the president's arm around him.

Twelve years later, Naveed bounced with the same gaiety to defend American journalist Daniel Pearl's alleged killers. In both Fauzia and Daniel's case, he exited once the media lights were turned off.

But, at Jamali's bail-before-arrest hearing, Naveed's theatrical performance was heard in all seriousness. Although he merely read the evidence recorded by Jamali's driver, Mohammed Ishaq in front of a judicial magistrate, the facts of the case were dramatic enough to keep everyone's attention. With eager scrutiny, men and women watched Judge Rehmat Hussein Jafri ponder the merits of the case. The accused stood sullenly – aware that the Sindh police waited outside in full force to arrest him.

The deliberation took several hours. The overflow turnout of the crowd and their interest bowled me over. I never imagined that the city elite would wait for hours to hear a judgment from the court. Finally, the judge looked up from his pince-nez spectacles and pronounced the verdict: "Bail denied."

Photographers and reporters struggled to capture Jamali's response as he was handcuffed and led to the awaiting police van bound for Karachi Central Jail. History had been made as a sitting MPA was sent to prison.

There was huge relief on Javed's face as the verdict was announced. His was a Herculean task: to achieve what the civilized world takes for granted – getting justice through public institutions. Instead of retaliating with a tribal act of revenge, the victim's brother had mobilized society to follow the rule of law.

Buoyed by the victory, human rights organizations rallied around Javed to find him a lawyer. The Citizens Police Liaison Committee (CPLC) – a powerful organization, initiated by then PPP Governor, Fakhruddin G. Ebrahim to fight crime – used its leverage with the government to secure the appointment of a trusted high court lawyer, Syed Sami Ahmed as special public prosecutor to argue on behalf of the victim's family.

A senior, capable lawyer, Sami Ahmed brought an imposing presence to the lower courts – impressing judges who were far junior to him in the profession. Tall, well-built and always impeccably dressed in well-tailored suits, he spoke in clipped sentences. His special appointment had done away the need for public prosecutors, whose pittance earnings from the government made them a rapacious breed.

The first sign of the rotting system came when police took the jailed Jamali for two weeks of questioning. This process, called a police remand, is routinely followed to extract information from the accused. The application for police remand had been moved by Sami Ahmed to lay the basis for trial.

To everybody's shock, after the two weeks of "questioning" Jamali came to court looking fat and rested. "It's as though he had gone for a sauna," – a bewildered Javed said.

Human rights activists came to the hearings, their presence meant to monitor the proceedings. But Jamali refused to sit in the prosecution box. Instead, he wore a black coat worn by all lawyers and sat in the front row – reserved for attorneys. On occasion, I saw an honest judge snap at him and warn him to take the designated stand.

Still, the accused sidled up to the human rights activists. As they moved away, he told a woman friend, "You all look at me as though I'm a murderer."

Using one pretext or another, the accused continually managed to get the hearings adjourned. Almost effortlessly, it seemed, he manipulated jail officials, doctors, witnesses, police and government prosecutors. Often, he would not be brought from Karachi Central Jail…the excuse being that jail vehicles or police escorts were not available. At other times, his lawyer didn't show up or came with a medical certificate that claimed that the accused was too sick to come to court.

Even judges were occasionally frustrated by the corruption and inefficiency in the judicial system. Like pieces of a jigsaw puzzle, the players in the trial – complainant, accused and witnesses – have to be physically present in court for a hearing to take place. By playing the system, the accused managed to get repeated adjournments, resulting in the production of only one or two witnesses in an entire year.

A Woman is Offered in Exchange

As Jamali went to prison, members of his clan visited the aggrieved Bhutto family to mediate an age-old solution to a modern crisis. They told Javed – the head of the Bhutto household – that the MPA had confessed to having murdered Fauzia and now wanted to pay the price.

The "price" according to the Baloch tribal custom, would be decided by a *jirga* – a council of tribal elders. Among their suggestions for this price was to offer a woman (or women) from the Jamali family to the Bhuttos in "exchange" for Fauzia's murder. They suggested that Javed or one of his brothers marry a woman from the Jamali tribe and treat her in the way they saw fit.

These are the horrifying traditions that the tribal societies have lived with for centuries. I encountered cases in rural Sindh where a tribesman who murdered his wife on suspicion of infidelity could get a woman from the "offending tribe" to serve as his wife or slave. With endemic corruption, the murderers simply paid off the police and escaped punishment.

But the Jamali tribe was barking up the wrong tree. Javed showed the tribesmen the door, saying that as a modern man he had no place for such anachronisms. Although born and raised in a small town in Sindh, he believed in the equality of women. More practically, he had joined hands with civil society in Karachi to make public institutions work for the common good.

By 1991, a year after Jamali was indicted, Javed taught in the philosophy department of Sindh University, Jamshoro. His university was about 150 km from Karachi. He had built the department by convincing students from Sindh to become interested in studying western philosophy.

The hearings brought him regularly to Karachi. Afterwards, the two of us would meet for lunch at the Karachi Press Club, sip tea on the lawns and in addition to the case discuss the history and politics of Sindh.

In those days, Javed was a chain smoker who thought in an almost cyclical fashion, as he reached out for a match and lit up before he started a new sentence. Although I was opposed to smoking, I put that aside for the time being and listened to him in fascination. We both looked forward to the time together as a respite from the somber reality of the trial.

"Follow Your Heart" – A Friend's Advice

Every year or so, I would try to visit friends in the US to keep in touch with my old university life in Boston. When I went for a visit in 1991, I confided in a dear American girl friend about my feelings for Javed.

I had met Jane Pipik when she and I had both volunteered for a bi-weekly radio show called Women's Network News at *WBAI* radio station in New York. I was one of its reporters and she was the sound engineer for the show. Although we were raised on opposite ends of the world, we bonded as women working in male-dominated professions.

Jane encouraged me to follow my heart. Then in my thirties, I had long diverged from the marital path followed by my school friends and invested instead in my career. Reporting – and its importance in bringing change in a developing country like Pakistan – was so overpowering that I was not ready for another dramatic change. Moreover, though Javed and I had moved toward a new level of friendship, his shy, introverted nature never let me glimpse what he actually thought.

Jane – whose own marriage was a success – passionately tried to convince me across long car drives in Boston to probe into whether my relationship with Javed could grow into a life-long relationship. I was still thinking about the possibilities when I received a postcard from him in New York.

"Nothing is the same at the old haunts in Karachi without you," he wrote – signed J. B.

Electrified, I suddenly realized that life many not be the same anymore. I called up Jane. She knew what it meant. Given Javed's quiet, reserved nature, we talked about what a leap it must have been for him to have written such a card.

When I flew back home and we met, he seemed visibly overjoyed to see me. Still, neither of us would express our feelings.

I took a bold step. As I drove my car in Karachi...with him sitting besides me... I glanced over and asked,

"If the case ends, will you ever call me again?"

"Of course," he said.

He said it with so much emotion – I knew it to be true.

Tying the Knot

After so many years, neither of us honestly remembers who proposed. My family, who had resigned themselves to my independent high-wire acts, was convulsed with happiness as I announced I had found the right person.

True to his nature, my father wanted to show he was still in charge. In a society where marriages are arranged, or only take place with family consent, he said he would have to meet Javed before agreeing to my choice.

On that fateful day, Javed, slender and youthful, arrived with his hair brushed back – hopeful of making a good impression on my family. Seated across from him, I saw his trepidation as my father grilled him about his family background. My father would leave me on tenterhooks even after Javed left, saying he would take some time to give his "considered verdict."

Of course, my father gave the nod that Javed's family could come to our house to talk about the potential for the marriage. In that unforgettable meeting between both families, my father talked about everything on earth except the subject at hand. My sister and mother were growing nervous. My father always did love to extend the drama of the moment. He ended it with a flourish by saying, "Congratulations on the engagement of Javed and Nafisa."

The next six months of my life would be the happiest. We strolled along the Arabian Sea, where even the usual sight of the waves that ran amok under clear blue skies filled me with a joyous sense of well being.

Mostly, I was busy working – but at home, my family planned a big wedding. My father daily drew up guest lists and then tore them up as the family argued over whom to invite. Given the size of our family, it was no easy feat and we had to reduce the guest list to 600 people. The wedding reception was to be held in a huge football field. My father took volunteers on site for months ahead of time and made sure everything was perfect on the big day.

"Caught Taking Bribe, Released Giving Bribe"

In August 1990, as Benazir Bhutto's government was sacked, the incumbent PPP legislators were automatically unseated. It was a bad year for Jamali. Not only had he lost his seat in parliament, but he was also in prison for murder.

Under Pakistan's legal code, an accused is entitled to bail within two years unless it can be proved that he performed a heinous crime. While Jamali was in prison, he tried to use money and influence to secure his release through the high court. But his attempts were blocked by human rights activists, whose lawyer, Syed Sami Ahmed skillfully convinced the judge to deny him bail. Jamali remained in prison for two years for Fauzia's murder.

In early 1992, a district and sessions judge had solicited Javed, saying he had received Jamali's bail application seeking release through the lower court.

"What do you think I should do with it," the judge asked Javed in the presence of a court clerk.

It was clear to Javed that the judge would rule in favor of whoever paid him the most money. Bravely he replied, "I came here to get justice. I expect to get justice from the court."

But such words have become irrelevant in a society mired in corruption. Unable to "sell justice" to the aggrieved party, the judge turned a deaf ear to the eloquent arguments raised by Javed's lawyer about the heinous nature of the crime. Instead, he granted Jamali bail and enabled him to be released a few months later.

What had transpired between the judge and the accused? It was anyone's guess. Once in a while, the anti-corruption task force would mark hundred rupee notes and catch a judge red-handed accepting a bribe. But as the popular Pakistani saying goes,

"He was caught accepting a bribe and released giving a bribe."

Still, in the two years that Jamali was in prison, the world outside had changed. Political parties treated him as a pariah. In 1993, as the PPP began awarding tickets to candidates, it refused to give him a ticket for the second time. Newspapers refused to publish his statements. Society treated him as a common criminal.

Hope Arrives in the Form of a Muslim Cleric

Married to Fauzia's brother, I voluntarily stopped covering the trial. I knew it was not right to cover a trial in which I was emotionally invested. My editors seemed to think so too and reassigned the case to another male reporter.

Lengthy court delays gave the defense enough time to work on their witnesses. As expected, the driver Ishaq – the only eyewitness to the murder – reneged on his testimony to the magistrate. I had seen the scared look in the scrawny fellow when I questioned him point-blank in his hometown in the early days after the murder. Now, as Ishaq came to court, slinking into Jamali's shadow, he avoided meeting the gaze of the activists. Predictably, he told the court he had seen "Nothing."

Hope finally arrived five years into the trial in the form of a Muslim cleric from Nawabshah, Maulvi Faiz Mohammed Sahto. The elderly, white-bearded cleric told the court that he had been horrified to discover through the newspapers that Fauzia was already dead on the date he had performed her marriage in absentia to Jamali.

Apparently, the innocuous paragraph I had inserted in *Dawn* on January 12, 1990 – linking Jamali to Fauzia – had pushed the accused toward the marriage. Petrified that I had referred to Fauzia as his "girl friend," Jamali had, after my news item, contacted the Muslim cleric and given the impression that he was marrying Fauzia in absentia.

Maulvi Sahto testified in court that Jamali had tricked him into preparing a fake marriage document. He testified there was a discrepancy in the marriage dates. The cleric's official records showed that the accused had contracted the fake marriage after Fauzia's murder but forced the registrar's office to back date the marriage certificate. A handwriting expert brought into court confirmed that Fauzia's signature had been forged on the marriage document.

The humble cleric's insistence on speaking the truth in court was an affront to the influential and well-connected Jamali. The accused had managed to get several adjournments to prevent the cleric from testifying. He even sent his men to the Nawabshah mosque, where the cleric led the prayers of the male congregation. There, the cleric said he had been alternately cajoled and threatened against testifying.

Even under these threats, Maulvi Sahto made numerous trips to Karachi. After a year of adjournments, he finally testified against Jamali. The testimony obviously lifted a big weight from the conscience of a deeply religious man. It also kept alive the spark of hope among activists fighting for justice in the Fauzia Bhutto murder case.

In January 1996, office-bearers of the Pakistan Medical Association nominated Maulvi Faiz Mohammed Sahto for the Sughra Rababi human rights award – instituted in the name of a late woman artist. Large numbers of people came to the PMA House in Karachi to applaud the presentation of the award by a former Supreme Court judge and Chairman Emeritus of the Human Rights Commission of Pakistan, late Justice Dorab Patel to the humble but upright Muslim cleric.

But four years of repeated court delays wearied the special public prosecutor and caused him to withdraw. The trial would now be conducted by poorly qualified government prosecutors. At times, Javed walked into the office of the state public prosecutor and found the accused sharing cups of tea with those appointed to try him.

As the case proceeded, a piece of the bloodstained carpet – recovered from the apartment used by Jamali – mysteriously disappeared from the storage rooms of the court. That had been a key part of the evidence. Earlier, the laboratory report presented to the court had confirmed that the blood on the carpet matched the bloodstains on Fauzia's clothes at the time her body was found.

A number of district level judges heard the Fauzia Bhutto case. In more than one instance, Jamali appeared to have won them over. At times, he was the only one invited into the judges' chambers while everyone else waited outside the courtroom.

The accused also maneuvered the law department to block the appointment of another special public prosecutor. It became another uphill battle for the Citizens Police Liaison Committee to coordinate with the women and human rights groups to get their nominee, Shaukat Hayat appointed as the prosecutor.

But 14 years of repeated court adjournments would give the accused ample time to tamper with the evidence. In June 2004, additional district and sessions judge in Karachi East, Nadeem Ahmed Akhund ruled that there was "insufficient evidence" against Jamali and acquitted him along with his driver.

In December 2004, human rights activists pressured the Sindh government to appeal against the judgment. The state filed a case in the high court, challenging the lower court's acquittal. But the high court upheld the lower court's judgement and dismissed their appeal.

The Past is Never Forgotten

Fauzia's murder was a devastating blow for the family. Years later, the victim's mother still weeps, remembering how she would wait by the door for the train to bring her daughter home to Shikarpur for the holidays. Fauzia's sister, Sofia – two years her junior – her eyes a deep well of tears, wanted to know, "Why, why would anyone want to murder my dearest sister?"

These are the questions that victims in Pakistan ask from a legal system that has practically collapsed. When Fauzia first disappeared, it was she who was judged for being young and unmarried. It was a Herculean battle to chase the Machiavellian assembly member of the PPP and force the politicians, bureaucracy, police and judiciary to take note of the heinous crime.

Today, if there is any comfort for the family, it is that Jamali has been discredited in the court of public opinion. In 1998, the Sindhi press carried the dramatic news that Jamali's son had committed suicide. The response was predictable: there were many in the community who called the incident an "act of God" and "*Makafat-i-Amal*" – the Persian term for "What goes around, comes around."

In the small towns of Sindh, speculation was rife that it had been difficult for a young man to live with a father who had the reputation of a murderer. The irony of it all was that the son had used his father's gun to kill himself.

Today, Fauzia's murder is an example of the criminalization of politics in Pakistan: a masterful manipulator within the ruling party who exploited the corrupt system to roam free in society. It has also exposed the weak judiciary in Pakistan, where money and influence allow the corrupt to buy their way out of punishment.

On the other hand, late Fauzia Bhutto's case is symbolic of the power of the people, which rose above government weakness and a broken legal system and obtained a semblance of justice.

PART III

Terrorism in Pakistan

Chapter 6

PAKISTAN IN THE SHADOW OF 9/11

"Why do They Hate US?"

It was 9.15am on September 11, 2001 when the phone rang. There was a strange urgency to the ring. It made me spring out of bed in my tiny apartment in Sunderland, Western Massachusetts and run to the other room to quiet it.

It was my relative, Shabnam, who had left Pakistan decades ago and lived in Houston, Texas. In the instances when we met on either side of the globe, I shared with her my adventures as a journalist. Given our mutual background, she reveled in the exciting stories I told her as a reporter for the nation's leading newspaper.

Evidently, she knew me well enough to sense that this day – a day that changed the US – would change my life as well.

"Quick, turn on the television," she said.

Alas, I told her, we didn't have a television. My husband and I lived in a one-bedroom apartment and had only the sparse belongings of new immigrants. We had arrived about a year ago from Pakistan and I had just finished teaching a course at the Women Studies Department in Amherst College, Massachusetts on gender politics in Iran, Pakistan and Afghanistan.

"The trade towers in New York are burning. They say it was hit by an airplane," she was saying.

Sensing it was a terrorist act, I rushed to turn on the radio. I was immediately drawn into the drama unfolding in downtown Manhattan, where I had worked as a journalist for two years during the 1980s.

National Public Radio contributor, Ginger Miles, whose apartment overlooked the World Trade Towers, was on air. I knew Ginger from my reporting at *WBAI* radio in New York. There was unmistakable excitement in her voice, sounding like journalists do when they inadvertently turn into part of the story. Ginger fought her way through the smoke and debris blowing in through her windows as she spoke. Her commentary about thick ash, which blew into her apartment from the collapsing trade towers, conjured up vivid images of the attack into the heart of capitalism.

My mind flashed back to 1993, when I had visited the US from Pakistan. Then, I had stood on the balcony of a British writer's high-rise apartment near the UN building in New York, which faced the World Trade Towers. Arms outstretched, Jan Goodwin had dramatically described it as the site where an Al Qaeda operative Ramzi Yusuf, linked with militant terrorist groups in Pakistan, made the first unsuccessful attempt to bring down the towers.

On the day that would come to be known as 9/11, as the fall colors enveloped the picturesque Amherst valley, the radio reported that thick, billowing smoke had enveloped the World Trade Towers and the towers had begun to collapse. People trapped inside faced the horrifying choice of being burnt alive or jumping to meet a faster death.

At Amherst center, bewildered American students milled around in a candle light rally to show solidarity with the families of the victims. Many of the students who subsequently enrolled in the post-9/11 course I taught at the University of Massachusetts,

Amherst told me that they had joined to learn the facts that were kept secret from them by the US government, and which had resulted in such a terrifying and heartless attack on their soil.

Knowing the longstanding relationship between the US government and the Islamic militants in my region, it was clear to me that the finger of guilt would point to Pakistan and its neighbors.

I had left Pakistan just as the primordial Taliban fastened their tentacles around it. In 1999, *Dawn* had published my investigative report on the terror links between militants who bombed the US embassies in Africa and the Pakistan's north-west region. In that front-page report, I wrote that the militants were foreigners who traveled to Kenya and Tanzania through Karachi, using fake passports and Pakistani identities.

It was a time when the tail had begun to wag the dog. The Taliban had taken over Afghanistan in 1996 and were spreading in Pakistan. Shortly before I left for the US in 2000, the sectarian Anjuman Sipah Sahaba Pakistan (ASSP) – which translates as "Army of the Friends of the Prophet" – had shut down Karachi after an Islamic scholar, Maulana Mohammed Yusuf Ludhianvi and his driver were killed by rivals near the Binori Town mosque.

In early 2001, I taught at the secluded Amherst College with a sense of despair at the "Talibanization" of Pakistan. I was making my first break from reporting and it was an uphill task to explain its stormy cross-currents to my small class of mostly elite American students. The region's politics felt even more remote in the snow-covered hills and valleys of the Five College area.

After the semester ended, I moved a few yards down the road to work for the *WFCR* radio. The station was affiliated with the National Public Radio. My co-workers eyed me curiously and with an element of surprise because of my passion for coverage of the Pak-Afghan region. Occasionally, I overheard them mumble that scarce dollars were being squandered to cover my unusual interests.

As public funding was a big issue, it became harder to commission reports on my region. Only days before the 9/11 attacks, I had with difficulty convinced my program director to allow me to report on the Taliban's kidnapping of foreign Christian aid workers in Afghanistan. It grew harder to secure funds for such foreign programming since the audiences were a select group with esoteric interests.

And then the biggest attack on US soil in recent history occurred – and changed the direction of my life. Suddenly my telephone rang off the hook. Radio stations interviewed me on my cell phone. Television stations sent chauffeured limousines to interview me. Newspapers reporters arrived for interviews at my campus office. I spoke at impromptu meetings, seminars and question and answer sessions – organized by teachers and students in both the Five College and Boston areas – on why America had been attacked.

All of a sudden, people hung on to every word I said about the Taliban and growing Islamic fundamentalism in my region.

"Why do they hate us?" was the common refrain I heard all around me.

My mind was captivated by the image of powerful stones breaking through America's formidable ivory towers – and leaving massive debris all around.

The Chickens Were Primed to Come Home to Roost

The terrorist attacks of September 11, 2001 in New York and Washington DC – which provoked the US government to overthrow the Taliban government in Afghanistan – were for me a powerful reminder that the explosive situation building in my region had boomeranged to the world's super power.

As the planes ploughed into the World Trade Towers, I felt my experiences of terrorism resonate among Americans, for whom the battle had been brought to their doorsteps. When President George W. Bush took to the airwaves and challenged Pakistan's military ruler, Gen. Pervaiz Musharraf to make a stark choice, "Either you are with us or with the terrorists," I knew that my region would not be the same again.

In November 2001, a Washington based institute commissioned me to travel to Pakistan and study the media. It was the beginning of the transformation of the region. The US military had invaded Kabul, following disagreements with the Taliban government of Afghanistan that they had sheltered Al Qaeda. Although the 9/11 hijackers were Arabs, the US had been sufficiently involved in Afghanistan to follow their footprints.

As my plane flew over miles of contiguous rugged grey hills that stretch from Afghanistan to Pakistan, I saw why Al Qaeda had selected the settings. In this formidable moonscape, the militant Pashtun tribesmen who straddle the Pak-Afghan border had, in 1996, ousted the Afghan Mujahideen to form the Taliban government. They went on to host Al Qaeda Arab militants like Osama Bin Laden, as well as Chechens, Uzbeks and Uighurs, who had during the Cold War helped the US drive the Soviets out of Afghanistan.

From Pakistan's western city of Quetta, I traveled in a convoy of Western journalists through the dry winding hills to the Weish border of Afghanistan. We were headed to the tented city, set up by the United Nations for Afghan refugees. As our convoy wound around the hills under the bright November sky, Kalashnikov-hugging guards trailing us in open jeeps swung into view. It was like being part of a Western action movie, only this was real life.

We passed the ramshackle huts of the tribal Taliban, where angry tribesmen stared at our motorcade with suspicion and hostility. At one point, our vehicles were pelted with stones. It forced our driver to gather speed and drive frenziedly through swirls of mountain dust. Later, when I saw British journalist, Robert Fisk at the Serena Hotel in Quetta, a bandage around his head and locals in tow, I guessed he had been part of our motorcade.

My Australian colleague, Kathleen Reen and I stopped at the UN refugee tented city at the Weish border. Outside the tents were elderly Afghan men and children with dirty blond hair, green-gray eyes and runny noses. Their mothers wore voluminous *burqas* (encompassing veils) inside the tents. They were part of the Pashtun families who had fled US bombing in the southern Afghan town of Qandahar, walking for days to cross over to Pakistan.

From afar, I saw swirling clouds of dust, created by what looked like people chasing a vehicle. Hordes of Afghan children – and even grown men – ran after the UN truck that carried food and rations for them. The truck stopped and we watched. As the driver jumped down to distribute rations, he was mobbed and practically carried on the shoulders of the hungry crowd.

On the way, Kathleen and I stopped briefly at the home of a local journalist. If we had any hopes of meeting the family, these were dashed when the Pashtun women took one look at us and dashed out of the room. We were perplexed. Neither of us was veiled, yet neither did we look frightening.

As we walked down the street, our male companions explained, "Now that the Taliban government has been ousted, they are terrified you will force them to unveil."

It was evidence of the deep social conservatism of the millions of Afghan Pashtun tribesmen who fled to Pakistan and resettled here after it was invaded by the former Soviet Union in 1979. In Afghanistan, Pashtuns had reacted to Soviet-backed reforms by killing social workers who taught literacy and education to women. These conservative Pashtun Muslims would lay the basis for the Mujahideen, funded by the US, to drive the Soviets out of Afghanistan.

The Mujahideen in Pakistan

Seeing the Afghan refugees in 2001 was déjà vu for me, for I had visited the UN refugee camps in Pakistan during the 1980s after three million Afghans fled the Soviet invasion of their country. Then, the UN had resettled them in billowing white tents in the outskirts of Karachi in a settlement called Sohrab Goth. Hordes of boys and fierce-looking, bearded men roamed the tented settlements. Growing increasingly restive in an overcrowded city, the refugees told me they longed to fight against the Soviet occupation of their country.

In April 1988, I met a key Mujahideen leader and head of the Hezb-i-Islami, Gulbuddin Hekmatyar, as he arrived at a rally at the refugee camp to speak about the Geneva Accord – in which the UN had set a timetable for the Soviets to withdraw from Afghanistan. He was then a key recipient of US aid, funneled by Pakistan's Inter Services Intelligence (ISI).

Dressed in an immaculate white *shalwar kameez* (baggy tunic and trousers), Hekmatyar had a striking long face, tapering fingers and a beard. He spoke to me in well-articulated English, all the well that he kept an intent expression. "We Afghans have to unite in order to get rid of Russian occupation."

In mid April 1988, there were other Mujahideen leaders who had turned out to demand an early withdrawal of the former Soviet Union from Afghanistan. Dressed in Afghan gear, replete with a shawl across their shoulders, the leaders denounced the UN for laying out such a lengthy time frame for Russian withdrawal.

Their speeches rang out in the air, "Even if the Americans stop assistance we will snatch weapons from the Soviet army and turn it against the government in Afghanistan."

The View from Soviet-Dominated Kabul

In November 1989, I flew from Pakistan to Afghanistan as part of a delegation of journalists invited by the Soviet-backed Najibullah government – and saw the Mujahideen from the Afghan perspective.

The Soviet Union had fulfilled the Geneva Accord and pulled out of Afghanistan that year. Still, there was no let up in the Mujahideen's attacks on Najibullah's government. Barely had we arrived at the Intercontinental Hotel in Kabul when we heard that rocket missiles had killed 13 members of two Afghan families across from the hotel. The victims' families, who lived in homes atop the hills, were furious that the government failed to protect them and refused to meet us to tell their story.

Still, with the departure of Soviet troops, many Afghans had begun to own the fledgling government. Our Afghan hosts took us to Kabul University, where we found women to be among Najibullah's biggest supporters. Almost 60 per cent of the 9,250 students at Kabul University were women. Dressed mostly in long skirts and clutching notebooks, they imbibed modesty with modernity.

Even so, the Mujahideen were never far away from the minds of the Afghan students. It was hard not to think about the Islamic militants, given the occasional gunfire and bomb blasts that rent the air. On that bright, sunny November day, the women's spirits clouded over as one young Afghan said, "If the Mujahideen take over, they will force us to veil."

Under these circumstances, our hosts told us that Afghan women had volunteered to join the 200-member women's battalion, set up by the government to combat Mujahideen attacks. A group of Afghan male trainers had been assigned in a residential home in Kabul to equip women to defend against Mujahideen attacks in Nangarhar, Khost and the Salang Highway – the routes charted by the Islamic militants to take over Afghanistan.

The chief of the Women's Battalion, Major Saleha – a tall, slender woman – told me that the women were trained to handcuff the Mujahideen and hand them over to the police if they were suspected of planting bombs in the market place. In one recent incident, she told me that when the Mujahideen attacked, "They were aghast to find that the entire area was defended purely by women!"

We were flown to Qandahar, which shares a long border with Pakistan. I broke away from the main delegation to speak in Urdu to Afghan shopkeepers. The Qandaharis normally speak Pushtu, but their access to Pakistan's open borders had made them familiar with its national language.

A shop-owner in Qandahar, Abdul Ghaffar Waheedullah told me in halting Urdu, "Formerly, the Mujahideen would come out of their hide-outs to kill Kabul officials and get away with it because of support from the local families. But now they come like thieves."

The besieged President Najibullah invited our delegation of journalists to his imposing palace to appeal for an end to the Mujahideen's attacks from Pakistan. Heavy-set and clean-shaven, he entered the room in full military uniform, looking calm but wary. Seated at the head of an elongated mahogany table, he spoke through an interpreter to say that the Afghan government had fulfilled its promise and negotiated the withdrawal of the Soviets nine months before.

"Now it is up to the US, Saudi Arabia and Pakistan to keep their promise and stop the Mujahideen from launching attacks on our territory from your country."

He made a prophetic appeal to Benazir Bhutto, who had barely been in office for a year. "If Prime Minister Benazir Bhutto allows her country to be used to launch attacks against our government, one day she will be ousted by the Islamic fundamentalists."

We were in Kabul when our hosts informed us that the Afghan military had foiled a major offensive in Jalalabad, south of Kabul. The prisoners were brought to Kabul, where we could interview them. We were taken to a huge hall in which the Afghan foot soldiers of the Mujahideen, dressed in army fatigues, squatted on the floor. These prisoners were a breakaway faction of the Mujahideen groups based in Pakistan – the Hizb-i-Islami and Mahaz-i-Milli. They looked dazed but ready to cooperate.

Afghan Lt. Gen. Mohammed Anwar told us that the Mujahideen offensive in Jalalabad had been commanded by ISI's Colonel Sultan Mir and assisted by Major Bashir from Kohat with the help of "foreign advisors." These Mujahideen soldiers told us that they had been "brainwashed" into believing that Najibullah's cabinet consisted of *"kafirs"* (infidels), who would have to be killed in order to bring Islam back to Afghanistan.

It was a public image that President Najibullah struggled hard to dispel. The government had reconstructed many of the mosques destroyed during the war and one heard the *azaan* (call to prayer) during the day. A photograph of Najibullah, bent on a prayer mat, was pasted around Kabul to "prove" that the leadership consisted of God-fearing Muslims.

A team of skeptical team of Western journalists was also on hand to cross-question the prisoners of war. "How much does Najibullah's government give you to join them?" shot an English woman reporter. She was part of a British team that had filmed the Afghan Mujahideen in Pakistan's refugee camps. One of the

Afghan tribesmen captured by Najibullah's army had identified her from that encounter.

I had also come to know her as among the few European journalists we bumped into at breakfast in the otherwise empty Intercontinental Hotel. At times, I joined the British and Swiss reporters for coffee in the dining hall that overlooked the distant hills, which intermittently resounded with gunfire.

The British woman was full of scorn for the "propaganda" put out by our Afghan hosts. "Najibullah is a Russian puppet," she told me in her definitive tone. Seeing that I didn't look fully convinced, she went on, "Did you know that he was the head of the Afghan secret police – KHAD – and has a reputation for torturing Afghan dissidents?"

I didn't know that. But her conversations convinced me she was among those who had cast their lot with the Mujahideen – then portrayed by the West as the "freedom fighters."

Knowing that in those days Western journalists were a rare breed in Afghanistan, it was my turn to ask the foreign reporters, "So why are *you* in Kabul?"

They told me that they had arrived because there was a huge Mujahideen offensive underway, which given the massive US support funneled through Pakistan was expected to soon force out Najibullah's government. I had correctly surmised that they had traveled from neighboring Peshawar where most foreign journalists based themselves during the Cold War.

For the Western media, the Mujahideen were the key to dismantling the Soviet Union. The foreign media had begun the count down to President Najibullah's downfall nine months earlier, as the Soviet Union complied with the Geneva Accord and withdrew its military forces from Afghanistan.

That day – February 15, 1989 – I flew from Karachi to Islamabad to witness the Afghan Interim Government outline its plans for the take-over of Kabul. Western reporters asked few questions from the bearded, turbaned Mujahideen commanders who sat on stage. Instead, photographers clicked away at the US's unlikely allies – the seven-member coalition of Islamic political parties poised to form a Sunni Muslim state in Afghanistan.

Looking at the Mujahideen commanders on stage, I felt my heart sink. My instincts told me that their take-over of Afghanistan would be bad news for Pakistan. It was a Western planted sapling for a fundamentalist Islamic movement that threatened Muslim sects and non-Muslims in the region and paved the way for the Taliban.

After 1991, when differences emerged between the Mujahideen – and Gulbuddin Hematyar's hardline Hezb-i-Islami party rained missiles on Burhanuddin Rabbani's government in Kabul, the Pakistani military stepped in. They were aided by Islamic political parties like the Jamiat-i-Ulema Islam (JUI), who trained the young orphans of war in Pakistan's refugee camps in *madressahs* (Islamic schools) on concepts of *jihad* that would serve the military's strategic objectives in the region.

In 1996, Pakistan's military helped the Taliban to oust the Mujahideen and take Kabul. It was a government that was recognized only by Pakistan, Saudi Arabia and the UAE. Over time, the Taliban would allow Al Qaeda to ensconce itself more firmly into Afghanistan and launch the 9/11 attacks.

Fleeing Militants Massacre my Christian Friends

As President George W. Bush blamed the loss of 3,000 American lives on the Taliban, Pakistan's army, headed by Gen. Pervaiz Musharraf, backed down from their overt support for the Taliban. Instead, Pakistan made a prima facie U-turn against the government that it had helped to establish in Afghanistan.

For the Taliban and its Al Qaeda benefactors, their abandonment by the Pakistani military was a cue to attack anything remotely Western. Driven out of Afghanistan, these militant groups headed straight to Pakistan where they went on a killing spree against non-Muslims.

On September 25, 2002, the terrorists massacred eight of my Christian friends and colleagues from the Institute for Peace and Justice in Karachi. They tied up eight people with tape and shot them in cold blood – leaving a ninth struggling for dear life.

As the news filtered into my apartment in Sunderland, Massachusetts on September 25, 2002, it made my blood curdle. Their faces flashed before my eyes: Aslam Martin was a broad-shouldered, strong man who would enter our reporter's room with a diffident smile. Making a beeline for my desk, he would put his heavy motorcycle helmet on my table and discuss his institute's press release.

The murder of the gentle and innocent Johnny Mascarenas, who was known to our family, was no less painful. Johnny was a tall gangly youth with a shy laugh, who worked for just causes. He was so gentle and innocent that it made me wonder about the savagery of the terrorists who had killed him.

My niece, Nadia – who then studied at Columbia University, New York – had telephoned me right away after the incident. The moment I picked up the phone, I heard her sob. Struggling with bewildered grief, she asked me a question for which I had no straight answer: "Why, oh why would anyone want to murder Uncle Johnny?"

I reflected with a heavy heart. For me, who had grown up in a multi-religious Karachi that also included Christians, Hindus, Zoroastrians and Jews, our non-Muslim neighbors were a bigger extension of our family. In the 1960s, as our Christian neighbors left our neighborhood and migrated to the West, Martin and Johnny had remained among the few brave souls who mobilized to make Pakistan a religiously tolerant society.

I covered their protests against the blasphemy laws, passed in 1984 by Gen. Zia ul Haq. These laws have led to the persecution, imprisonment and murder of thousands of Muslims and non-Muslims on suspicion of defamation of the Prophet of Islam. Benazir Bhutto, for all her personal liberal beliefs, dared not touch the blasphemy laws and Gen. Musharraf hastily revoked pronouncements to undo them in 1999 when the Islamic parties growled at his attempts.

Ten days after my Christian friends were murdered, I visited Karachi – where a year of terrorism had made the political climate hotter than the weather. It had been only a year since the US invaded Afghanistan, but Karachi already had a new and dangerous feel to it. As a former reporter with my finger on the pulse of the city, I witnessed how the waves of change had washed down to the nation's southernmost shores.

In the middle of Karachi, giant Armored Personnel Carriers (APCs) and police mobiles had cut off entry to the American consulate. The embassy had already stopped its sought-after visa services since 1997, when a terrorist attack had killed four American employees. Still, shortly before my arrival, the militant Harkat-i-Jihad-i-Islami had crashed an explosives-packed vehicle into the building and killed over a dozen local pedestrians.

Only a couple of blocks away another Kashmiri militant group – Harkat-ul-Mujahideen – had exploded a car bomb next to a bus parked across the Sheraton Hotel. It killed French naval engineers who had arrived that summer to help Pakistan build a naval submarine. Following the tragedy, the French prime minister immediately recalled the remaining engineers.

In the aftermath of the murders of French engineers, the Harkat ul Mujahideen chief, Asif Zaheer had said with a tinge of regret, "We had been led into believing they were Americans."

But today many French people are not convinced that the engineers were killed in the post-9/11 wave of terrorism. Instead, a lawsuit filed by the victims' relatives has forced the French government to investigate whether the attack was carried out because its previous government cancelled commissions for the arms deal with Pakistan. The case involves both French President Nicolas Sarkozy and President Asif Zardari as the beneficiaries of the commissions.

I met up with the sole Muslim survivor of the massacre, Rahim Baksh Azad, who worked at the dirty, congested Rimpa Plaza building where the Christians were murdered. That fateful morning Azad had arrived late at the Institute, knocking the door to find a watchman gagged with tape stagger to open the door. The watchman had been knocked unconscious by the fleeing terrorists and apparently left for dead.

Azad told me when he ran toward the library, he found some of his colleagues on chairs and others lying on the floor – blood dripping from them. Two of the Institute's members, Edwin

Foster and Robin Sharif were barely alive and writhed like fish, just pulled out of water. Seeing his colleagues wallow in a pool of blood stunned Azad. He grew confused and kept dialing 15 – the police emergency number – forgetting that he needed to dial 9 first to get an outside line.

Edwin Foster did not survive. Robin Sharif recovered in hospital and narrated to the local press that the terrorists – later identified as the Lashkar-i-Jhangvi, a sectarian form of the Punjabi Taliban – had barged in and asked for Aslam Martin and Father Arnold Heredia. The slender, bespectacled council member of the Human Rights Commission of Pakistan (HRCP), Father Arnold would speak passionately at the Commission's meetings against the growing cancer of fundamentalism in society. Luckily for Father Arnold, he had already migrated to Australia.

At the HRCP, its prominent leader, Asma Jehangir – who then also served as the UN Special Rapporteur on Extrajudicial Killings – told me in her clear, forceful and unblinking style that she held the military government responsible for its failure to put extra security on a predominantly Christian organization like the Institute. "We had repeatedly asked them to do so, but they refused," she said.

The murders of the Christian activists sent shock waves in the community. There were touching scenes of anger, mixed with sorrow as thousands of Christians, Muslims, Hindus and people of all faiths lowered the human rights activists into the ground.

At a memorial meeting for the slain Christians, the executive director of Aurat Foundation (Women's Foundation), Anis Haroon reminisced: "When I went to the Church services for our friends from the Institute, it was a bit like going to my own funeral."

A hush fell over the room as the Women's Action Forum – which had, for decades, fought alongside the Institute for Peace and Justice against discriminatory laws – reflected over her heartfelt sentiment.

While Christians became prime targets, the militants who fled Afghanistan next picked on Shia doctors. The Pakistan Medical Association's secretary general, Dr Shershah Syed – an energetic gynecologist, driven by social concerns – and his staid colleague,

Dr Mirza Ali Azhar told me that in 2002, medical practitioners removed billboards from private clinics which displayed Shia names like Husseini and Ali. Apparently, the militants had been breaking into clinics and killing doctors, merely because they did not belong to their Sunni Salafi sect of Islam.

"Why kill doctors?" I asked.

"Because they are high profile members of society and by targeting them the militants terrorize society," they answered.

The terror tactics seem to have worked in the society where news spreads through word of mouth. Doctors felt threatened, not just because they belonged to the "wrong" Muslim sect, but because high-profile Sunni doctors were killed in reprisals. Panicked doctors refused to accept police assurances that these were "isolated incidents" and quietly packed their bags to resettle overseas.

The Pakistan Medical Association office bearers began serious negotiations with the administration to change the situation. Aware that the Musharraf administration had given a free hand to sectarian outfits like the Anjuman Sipah Sahaba (ASSP) to hold public rallies, intended to mop up anti-US sentiment, they were not convinced by the administration's argument that it did not have sufficient police force to catch the criminals.

"We told him that was their problem and if they did not catch the culprits, we would bring out doctors on the streets," Dr Azhar told me. The pressure worked and the killings stopped.

During my three-week sojourn in Karachi in 2002, I did not see a single European face. For someone used to the occasional Western journalist popping in and out of the Karachi Press Club, it was strange that even a major event such as the October 10 elections, introduced by Musharraf to bring back "phased democracy," had failed to attract Western reporters. Instead, 9/11 ushered in a season of discontent between the US and the Musharraf administration.

9/11 Gives License for Disappearances

In 2001, as Al Qaeda militants fled from US bombing in Afghanistan, they crossed over into Pakistan. There they found safe refuge not only in the tribal Waziristan belt but their top leadership relocated to urban areas of the north-west and down south. They were selectively caught in lieu of reward money offered by the US, as were some of their local abettors in the Islamic parties.

Musharraf's autobiography offers a glimpse into the role he played in catching some of these high value targets. "Since shortly after 9/11 – when many Al Qaeda members fled Afghanistan and crossed the border into Pakistan – we have played multiple games of cat and mouse with them. We have captured 672 and handed over 369 to the United States. We have earned bounties totaling millions of dollars…"

For relatives of families who were disappeared under Gen. Musharraf, his words are no less than a confession. Amna Masood Janjua, a petite woman in headscarf, whose husband Masood – from the prosleytizing Islamic group, Tablighi Jamaat – mysteriously disappeared in 2005, has presented Musharraf's quotation to the Supreme Court as self-incriminating evidence. The former housewife, who denies that her husband engaged in militant activities, says that the former military ruler can scarcely deny he caused people to disappear when he admits to their capture and "sale" to the US.

Amna's husband was scheduled to depart from their home in Rawalpindi for Peshawar on July 30, 2005 when he was picked up. As she searched for him, she was mystified to find an army man spying on her family home and the college, which was run by her husband. Acting on a tip off from a member of the intelligence agencies, she discovered that her phone was bugged. Amna – who had, by then, taken over her husband's travel agency in Islamabad – hired a lawyer.

When she approached the Supreme Court as a wife and a mother, Amna was contacted by a growing number of family members whose loved ones were disappearing in Pakistan after September 11. It would lead her to form the Defense of Missing Persons, which by 2010 included 788 families whose members were held in illegal detention.

Many of those on Amna's list were Baloch nationalists who had nothing to do with Al Qaeda or Taliban and were picked up by the intelligence agencies for their alleged links with India and other spy agencies which support the Baloch armed struggle for secession.

Amna says that US agencies in Pakistan partnered with local intelligence agencies to interrogate suspects through torture methods that included beatings, isolation, sleep and toilet deprivation and repeatedly questioned them about their alleged meetings with Osama Bin Laden. Detenus wore orange jump suits at detention centers located in Pakistan's garrison city of Rawalpindi, Bagram air base in Afghanistan and in US-administered Guantanamo Bay.

When Amna contacted former US ambassador to Pakistan, Anne Patterson and told her that her husband was missing, the ambassador reportedly replied, "I know nothing about the case."

But Amna says that US intelligence agencies had also denied knowledge of the whereabouts of Saud Memon – the businessman who owned the shed in Karachi where Daniel Pearl's body was found. In 2003, the FBI picked up Memon and moved him to Guantanamo Bay. Four years later, he was produced in Pakistan's Supreme Court emaciated and with memory loss after no evidence was found to tie him to Pearl's murder. His family claims he had been "severely tortured." Memon died shortly afterwards – a victim of "collateral damage."

Her group also lobbied for the release of suspected jihadist, Dr Aafia Siddiqi, who went missing in Pakistan. The Human Rights Commission of Pakistan highlighted Dr Aafia's case among the disappearances under Musharraf. When a New York court eventually sentenced her to life imprisonment – in spite of the fact that she was suffering from a confused mental state – Pakistan reacted with a wave of sympathy.

In 2007, the HRCP presented the cases of 200 missing persons in front of the Supreme Court with an appeal to investigate the disappearances. But on March 3, 2007, when Chief Justice, Iftikhar Chaudhry summoned the intelligence agencies to elicit a report on the disappeared persons, he was put under house arrest by Gen. Musharraf. Given the tumultuous political events of 2007, it was not until two years later that the Supreme Court held its next hearing on missing persons.

Running with the Hare and Hunting with the Hound

While President Gen. Pervez Musharraf got prize money for handing over high value Al Qaeda militants to the US, the military never really cut ties with the Taliban. Even as Musharraf made a U-turn to align with the US in the "War on Terror," he encouraged an electoral alliance of Islamic political parties that were banded in the Mutehidda Majlis-i-Amal (MMA), the United Council for Action and the sectarian ASSP to soak up the anger caused by the aftermath of the US bombing in Afghanistan.

It was an old nexus between the military and the Islamic parties banded in the MMA – the Jamiat-i-Ulema Islam (F – Fazlur Rehman) and the Jamaat-i-Islami, led by Qazi Hussein Ahmed – which secular politicians cynically dubbed the Mullah Military Alliance. Mindful of the military's larger goals of keeping the Taliban intact for future use in Afghanistan and Kashmir, Musharraf weeded out foreign Al Qaeda militants, putting bounties on their heads, even as he used the MMA to keep a light hand on the Taliban.

The secular Awami National Party (ANP) chief, Asfandyar Wali Khan – whose party was routed by the MMA in Khyber Pakhtunkhwa province in the October 2002 election, told me that the ISI had openly rigged that election. Under Musharraf, the secular ANP was sidelined in favor of the bearded, turbaned JUI chief, Maulana Fazlur Rehman whose party trained the Taliban in *madressahs* (Islamic schools) for *jihad* in the 1990s.

When the Taliban began suicide attacks to avenge military action, parliamentary opposition leader, Maulana Fazlur Rehman denied there were suicide bombers in Pakistan. Instead he referred to the blame on Islamic extremists as "a Western conspiracy to malign Pakistan."

In 2006, as the Bush administration claimed the elimination of Abu Musab Al-Zarqawi in Iraq as a great victory, the

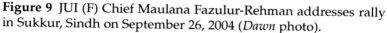

Figure 9 JUI (F) Chief Maulana Fazulur-Rehman addresses rally in Sukkur, Sindh on September 26, 2004 (*Dawn* photo).

JUI (F) tried to offer prayers for him in the National Assembly. One of their top Islamic leaders, when questioned about the move to offer prayers for Zarqawi, who was deemed to be a terrorist, responded, "A terrorist for some is a freedom fighter for others."

The Musharraf government entrusted the JUI (F) leadership to persuade tribal leaders in Pakistan's Federally Administered Tribal Areas (FATA) to hand over foreign militants who had reconverged after their exodus from Afghanistan. The Taliban saw little need to make concessions in *jirgas* (tribal meetings), led by sympathetic Islamic party leaders. Instead, their militants closed off FATA to outside forces and implemented harsh Sharia laws to govern the local tribesmen.

As the Taliban leadership grew in the FATA areas, the JUI (F) leaders praised them even louder. They had a reverential attitude toward Baitullah Mehsud, who first fought against the Soviets and later became a protégé of Afghan Taliban leader, Mullah Omar. In the words of a tribal leader from the JUI (F), "Baitullah Mehsud

Figure 10 Tehrik-i-Taliban Pakistan Chief Baitullah Mehsud in Sararogha, South Waziristan on February 7, 2005, shortly before he signed the peace deal with the Musharraf administration (*Dawn* photo).

is a commander who has a huge following not only in Waziristan but in the entire tribal area."

Although the Pakistan military kept up its offensive against the Taliban militants, the MMA Islamic coalition argued in favor of peace deals. Whenever their *jirgas* failed to keep the peace, the Bush administration demanded that the Pakistan military launch an offensive against the militants. The military offensives were followed up by fresh peace deals, which, like the ones signed with the Taliban in South Waziristan in 2004 and 2005, only allowed the Taliban militants to grow stronger.

As the armed militants from the Pashtun tribe operated between the seamless hills on the border of Pakistan and Afghanistan, President Gen. Pervaiz Musharraf and President Hamid Karzai hurled accusations and counter accusations at each other as to *who* was responsible for the resurgence of the Taliban. The army spokesman, Maj. Gen. Shaukat Sultan admitted that while militants came from Afghanistan to engage in subversive

Map 2 Map of FATA.

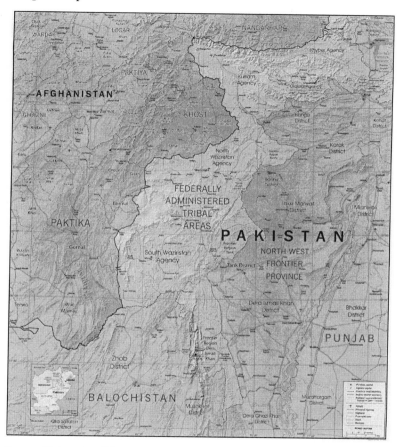

Source: University of Texas.

activities inside Pakistan, they also ran across the 1,200-mile border to create trouble for the Afghan government.

The Pushtun ethnicity of the Taliban – who straddle the seamless Pak-Afghan border – and their common objective of fighting US occupation forces in Afghanistan helped the leaders of both nations – Musharraf and Karzai – to avoid taking direct responsibility for the resurgence of Islamic militancy in the region.

The Taliban Sets up Shop in Pakistan

With stepped-up US and NATO patrols in Afghanistan, the Taliban and Al Qaeda found Pakistan's tribal Waziristan belt a much more hospitable terrain to resettle and reorganize. The Al Qaeda's militants, who were welcomed by the US to fight against the Soviets during the Cold War, had already integrated through marriages within the local tribes. In the post-9/11 era, the peace deals offered by Musharraf allowed them to recreate a Taliban state that mirrored their fallen government in Afghanistan.

Over time, the Taliban murdered hundreds of *maliks* (tribal landlords) in FATA, accused of spying for Pakistan; beheaded drug peddlers, kidnappers, looters and dacoits and collected *jaziya* (taxes on non-Muslims) to establish their rule. It would change the traditional social structure and hierarchy and cause an exodus of landlords, political agents and secular communities to Khyber Pakhtunkhwa's settled areas.

In Khyber Agency, the main artery connecting Peshawar to Kabul, a running battle between two religious groups – led by Mufti Munir Shakir and an Afghan, Pir Saifur Rehman – in 2005 resulted in a heavy loss of life. Shakir's group spawned the Lashkar-i-Islam (Army of Islam), whose leader Mangal Bagh used FM radio stations in the *madressahs* (Islamic schools) of the tribal belt to incite listeners into acts of sectarian violence against the local Shia population. From time to time, they blew up transmission towers of FM radio stations to stop the government from broadcasting music and information.

While the government encouraged the predominantly Shia population of the surrounding Kurram agencies to form tribal armies – or *lashkars* – for self-protection, the militants responded by suicide missions that included ramming explosive laden vehicles into *jirgas* (tribal councils). These militants banded under the ASSP and LEJ also found ways to attack Shia refugees and their congregations in prayer houses, shrines and mourning processions that stretched all the way from Khyber to Karachi.

Although Shias did not turn against Sunnis on a large scale, as has been the case in Iraq, these attacks led to steady stream of retaliation. Where the military took on the Taliban, their sectarian affiliates responded with growing attacks on non-Muslims, surpassing the sectarian violence witnessed two decades before.

As the Bush administration mounted pressure on Pakistan to "do more" in the "War on Terror," Pakistan's army soldiers came in the front line of fire. Being poorly equipped and trained, the conventional army was no match for the well-armed Taliban who fought with guerrilla tactics that included improvised explosive devices (IEDs), suicide attacks, kidnappings and beheadings. It led to situations in which entire contingents of soldiers were kidnapped and several were beheaded. Others were either forced to surrender or voluntarily deserted the army.

In 2006, matters reached a point where Musharraf was forced to make a deal with Taliban militant Hafiz Gul Bahadur in North Waziristan that his tribesmen would expel foreign fighters from the tribal belt and refrain from attacking the Pakistan military in return for the administration's movement of 80,000 troops from check posts in Waziristan to the Afghan border. The deal succeeded in getting rid of Uzbek fighters – subsequently leading to the assassination of their chief, Tahir Yuldashev, through a drone attack.

But the North Waziristan deal would eventually turn the area into the last refuge for jihadists. As late as 2010, Awami National Party Senator, Afrasiab Khattak admitted to me that Gul Bahadur's forces had become a "problem" for his government.

Meanwhile, tribesmen were eyewitnesses to the return of Afghan Mujahideen commander Jalaluddin Haqqani and Gulbuddin Hekmatyar in North Waziristan. In December 2009, these former CIA-funded Mujahideen gave sanctuary to a Jordanian double agent who used suicide bombing to wipe out a sizeable portion of US intelligence officials who were posted at Khost, Afghanistan.

Former FATA security chief Brig Mahmood Shah, who quit his post in 2005, calls the North Waziristan accord "a bad deal" that enabled the Taliban to consolidate its position. While initially the Afghan Taliban did expel foreign fighters from the region, soon it was back to square one as the Haqqani network attracted foreign jihadists and launched increasingly daring attacks against NATO forces in Afghanistan.

Drones Attack Last Refuge for Jihadists

During Musharraf, the Bush administration worked out a deal with him to allow drones to take out "high value targets" in the FATA areas bordering Afghanistan. Both sides kept a high level of secrecy about the drone attacks and for years the Pentagon refused to acknowledge them. Musharraf's media spokesmen were given the difficult task of answering to civilian deaths in drone attacks, even while his administration scuttled the issue.

The US gradually increased drone attacks in FATA to counter growing insurgent attacks on NATO troops in Afghanistan. By 2007 drone attacks were frequently used against the Tehrik-i-Taliban (TTP), which surfaced under the leadership of Baitullah Mehsud and was found responsible for a substantive increase in the Afghan insurgency. That year, as Pakistan buckled under US pressure and killed Taliban militants in South Waziristan, Baitullah's response was to launch a spate of suicide attacks against military and police targets in Pakistan.

Still, careful not to antagonize Baitullah, the Musharraf administration sent delegations led by JUI (F) Senator Saleh Shah and the late Maulana Merajuddin to negotiate with the TTP militants. These leaders were ever-ready to defend the fire-brand militant. They held Baitullah Mehsud in awe, notwithstanding the fact that the militant had let fall all pretenses and declared open war against Pakistan.

On the other hand, the Afghan Taliban led by Afghanistan's deposed Taliban leader, *Amir ul Momineen* (Leader of the Pious), Mullah Omar, assiduously avoided attacks on Pakistan and instead used its territory to launch attacks against NATO troops in Afghanistan.

As the CIA became more vocal about the ISI's role in shielding the Afghan Taliban, the US threatened to take drone attacks deeper into Pakistan's territory. Talk of an Afghan government in exile – notably the Quetta Shura – gained currency as the US alleged that Mullah Omar and his coterie had formed a government-in-exile in Balochistan. Even if the US threatened to carry out drone attacks in Quetta, merely to test the waters, anxious residents expected the missiles to rain on them any day.

In Quetta, it is an open secret that Mullah Omar's fighters often travel to neighboring Qandahar in dark-tinted vehicles, laden with weapons. From time to time, they ambush the NATO supply trucks at Chaman, bordering Qandahar. Those wounded by NATO troops are brought back by popular routes for treatment to Quetta's hospitals. Still, the Afghan Taliban refrain from attacking targets inside their host country and instead keep a good relationship with the Pakistan army, which in turn looks the other way for its broader strategic objectives.

On the outskirts of Quetta lies a well-lit colony for the Afghan Taliban called Kharotabad. This base camp in the hills sparkles amid otherwise dark surroundings. Apart from Pashtuns, the three other ethnicities of Afghanistan – the Uzbek, Tajik and Hazara – are frequent visitors. The colony has become a notorious focal point for the smuggling of heavy weapons, narcotics, as well as vehicles and tunnels that enable a quick getaway.

But even as the US-leaked memos and statements accused the ISI of secretly supporting the Afghan Taliban, Pakistan put its foot down on allowing the US to operate inside settled areas. While US drone missile strikes grew more frequent, they were only allowed to operate in the FATA belt along Afghanistan. Drones became a weapon of choice in North Waziristan, where Al Qaeda's foreign fighters and Taliban congregated but where the military held off from conducting any operation.

The UN has questioned the legality of drone attacks because of the highly covert nature of the strikes. Although the true extent of civilian casualties are unknown, a study by the New America Foundation shows that while drones have killed more than 1,300 people, the civilian fatality rate is approximately 30 per cent of that figure.

On the other hand, Washington has ramped up drone attacks because they avoid the loss of US lives, and there is no media to record the blood spilled on the ground. But the strikes remain highly unpopular in Pakistan, where common people pay the ultimate price. These drone attacks have been avenged by the militants through a spree of almost indiscriminate suicide attacks in Pakistan.

Pakistan in 2007 AD

In 2007 – the year that gave birth to the current situation in Pakistan – alarm bells rang in Washington that two firebrand clerics – Maulvi Abdul Aziz and Abdur Rashid Ghazi – planned to "Talibanize" Pakistan through their state funded Red Mosque in Islamabad.

There were real fears in the US that the speed with which the Taliban had grown under Gen. Musharraf had reached Islamabad. In Washington, think tanks had begun to speak out that the sons of the late Islamic radical Maulana Qari Abdullah – who had managed to collect rabid militants in the capital of nuclear-armed Pakistan – could usher in a horrific attack on the West that would make 9/11 pale in comparison.

The Red Mosque was emblematic of the dual character of the Musharraf administration. The mosque was patronized by senior government and intelligence officials, even as its clerics were known to keep close links with the Al Qaeda and the Taliban.

On a visit from Washington DC to Islamabad, I came face to face with how the influx of foreign money, massage parlors and video shops had sharpened the contradiction between poor Islamic militants and the corrupt ruling military elite and provoked the puritanical Red Mosque clerics to take on the administration.

Red Mosque cleric, late Abdur Rasheed Ghazi asserted that he and his brother had repeatedly asked the Musharraf administration to clean up the trash – i.e. close down the brothels and the massage parlors – but without success. In his words, "We are now tired of asking and have decided to take out the trash ourselves."

Thereafter, *burqa*-clad female students of the Red Mosque's sister seminary, Jamia Hafsa began a "purification drive" in Islamabad by kidnapping three women accused of running a brothel. Word had it that the brothel was patronized by senior government officials. Ghazi's activism temporarily paid off and he forced the foreign women and their children to close shop before they were released.

Under US pressure, Musharraf ordered the demolition of a mosque being illegally constructed by the Red Mosque clerics. At that stage, television images captured tall, *burqa*-covered students in dark glasses and armed with machine guns as they occupied a children's library next door. It made civil society wonder aloud whether these were really women or tall men in women's clothing.

Washington watched with unease as the Red Mosque clerics carried out their militant activities right next to Islamabad's diplomatic enclave. It was strangely reminiscent of 1992, when the military had let dacoits rampage through Sindh without lifting a finger. There was a brief lull as Gen. Musharraf sent senior leaders of his party to negotiate with the militants.

And then came the storm.

Ironically dubbed "Operation Silence," the encirclement of Red Mosque by 12,000 army men turned into a deafening war between the army and 600 heavily armed militants holed inside. Red Mosque cleric, Maulana Abdul Aziz fled wearing a *burqa* while his brother, Abdur Rashid Ghazi, a loquacious speaker, held the fort for hours before he was killed with some 84 militants – and promptly dubbed a martyr.

The siege of the Red Mosque proved to be a turning point for Pakistan. Betrayed by the army, the militants fled to North Waziristan where they swelled the ranks of the Tehrik-i-Taliban Pakistan (TTP). Apart from the Punjabi Taliban, based on sectarian groups, former state-sponsored elements reinvented themselves under the Asian Tigers.

The connection of Red Mosque militants with North Waziristan came to the fore when the Asian Tigers killed former ISI officer, Khalid Khawaja who had boldly accompanied a British journalist of Pakistani origin, Asad Qureishi, during his investigative reporting into the tribal areas. Khawaja was accused by the Taliban of double-dealing in the Red Mosque episode. At the same time, the TTP kept an accompanying army officer, Col. Inam in capitvity as they debated whether or not to kill him for espionage. He too was eventually killed.

A General Loses Face

When Gen. Pervaiz Musharraf ousted Prime Minister Nawaz Sharif through a military coup in October 1999, he had managed to convince a number of people that democracy spelt anarchy. For a while the popular wisdom was that tried and tested politicians were "corrupt," and that the military was the only institution that could bring stability and relief for people suffering from the greed and chaos of politicians.

But as the Al Qaeda and Taliban introduced suicide bombers on the Iraq pattern, new forms of terrorism manifested in Pakistan. The situation in Balochistan, never good under previous rulers, saw an escalation in violence. Disappearances, torture and an absence of freedom of expression became the order of the day. As poverty showed no sign of abating, people began to clamor for a return to democracy.

In my visits to Pakistan, I saw how Musharraf had attempted to strengthen the military at the expense of the people. The roads were full of potholes, there were many more beggars on the streets and the chaos of people and traffic was more unseemly. The trade deficit had grown by several million dollars. Billions of rupees had been loaned to highly connected people, who had defaulted on payments. While US annual military aid of USD 1 billion was unaccounted for, the Taliban had grown with a vengeance.

In Karachi's Defense Housing Society, which catered to the privileged military elite, there were new hotels, expensive golf courses and private clubs that catered exclusively to the ruling elite. The armed forces reclaimed land from Clifton beach, where multinational franchises like McDonalds and Kentucky Fried Chicken sprung up for a class which could the afford the dollar rates. New roads, bridges and roundabouts had grown Karachi into a mega city and changed it beyond recognition.

Under Musharraf, army and naval chiefs, as well as intelligence officers – retired and serving, were appointed as heads of the government corporations. They controlled transportation, communication and education at the federal and provincial levels. At the same time, tax exemptions to military personnel had enabled them to invest in national industries and turn it into a profit.

Militaristic responses to political problems, unfair allocation to the provinces, widespread unemployment and a yawning gulf between the rich would motivate poor people to cry for an end to military rule and the return to democracy.

As the Taliban grew more powerful, the US Congress forced Musharraf to release his chokehold on political parties. At the same time, it made contact with secular parties that could play a role in the future set-up. The Awami National Party, based in the Khyber Pakhtunkhwa province bordering Afghanistan – came up for air. The ANP, which had been sidestepped by Musharraf in the 2002 election, told US leaders that the resurgence of the Taliban was a "ticking time bomb" for the region.

The biggest beneficiary of Musharraf's fall from grace would be the Pakistan Peoples Party, led by Benazir Bhutto. Educated in the West and keenly attuned to Western needs, Benazir was aware that her fortunes were knitted into Washington's post-9/11 framework. As the only female prime minister of Pakistan and indeed the Muslim world, Benazir pledged to free her country from Islamic extremism.

Still, the Republican administration led by George W. Bush stayed skeptical of Benazir, aware that only the army could deliver vis-à-vis US strategic interests. Moreover, as chief of army staff and president, Musharraf had since 9/11 enjoyed a special relationship with President Bush. In 2007 however Bush's fortunes were on the decline and the Democratic Party, aware that Musharraf's sagging profile needed a facelift, understood the logic of putting Benazir Bhutto in the picture.

And yet, it was nearly decade since Benazir had left Pakistan. During this period, Pakistan had grown vastly more dangerous because of the resurgence of the Al Qaeda, Taliban and its sectarian affiliates. Moreover, being the largest political party, the PPP had been infiltrated by the mafia. The contradictions sharpened because, while the army secretly held on to its policies of strategic depth, Benazir pledged to go the extra mile in crushing the Taliban.

All her life, Benazir had been dogged by the non-transparent dealings of the military's intelligence agencies. Indeed, as a young prime minister, she had asked us how she could control the agencies. Some two decades later, her sixth sense made her reach out to world that, should anything happen to her, she would hold Musharraf directly responsible for the consequences.

The more things changed, the more they stayed the same.

Chapter 7

THE DEMOCRACY TRAIN REVS FOR MOTION

A Prime Minister in Waiting

Some two decades may have separated President Gen. Zia ul Haq and President Gen. Pervaiz Musharraf's military rule in Pakistan, but they had one person in common – Benazir Bhutto. The twice-elected woman prime minister of Pakistan took on both military rulers, one by one, with a promise to take the nation from dictatorship into democracy.

Ironically, on both occasions – 1988 and 2007 – Benazir went to Pakistan with a commitment from officials in Washington at a time when the US needed Pakistan to achieve its strategic objectives in Afghanistan. Never mind the fact that millions of people were ready to vote for her, realpolitik demanded that the road to Islamabad be traveled not through the dusty villages of Pakistan but through the power corridors of Washington DC.

In 2006, as Benazir solicited US help to return to power, I went from DC to Maryland to hear her address a rally – organized by

PPP workers. That cold February afternoon, she told expatriates gathered in a hotel around lunch tables in a speech in English, intended for the consumption of the US government,

"One crucial reason Gen. Musharraf gets so little pressure from the Bush administration about restoring democracy is the assumption that only a dictator can deliver military cooperation. That had better not be true."

Benazir made the sales pitch to Washington at a time when its "blue eyed boy," Gen. Pervaiz Musharraf – who then wore two hats as chief of army staff and president – prosecuted President George W. Bush's "War on Terror." Western pressure on Musharraf to relax his chokehold on politicians had led to the release of Benazir's husband Asif Zardari in 2004. Pakistan's former woman prime minister followed it up with a visit to the US capital to test the waters for her return to power.

Asif, who underwent medical treatment while he lived in an apartment in New York, joined Benazir after the speech. High-spirited and cheery, he flashed his familiar grin as he met expatriates. Out of Benazir's earshot and away from the public milieu, I asked him with an informality that came from long years of acquaintanceship.

"So, you need to come to Washington to get back into power?"

"Of course, it is after all the world's only super power," he shot back.

We had the conversation at PPP senator, Khawaja Akbar's home in Virginia after Benazir had sent word to me to join their private gathering. After her speech, I had walked to the stage where she signed autographs for a bevy of admirers. It had been more than a decade since I came face to face with Benazir. Still, her look of genuine surprise at seeing me in the US – as opposed to familiar surroundings in Pakistan – came with a warm response.

"Wait, I want to see you," she said.

Minutes later, she had sent her senator to my table with a message to follow her small entourage to his Virginia home. It was an occasion to have a close sitting with Benazir and Asif, away from the public glare and in a small homely setting. Benazir looked different without her head cover, with shoulder-length light brown hair and a heavier physique, but she still had the same twinkling eyes that reflected her deep self-assurance.

She picked my brains on a drone missile attack that had then occurred in Damadola in Bajaur tribal agency.

"Do you know if the missile attack actually killed Ayman Zawahiri's nephew as the government claims?"

I told her that it did not appear so, and that there were contradictory statements about the incident in the US newspapers as well.

Benazir had read with interest the Washington Post's editorial, which cast aspersions on Gen. Musharraf's role in the "War on Terror" and questioned the effectiveness of keeping him as an ally. As early as 2006, the US media's critical comments that Musharraf could be engaged in double dealing with the West had obviously presented itself to her as an opportunity.

At that juncture, Benazir's relationship with Musharraf was one of spy versus spy as both seasoned politicians – one civilian and the other military – worked to outfox each other. While Benazir gathered information on how Musharraf fared in the US, his administration followed her activities in Washington, DC with eagle eyes.

Only a few weeks earlier, Interpol had issued a red alert against Benazir and Asif on money laundering charges. Musharraf had shifted the responsibility of the alert on the National Accountability Bureau (NAB), allegedly set up to fight corruption among public officials and politicians. But just that morning, Federal Minister for Information and Broadcasting Shaikh Rasheed Ahmed had delivered a cold warning from the general, "Benazir will be arrested the moment she lands in Pakistan."

Coincidentally, the same day that the Interpol alert was issued, I heard Benazir at a public forum in Washington, DC. As I reiterated the threat conveyed by Musharraf's information minister to Benazir and asked her what she planned to do about it, she seized on the chance to criticize Musharraf and declare that "such tactics will not stop me from returning to Pakistan to bring democracy."

At the home of the PPP senator, Benazir waxed casual as I reminded her of the Interpol alert. She began to ask party leaders about individuals in Pakistan's establishment who might have been responsible for issuing the red alert against herself and Asif.

"Can you believe it, they are equating me with terrorists like Ayman Al Zawahiri," she turned to me with a twinkle in her eyes.

Asif, too, was relaxed in the homely settings and more chatty than usual. It was a contrast to his behavior a few weeks ago when he had dodged my questions by saying he was under a "gag order." Instead, he had passed the buck rather nicely:

"Why don't you ask Benazir? You've known her longer than I have."

Now on a one-to-one level, he volunteered to explain that he had been released from prison without striking a back room deal with Musharraf.

"You never thought I would get out of prison did you," he chuckled.

To my surprise, Benazir talked of her erstwhile rival, former Prime Minister Nawaz Sharif, with camaraderie. It was a far cry from the Benazir I knew in Pakistan's last decade of civilian rule, when the two former prime ministers were bitter rivals and worked at cross-purposes. Instead, a year ago Benazir Bhutto and Nawaz Sharif had come together in London to frame a "Charter of Democracy" that promised to force Musharraf to hold "free and fair" elections and enact constitutional reforms.

Long years of exile suffered by Nawaz and Benazir under Musharraf had convinced the ousted prime ministers to agree on a charter that would prevent military rulers from overthrowing elected leaders like themselves.

In London, the politicians did the spade work for the constitutional package, passed by the Zardari government in April 2010, which undid the constitutional amendments passed by two former military rulers – Gen. Zia ul Haq and Gen. Pervaiz Musharraf – and curtailed the power of the president. The "Eighteenth Amendment," as it is called, has been largely welcomed in Pakistan, even while some sections have been challenged in the Supreme Court.

More western savvy than Nawaz, Benazir had after 9/11 correctly surmised Pakistan's importance for the US. Although President Bush had developed a one-on-one relationship with Musharraf, American voters were growing disillusioned with a sagging economy and a seemingly unending war in Afghanistan. Taking advantage of the swing of voters toward the Democratic Party, Benazir put her foot in the door and worked to prize it open for her reentry to power.

A senior journalist seated at our small table suggested to Benazir that her goals may be better served if she moved from Dubai to the US. Benazir demurred, not just because it would make her US connections far too obvious, but because she said she was concerned about the education of her children enrolled in Dubai's schools.

Instead, Benazir went on to work with Democratic members of the US Congress to broker the National Reconciliation Ordinance (NRO) deal with Musharraf, which granted amnesty for herself, husband Asif Zardari and thousands of other politicians and businessmen accused of corruption. PPP sympathizers say it was Benazir's way of ensuring that the "politically fabricated" cases did not stand in her path to return to Pakistan.

Among those who got former President Musharraf to sign the National Reconciliation Ordinance was Democratic Senator John Kerry. Kerry's advisor Shahid Ahmed Khan accompanied Benazir and Kerry to the office of Tom Lantos. The latter, a Jewish Holocaust survivor, knew Musharraf in his capacity as the head of the House Foreign Affairs Committee.

As Benazir telephoned Musharraf, Khan stated that he had stepped out of the office "to give them some privacy."

Afterwards, Khan said that Senator Kerry told him that he had talked briefly with US Under Secretary of State for Political Affairs R. Nicholas Burns to ask that he telephone Musharraf to ensure security arrangements for Benazir's return. Khan said that Senator Kerry subsequently asked the Republican administration's US Secretary of State Condoleeza Rice to ensure that Benazir was provided with proper security while she was in Pakistan.

In 2007 Benazir met President Gen. Musharraf in Dubai to work out her quid pro quo arrangement with him. It culminated on October 4, 2007 with Musharraf's signature on the NRO – which paved the way for Benazir, Asif and several party officials to return to Pakistan. Two days later, as Gen. Musharraf presented himself for presidential reelection the PPP members permitted him a façade of legitimacy by remaining in parliament while other political parties boycotted the vote.

That cold February afternoon, as Benazir and I stood alone at the refreshments table in the Virginia home of her party senator, she picked away disinterestedly at the lavish spread. She was in a pensive mood, apparently reflecting on the gravity of her decision to return to Pakistan. Instinctively, I said to her,

"It's very brave of you to go back."

She dropped her gaze still further and became still. It would be many seconds before she turned to me and we rejoined the rest of the group. Perhaps she knew that this would be her last battle.

"Democracy is the Best Revenge"

In Pakistan, the body politic was divided on whether Benazir should return before the elections announced by Musharraf for January 2008. The secular Awami National Party (ANP) – which now heads the government in Khyber Pakhtunkhwa along the Afghanistan border – had had bitter experience of the rabid "Talibanization" under Musharraf. Through an emissary, its leaders conveyed to Bhutto's husband Asif Zardari that she should not return.

PPP stalwart and former senator Taj Haider went on a limb to beseech Benazir not to come back. He had researched the security situation for months, and had even asked former ISI chief Lt. Gen. Asad Durrani about Benazir's chances of survival if she were to return.

"Durrani had said 'zero'," said the white-haired party loyalist, visibly dismayed that despite his communication to Benazir, she had ignored the warning. Instead, she had quoted a line from a poem by Robert Frost that he wistfully recalled in its full verse.

The woods are lovely dark and deep, but…
"I have promises to keep"
And miles to go before I sleep
And miles to go before I sleep

As the PPP cadre festooned Karachi for Benazir's return on October 18, 2007, there were emotional scenes from the exile. Two days prior to her return, Benazir held a press conference to make the announcement in Dubai. There, an elderly Sindhi expatriate from Khairpur Mirs had wept and begged her not to leave. She, too, held his hand and cried. But her determination and apparent faith in the US had shone through her tears as she told supporters: "The West has assured me of my security."

But Benazir did not have a promise from the US government or even private security agencies in America that she would be protected in Pakistan. While Senator John Kerry and Senator Joe Biden supported Benazir's bid for power, returning home was clearly her own initiative. Boston-based consultant Shahid Ahmed Khan says that prior to her return, Senator Kerry had warned Benazir about the "volatile" situation in Pakistan and told her she should not go.

As though the challenges weren't enough, Benazir braced for a new player in Pakistan's politics. He was Supreme Court Chief Justice Iftikhar Chaudhry, whose defiance of the ruling Gen. Musharraf had turned him into a folk hero. Only six days before her return, the chief justice had thrown a spanner in the works by suspending the NRO and declaring President Gen Musharraf's re-election as invalid.

But October 18 was the day Benazir was determined to tell the world that she still reigned over the hearts of the people. Indeed, some two decades after her return to Lahore, Pakistan was more populated, angry and desperate to find a leadership that could lift them out of poverty under quasi-military rule. Karachi's frenzied energy level had not diminished over time.

Instead, the crush of humanity looked for a political change to end grinding military rule and return the nation to democracy.

That afternoon, as Bhutto's plane prepared to land from Dubai to Karachi, a member of the PPP welcoming committee, veteran trade union leader Habibuddin Junaidi, arrived ahead of others at the airport. From the elevated Jinnah terminal, all he saw were waves of people. Not only had they packed the wide Shahrah-i-Faisal Road to the airport but also the arteries that ran into it. Startled by the panoramic view, he mumbled to his colleague: "There are so many of them, they can take over the sea."

As Benazir stepped off the plane after a self-exile of nine years, she raised her hands in gratitude for the opportunity to return home and tears of joy rolled off her cheeks.

The poorest of the poor had arrived to greet Benazir. They included people from remote corners of the country, with tattered clothes and without shoes, who had chased her "Democracy Train" almost two decades before. Some of the villagers in rural Sindh had sold their livestock to pay for their fare to Karachi. Others had traveled from Gilgit and northern areas of Pakistan just to catch a glimpse of her.

Thousands of people broke the security cordon at the airport and milled around her truck, where she stood amid party leaders to acknowledge their cheers. Even the MQM activists, then in coalition with the Musharraf government, had been unable to suppress their curiosity and turned up for the welcome.

PPP's information secretary Saeed Ghani looked at the sea of people and was briefly overcome by a sense of misgiving as to what would happen if there was a security breach. His cell phone had rung all morning – a sure sign that the bomb jammers promised by the Sindh administration did not work. For weeks, his enthusiastic party workers had clashed with police as they decorated the city with banners. The encounters had left him uneasy about whether Sindh Chief Minister Arbab Ghulam Rahim would provide Benazir with the security they had requested.

Still, like thousands of PPP devotees Ghani brought his family to celebrate Benazir's homecoming. His younger brother Fahad traveled in the third truck behind Benazir's bombproof

Figure 11 PPP Chairperson Benazir Bhutto is welcomed on her return at Karachi Airport on October 18, 2007 (*Dawn* photo).

vehicle. The sea of humanity forced Benazir's vehicle to crawl to Karsaz and the 45-minute journey stretched to seven hours. The "Janisaran Benazir" – a cadre ready to sacrifice their lives for Bhutto – ran along her truck and their Baloch members danced in joyous abandon to African drumbeats.

It was dark and the streetlights were off when the first bomb went off. "We stayed calm, imagining a tire had burst," said Fahad, whose voice choked as he recalled how the scene would turn into a massacre.

Apparently, the first bomb exploded when a man passed a crying infant swathed in a blanket over the heads of the crowd, with a request to Benazir to appease it. She did not take the baby, knowing it would not stop crying. Instead, her security personnel – among them, PPP's Agha Siraj Durrani – directed that the infant be moved along.

The crying infant was put on the lap of a party office-bearer, Rukhsana Farid, who sat in an accompanying police mobile. Moments later, the infant exploded and killed Rukhsana, along with police officials and an unfortunate cameraman.

Later, Benazir had a strong-willed argument with PPP's Taj Haider that the bomb had been delivered in a doll. Haider patiently told her that eyewitnesses had identified that it was an infant who wailed and cried as it was passed over the crowds.

"But Benazir stayed unconvinced," said Haider. Instead she argued, "Nowadays in the West, they make dolls that cry like real babies."

The second explosion shook Benazir's bombproof truck while she was inside. It sent a bolt of lightening across the sky, even as it threw human flesh in the air and scattered showers of blood. Hundreds of *Janisaran* Benazir, who had made a human shield around her truck, were instantly killed. Perched on a press truck a few vehicles behind Benazir's truck, Fahad saw the joyous PPP loyalists dancing one minute and the next – dead.

Ghani's wife Naila, who arrived at Karsaz with her six month old baby to catch a glimpse of Benazir, saw the sky light up in the terror attack and found her hair covered with bits of human flesh.

"My heart still pounds when I think of that moment," says the slender young woman, who has since renamed her daughter "Benazir."

Benazir clambered out of her bombproof vehicle with other PPP party office-bearers, alive, if somewhat bruised. Some 180 PPP supporters lay dead all around. The police van, which carried her back over the Clifton Bridge to Bilawal House, rushed in panic mode as though the assassins still chased them.

Flanked by loyalists at the Bilawal House, Benazir named three of President Musharraf's associates as suspects in the attack: former chief of the Inter Services Intelligence Hameed Gul; Intelligence Bureau chief in the Punjab Brig Ejaz Shah; and Chief Minister of the Punjab Chaudhry Pervaiz Ellahi.

Brig. Ejaz Shah, a friend of Musharraf, had come into the spotlight in 2002 for his role in sheltering the jihadist Omar Shaikh, currently serving time in Pakistan's prisons for his role in the kidnapping and murder of US journalist Daniel Pearl.

Benazir went on to write a letter to CNN anchor Wolf Blitzer through her lawyer, Mark Siegel. In it, she complained about the poor security situation and wrote that in the event that she was assassinated, she would hold Musharraf responsible.

"I have named three people, and more, in that letter to Gen. Musharraf. I have named certain people with a view to the attack that took place yesterday so that if I was assassinated, [it is they] who should be investigated."

Asif Zardari subsequently passed on the contents of the letter to the United Nations and asked that they investigate his wife's murder.

Squaring Off with a Potential Adversary

While the terror attack against Benazir was underway, Baz Mohammed Kakar – a key aide to Chief Justice Iftikhar Chaudhry – visited the Aga Khan hospital in Karachi, where he heard the sounds of the explosion.

The bustling Baz Mohammed – whose cell phone constantly rings – had been newly released from house arrest. As president of Balochistan Bar Association, he had mobilized lawyers around the chief justice who had made history by defying a ruling general.

At the hospital Baz Mohammed's ears were keyed to Benazir's procession, particularly because her emissaries had contacted him to secure a meeting with the chief justice.

But as the lawyer from Balochistan heard the bombs go off and news filtered in that hundreds of PPP workers in Benazir's procession had been killed, he wondered if that meant that the meeting would be put off.

Still, the bomb blast at Karsaz, which brought Benazir the certainty she could be killed any day, did not stop her in her mission. Instead, two days later, Benazir's emissary Farooq Naik met Baz Mohammed, where the Balochi lawyer had the opportunity to see the seven-point agreement negotiated between Benazir and Musharraf.

In that note, Musharraf reportedly wrote that if the duo shared power after the 2008 elections in Pakistan, Chief Justice Iftikhar

Chaudhry would have to be dismissed in the new arrangement. Benazir had rebutted Musharraf with the words, "I disagree."

But Baz Mohammed – who led the rallies to restore the chief justice after Musharraf dismissed him for "insubordination" – said Benazir was merely "point scoring." Still, he arranged for the chief justice to meet Benazir's emissary, Farooq Naik, where the two discussed the judiciary's role in a future PPP government.

Benazir clearly planned for difficult times ahead. In her second tenure as prime minister, she had been irked by the independence of the judiciary. At the time, she had clashed with her own appointed chief justice Sajjad Ali Shah after he refused to endorse her choices of judges to the Punjab High Court and instead laid down the principle for their appointments.

PML (N) chief, Mian Nawaz Sharif proved to be even less tolerant of an independent judiciary and in 1997 sponsored the storming of the supreme court when it was poised to give a verdict against him. But in 1999, Sharif was ousted in a military coup by Gen. Musharraf and forced to go into exile in Saudi Arabia. With both Sharif and Chaudhry falling victim to Gen. Musharraf's autocratic behavior, the ousted prime minister would use his clout to help reinstate the ousted chief justice.

For the newly-returned Benazir, it had become essential to square off with a chief justice who had become a folk hero in Pakistan. Even PPP's former law minister from the Punjab, Aitzaz Ahsan – who had in 1986 watched Benazir take his city of Lahore by storm – had in her absence aligned himself with the defiant chief justice. Not only did Aitzaz drive the ousted chief justice to massive public rallies because – as political commentator I. A. Rehman wrote – "he liked driving," but because he sought to bridge the espoused ideals of the PPP and an increasingly independent judiciary.

Anxious to show that she too considered the chief justice a hero, Benazir appeared to temporarily forget that she had returned to Pakistan through a quid pro quo deal with Musharraf. Instead, as Musharraf ousted Chaudhry for a second time in November 2007, she led a group of human rights activists to demand that he be released from house arrest.

The world saw Benazir stand outside the residence of the chief justice, where she bellowed into a megaphone, "He is our chief justice," and asked for bar cutters to cut through the barbed wires.

But an e-mail sent by Benazir to PPP loyalist Taj Haider only six days before her murder showed she remained privately skeptical of Chaudhry. In it, she wrote "Judges are highly politicized and need to be judged in light of their judgments."

Baz Mohammed said that when Benazir came to Quetta, she told him that once the PPP government came to power they would "restore all the judges except the chief justice." He says she was most concerned about the Supreme Court's ruling against the NRO, which threatened to reopen corruption cases against the PPP government.

Anticipating that the NRO would become the Achilles heel for the PPP government, in July 2007 Bhutto had secretly worked with President Gen. Musharraf to remove the wealth of her family and Zardari's close friends from Swiss banks. "There was pressure on her to do so from Zardari's "friends," who lived overseas and now form part of his government," sources close to her told me.

"Not so fast," said officials of the US government, who deployed their National Security Agency (NSA) – tucked away behind clumps of trees along the Baltimore Washington parkway – to wire tap phone conversations between Benazir and her son Bilawal. In them, she was alleged to have spoken to Bilawal about the family's secret bank accounts before she embarked on the dangerous trip to Pakistan.

Despite Benazir's best efforts, the reinstatement of Chief Justice of the Supreme Court Iftikhar Chaudhry and his revocation of the NRO would come back to haunt the PPP government long after she was gone.

The Chief Justice Notices the Disappeared

To understand why the chief justice from Balochistan was considered a hero at the time of Benazir's return, it is essential to put his actions in context. In a nation where supreme court judges have endorsed military regimes, Iftikhar Chaudhry's refusal to resign on President Gen. Musharraf's orders was unprecedented. Moreover, the Baloch insurgency had peaked when he summoned the intelligence agencies to produce persons "disappeared" by the military.

It was in Balochistan, whose capital, Quetta is nestled by hilly ranges lightly dusted with snow in winter, that the chief justice's ruling against disappearances received the widest acclaim. Balochistan has an undulating terrain of grey hills, which stretch seamlessly northwest into the Taliban insurgent areas of Qandahar and Helmand in Afghanistan. To the west of Quetta, the desert plateau meets the Taftan-Zahidan border – where the operations by the Sunni Baloch Jundallah against Iran's predominantly Shia population have created a new tension between Pakistan and Iran.

The convergence of "cross border intelligence agencies," in Balochistan has turned it into a hub of conspiracies and made governance from Islamabad an even more daunting task.

After 9/11, the Musharraf administration's alliance with the US in the 'War on Terror,' allowed the army to clamp down on a simmering Baloch insurgency with the type of secrecy they used to hunt down Al Qaeda militants. While the Afghan Taliban was left free to operate in Balochistan, the administration made Baloch secessionists disappear under the smokescreen of combating terrorists.

Fuelling Balochistan's insurgency was the fact that its disarming barren exterior hides rich deposits of minerals, coal and natural gas, which make a significant contribution to the nation's energy needs. Islamabad's failure to pay royalties and subsidies to Balochistan and its tight fisted control of the provincial government has fanned the tribal and secessionist movement, which reached a new pitch under Musharraf.

In 2005, when tribal leaders Nawab Akbar Bugti and Khair Baksh Marri mounted an insurgency against Musharraf, the army hunted down and killed their tribal fighters in the mountainous strong holds of Dera Bugti and Kohlu districts. In turn, the militant tribesmen ambushed and killed constabulary from the Frontier Corp, blew up gas pipelines and sabotaged train supplies to the province.

As rocket attacks accelerated, the Musharraf government set up a new military base and camps for army officers along the Sui gas field. The military and Baloch militant nationalists now engaged in a full scale war, backed by missiles and propaganda from both sides. From the government side, the District Coordination Officer Dera Bugti Abdus Samad Lasi told me that the tribal leaders like Nawab Akbar Bugti were responsible for keeping their people poor and backward, even as they used their tribesmen to fight their wars.

Enter a young woman doctor from Karachi, Dr Shazia Khalid, who then worked in Pakistan Petroleum Ltd, which manages the gas fields in Balochistan. Living alone at the company's onsite hospital, she was woken one night in January 2005 and reportedly raped at gunpoint by an army officer. Despite company directives to stay quiet, she testified against the offending captain.

Shazia's testimony to the media sent a match through the smoldering Bugti insurgency. Baloch insurgents intensified their attacks on army personnel and blew up gas pipelines, severing gas supply to the rest of the country.

Hustled into exile into London, Shazia spoke to me from her new location. Gen. Musharraf had rejected insinuations that *any* army man could be involved. However, annoyed by the negative publicity, Pakistan's officials had arranged for her to go abroad. As she awaited an immigration visa for Canada, Musharraf added insult to her injury with his remark, quoted in the *Washington Post* in September 2005: "If you want to go abroad and get a visa for Canada or citizenship and be a millionaire, get yourself raped."

The remark, obviously intended for a victim of rape, hurt the young woman. "It has made me lose hope of receiving any justice in Pakistan," Shazia told me in a voice muted with pain.

From his hiding place in Dera Bugti, the former governor of Balochistan and tribal chieftan, Nawab Akbar Bugti was livid that Shazia had been raped by an army man – and that he was being protected by the military president. In a voice that shook with anger, he told me that Baloch tribesmen would not rest until Shazia's rapist was brought to trial. Without waiting to differentiate, he declared, "You in the West may take rape lightly but we in Balochistan consider it a grave human rights violation of women."

On August 27, 2006, the army used satellite telephones to trace Bugti to an elaborate complex of caves he inhabited in Dera Bugti, where he was killed in a massive army operation.

In the US, where President Musharraf had managed to blur the lines between the terrorism launched by the Taliban and the insurgency by Baloch nationalists, Bugti's murder was lumped with Pakistan's ongoing war against the Taliban and Al Qaeda. The day after Nawab Akbar Bugti was murdered, an influential US newspaper cited Bugti's murder as the death of a "terrorist."

For a while Musharraf's operation against the Baloch nationalists broke the back of the insurgency. But in death, Bugti became a martyr. It rekindled memories of Balochistan's forced annexation to Pakistan and further provoked Baloch militants to seek arms and money from other countries in order to secede from the federation.

Around the time of the operation against Bugti, intelligence agencies secretly picked up secessionist leaders, locked them in 4×4 ft prisons without sunlight and tortured them in order to force them to "confess" their links with India and Afghanistan and foreign intelligence agencies. Baloch activists were picked up, blindfolded and thrown from a detention center across Balochistan's hot desert plateau – with their whereabouts kept secret from their families.

Balochistan Republican Party (BRP) leader Mir Wadood Raisani's mother has, for 14 years, campaigned against the intermittent detention and interrogation of her son. When I met her, Raisani was still missing. His nephew Nisar Ahmed – a young man with a proud demeanor – was angry with the run around given to the family. His spirit exemplified the new generation: "We are not going to beg them to release my uncle. We will keep on fighting until we get Balochistan liberated from Pakistan."

Around this time, Sindhi nationalist Asif Baladi was also kidnapped by military intelligence officials and questioned about his "Indian connections." Baladi was taken to Quetta, Balochistan where he saw hundreds of missing Baloch youth whose families had given them up for dead.

Figure 12 Protest rally against enforced disappearances of nationalist leaders of Sindh and Balochistan, taken in Hyderabad, Sindh on July 1, 2007 (*Dawn* photo).

Another activist from Baladi's *Jeay Sindh Qaumi Mahaz*, Dr Safdar Sarki, was also abducted by intelligence officials from his Karachi residence when he visited Pakistan in 2005. Sarki, a US citizen, was blindfolded and kept in detention centers whose locations he guessed at by their temperature or by the accents of his interrogators. Although US officials questioned his disappearance, military authorities in Pakistan shrugged off knowledge of his whereabouts.

Six months later, the chief justice of the Supreme Court managed to get Sarki produced before a Zhob magistrate in Balochistan. He was found sick and emaciated after being tortured. In May 2008, Sarki returned to the US to talk about his ordeal. He said that after his release, he had looked with trepidation at his image in the mirror: "The person who looked back at me made me break down in tears."

Dressing the Wounds of Balochistan

In November 2007, Benazir arrived in Balochistan with a message of reconciliation for the Baloch. In Karachi, she visited tribal chief, Sardar Khair Baksh Marri, to condole him for the death of his son, Balach Marri, who was killed during Musharraf's army operation in Kohlu. She also demanded the release of Baloch chiefs like Sardar Akhtar Mengal and Sardar Talal Bugti, who had been imprisoned in this period.

With the upcoming election in mind, Benazir worked to smooth anger against the federation and mobilize for a provincial PPP government in Balochistan. Much needed to be done to allay perceptions that she might follow in the footsteps of her late father, Zulfikar Ali Bhutto – whose dismissal of the National Awami Party government in Balochistan had, in 1973, triggered the Baloch insurgency.

The wizened PPP secretary general in Balochistan, Bismillah Khan Kakar – who sits in an unassuming party office in the crowded Quetta bazaar – shuddered at the way Benazir ignored security in favor of populism. As the trusted party official in charge of her security, in December 2007, Kakar vainly tried to dissuade Benazir from visiting the home of PPP worker, Azizullah Memon, who had recently passed away.

"We told her the security situation was not good but then she insisted that she would go on foot," said Bismillah Khan, the despair penetrating his sing-song Pushto accent.

Benazir went to address a rally in Afghanistan's border town of Quetta with the words people had come to hear: "Every dictator has to date been supported by the US. All we have got under Musharraf are dead bodies in Karachi and warlords in Afghanistan."

The US – which had negotiated the Benazir-Musharraf deal to allow their strong man to rule with a democratic face – was, by then, growing embarrassed by her public denunciations. The Bush administration's ambassador to Pakistan, Anne Patterson privately communicated to Benazir that she should tone down her rhetoric.

But Benazir had set a populist tone, which Asif Zardari too was obliged to follow. In the post-Benazir period, President Zardari apologized to the people of Balochistan for the military action under Musharraf. His government set up a commission entitled Aghaz-i-Huqooq-i-Balochistan (Initiation of the Rights of Balochistan), headed by PPP Senator Raza Rabbani, which promised repayment of billions in arrears owed for sui gas from the province, as well as royalties for its rich natural resources.

But although the tone of the PPP government had changed, the content remained the same. There was little follow up to ensure that the province received its due share. Instead, Balochistan remains economically depressed to this day: major power outages have undercut water provided by tube wells and damaged agriculture. Unemployment remains high – in 2010, nearly 40,000 graduates turned out to apply for 5,000 teaching jobs.

After Zardari took over as President, the chief of the UNHCR and American national, John Solecki was kidnapped in Quetta and the secessionist Baloch Liberation United Front claimed responsibility. Around that time, three Baloch nationalist leaders – Ghulam Muhammad, Sher Muhammad and Lala Munir – were abducted from a lawyer's office in Turbat, Makran. While Solecki was released, the bullet-riddled bodies of the Baloch nationalists were found in the desert.

In a small town like Quetta – where intelligence officials lurk in plain view outside the court where the nationalists were to be tried – people appeared to know their killers. When a shutter down strike ensued in the impoverished Balochistan province, it was not only a protest against the "hidden hands" but a referendum on the helplessness of the Zardari government.

Late Tahir Mohammed Khan – who had served as Zulfikar Ali Bhutto's federal minister and confidante – had watched Benazir try to dress Baloch wounds while she moved through his hometown in Quetta. Speaking with the considered wisdom that matched his experience he said, "Even if Benazir were alive today, she would have remained subservient, because the establishment and the bureaucracy remain very strong."

Musharraf's Emergency Breaks

On November 3, 2007, as President Gen. Musharraf lost his grip over power and imposed emergency, the frenetic pace of events only intensified Benazir's sense of mission. Convinced that the chief justice would not revalidate his second term as president, Musharraf put him under house arrest, removed 60 judges and curtailed civil rights, including media freedom.

As if sensing that everything would unravel, Benazir flew from Dubai to Pakistan the same day that Gen. Musharraf imposed emergency. Given that her deal with Musharraf was public knowledge, she took extra pains to distance herself from the general. It was, in every sense, like walking a tight rope. Benazir's association with Musharraf threatened to damage her vote bank as well.

Shortly after the emergency, I too flew to Karachi to a succession of unfolding events that would usher in the current political landscape. Thousands of lawyers, journalists and NGO leaders were under house arrest or jailed for their opposition to President Musharraf's Provisional Constitutional Order (PCO), which mandated loyalty to him rather than the constitution. In Sindh, 12 out of 17 high court judges had adopted the chief justice's directives and refused to take oath under the PCO – a pattern replicated by judges in the country's four provinces.

Among those who refused to take oath was the deposed chief justice of the Sindh High Court, the late Sabihuddin Ahmed. After the emergency, police had blocked the road to his home to stop him from officiating as chief justice. With his curling moustache and a habit of drawing puffs of tobacco smoke between short and often sardonic remarks, Justice Sabihuddin greeted me warmly at the door.

Inside, Justice Sabihuddin leafed through the constitution to show me the paragraph that read that it was illegal for the chief of army staff to declare an emergency when there was no external threat to the country.

Shortly after becoming a judge, Justice Sabihuddin had flagged me down from his official chauffer driven car. I had pulled over to the side of the road, wondering if I had violated traffic laws.

On my rolling down the window, he had walked up to my car – puffing away, with his big agreeable smile – to say, "Do drop by and see me sometimes. You folks have stopped seeing me since I became a judge."

But in November 2007, the legal community was in turmoil. A retired judge of the Sindh High Court, Justice Majida Rizvi was upset at Musharraf's novel methods to induct new judges. In Sindh, she said, lawyers received phone calls from the intelligence agencies saying that the government would revive cases pending against them in the National Accountability Bureau if they did not agree to become judges.

Only a month earlier, Musharraf had used NAB to take back corruption cases against Benazir, Asif and others in order to get the PPP to support his bid for president.

In the aftermath of the emergency, the electronic media was blacked out, their advertisements suspended and news anchors black listed. The Karachi Press Club became the center for the movement against Musharraf, where civil rights groups lobbied every day against the emergency. Military vehicles parked outside the KPC kept a watchful eye on lawyers, political groups, NGOs, labor groups and media organizations – even as their numbers grew too fast to be counted.

Musharraf's emergency also raised a red flag with the US. Despite the nomination of Gen. Ashfaque Pervaiz Kiyani on July 2007 as his successor, Musharraf refused to relinquish his position as general. His isolation was complete after his benefactor, US President George Bush, made a television appearance in which he called for Musharraf to take off his uniform.

Meanwhile, Benazir Bhutto and Nawaz Sharif met in Pakistan in December 2007 and reaffirmed their commitment to the Charter of Democracy. Benazir involved two prominent human rights activists, Asma Jehangir and Afrasiab Khattak – both former chairpersons of the Human Rights Commission of Pakistan – to work on a constitutional reforms package. It was designed to get rid of the constitutional amendments passed by former military rulers – Gen. Zia ul Haq and Gen. Pervaiz Musharraf – and strengthen the parliamentary system.

The Rawalpindi Conspiracy

Islamabad, in which Benazir Bhutto twice took oath as prime minister, had during her exile moved firmly into the US orbit of influence. It looked nothing like the provincial capital I had visited in 1991 or even 2001. Instead, toward the end of the decade it had become a cosmopolitan city where big money and an entrenched mafia had transformed it into a US outpost for Afghanistan.

Today, the Islamabad highway – which connects to the airport – has signs to Srinagar, Muzzafarabad, Lahore and Murree. The nouveau riche display their boorish mentality in high-speed, dark-tinted Mercedes cars, flashing lights to move drivers off the roads. Middle Eastern and foreign capital has poured in and influenced the architecture of banks, gas stations and mosques. Five Star hotels, amongst them the Marriot Hotel, are barricaded like massive fortresses.

Islamabad is the epicenter for CIA-ISI partnerships and betrayals in a growing battle for control over Afghanistan. As in the days of the Cold War, the US and NATO presence in Afghanistan has once again strengthened the Pakistan military. Like the Margalla hills, the war in Afghanistan casts its shadow over the National Assembly and Senate – which today sit amid a formidable ring of security check posts.

What has not changed is the presence of poor people, which Islamabad attempts to brush under the carpet. Behind the veneer of modernity, it is impossible not to notice common people at bus and wagon stops and impoverished wayside restaurants, bearded men in loose-fitting *shalwar kameez* or the few numbers of women in public. The feudal culture is evident in the peasants who trek from their villages to Islamabad, where they end up as domestic servants.

Islamabad – with its filthy rich and powerful – along with its poorer twin garrison city of Rawalpindi, was the perfect setting for the mafia to finally get Benazir Bhutto, who had cheated death from the day she landed in Pakistan. By publicly denouncing Musharraf, Benazir had simultaneously challenged the intelligence agencies and the Islamic militants secretly coddled by them for strategic purposes in the region. The prospects of a Bhutto rousing the masses riled the military, even as the militants were strongly opposed to being ruled by a woman.

That fateful day – December 27, 2007 – Benazir drove to Liaquat Bagh, Rawalpindi in a white Land Cruiser packed with eight people. They included the driver, Javed ur Rehman and a retired Major SSP, Imtiaz Hussain. Benazir sat behind them, between Sindh's leading feudal Makhdoom Amin Fahim and close companion Naheed Khan. The third tier consisted of Naheed's husband, Safdar Abbasi and security guard, Khalid Shahanshah. Benazir's personal attendant, Razak Mirani, occupied the last seat.

Eyewitnesses said that security was "very tight" that day at Liaquat Bagh, Rawalpindi. The rally participants were scanned at the rally entrance, even while armed police stood on rooftops. The crowd was small and, oddly enough, seated on chairs located a considerable distance from the stage.

Party loyalists and photographers swarmed the stage where Benazir – attired in blue with a white *dupatta* – talked energetically of how the militants had taken down the Pakistani flag in Swat, but "we will keep it flying."

While Benazir spoke, news filtered in that Nawaz Sharif's procession had been attacked in Islamabad. It created a commotion in the media stand and some of the journalists began to leave the rally. However, Benazir went on speaking.

Although PPP guards were deputed to guard Benazir, subsequent videos indicate that her internal security was compromised. *YouTube* videos show that Benazir's party member, Khalid Shahanshah gesticulated to "would be" assassins from the stage – a finger sliding across his throat and eyes rolling toward Benazir. Shahanshah was later killed by unidentified assailants in Karachi and the PPP failed to investigate his murder.

After her speech, Benazir walked on the staircase behind the stage and got into her Land Cruiser – parked within municipal precincts. Eyewitnesses said that police had, by then, secured the rally and did not let anyone leave.

Senator Safdar Abbasi, who was with Benazir till her last moment, recalls that she was "very pleased" with the reception she had received. There was a sense of abandon in her as she stepped into her white Land Cruiser and hugged Abbasi's wife, Naheed Khan – Benazir's life long protector and companion.

Their bombproof land cruiser made a right turn on Liaquat road and then on College road where some two hundred or so PPP supporters raced along, raising slogans. Subsequent video footage shows that among them was the killer – a sophisticated looking young man in dark glasses, white shirt and coat, with a gun and explosives. The video shows another man wearing a white hood stood behind him, believed to be his cover suicide bomber.

At that stage, the black Mercedes which carried Benazir's chief security officer, Rehman Malik – who had served Benazir and Asif well while they lived in exile – was nowhere to be seen. It was a departure from the normal drill, where Benazir's vehicle normally followed Malik's vehicle. Traveling with Malik was a former Musharraf loyalist, the retired Lt. Gen. Tauqir Zia – who had joined the PPP only days before – and party men, Babar Awan and Farhatullah Babar.

Blissfully unaware of the dangers lurking around and anxious to invigorate crowd support ahead of her forthcoming election, Benazir decided to respond to the PPP youth who ran alongside her white land cruiser while they cried "*Wazir-i-Azam – Benazir*" (Prime Minister – Benazir).

Abbasi recalls that at that point, "she turned to me and said, 'How about some political slogans like "*Jeay Bhutto*," [long live Bhutto] Safdar?'"

Acting on Benazir's wishes, Safdar Abbasi took hold of the megaphone from inside the cruiser and bellowed out the catchy slogan, "*Nara-i Nara-i Nara-i Bhutto...* [crying, crying, crying Bhutto]" to which the crowd frantically responded "*Jeay Jeay Jeay Bhutto*." That was the cue for a smiling Benazir to stand up from the sunroof of the vehicle and wave to the crowd. The frenzied crowd had by now forced the land cruiser to a crawl, giving the sharpshooter the opportunity to aim at Benazir's head.

Suddenly, shots rang out. Seconds later, Benazir had slumped inside the cruiser, and her blood had spilled all over Naheed's lap. The shots came from the left side, but the bullets pierced and left wounds on the right side of her head.

"She was instantly dead," Abbasi claims.

Immediately thereafter, there was a loud explosion that cracked the windows of the vehicle and caused the tires to lose air. Video footage later showed that the sharp shooter had fired three shots, looked down and detonated his explosives. Dozens of others were killed as well, at least 15 of whom were disfigured beyond recognition.

While the bombproof Land Cruiser did not explode, inside Benazir was lifeless. The tires of her vehicle had lost air. "We began to drive as fast as possible but the car began wobbling," says Abbasi.

At Murree road, they checked Benazir's pulse and found there was no beat. The backup car carrying Rehman Malik and three other men, deputed for security purposes, was nowhere in sight. It would force Benazir's entourage to make a U-turn on the road and transfer the nation's only woman prime minister – now dead – into the car of journalist-turned-PPP loyalist, Sherry Rehman, who took her to hospital.

Supreme Court lawyer Anis Jilani, who attended Benazir's last rally, was 15 ft away when he heard the gunshots, "followed by a huge fire ball and rush of air." While people and police ran away from the explosion, Jilani rushed toward the crime scene. He had arrived just in time to see Benazir's land cruiser wobble away from the road, strewn with the dead and wounded.

In the midst of the mass hysteria, Jilani saw people beat up the mask left over from a face that had blown off. He says that people suspected it was the suicide bomber – although it wasn't clear to him if it was really so. Within a few hours, he saw the fire brigade dispatched by the municipal corporation hosing down the scene of the murder.

Interior Ministry spokesman Brig. Javed Iqbal Cheema held a press conference in Islamabad 24 hours later, in which the government blamed Tehrik-i-Taliban chief Baitullah Mehsud for the murder. According to Cheema, who later confessed to holding the press conference on the instructions of President Musharraf, the military had obtained a tape recording of Baitullah congratulating another operator for "a job well done."

The United Nations investigation into Benazir Bhutto's murder, led by Chile's ambassador to the UN Heraldo Munoz, which submitted its investigative findings to the world body in its April 2010 report, called it "strange" that the Musharraf administration had such ready evidence of the assailants. The UN investigators, who interviewed 230 people over a nine month period, said that ISI officials had told them that they had been monitoring Baitullah Mehsud and recognized that it was his voice.

It was the same scapegoat named by Gen. Musharraf on October 18, 2007, when Benazir's procession was first attacked in Karachi. Even back then, she had rejected the government's claim. PPP insiders told me that when Musharraf called her and she named her three suspects – two intelligence officials and the Punjab chief minister – the general went "ballistic" and yelled at her for "playing politics."

The UN report, undertaken at the request of the Zardari government, turned out to be a damning indictment of the Musharraf government and the intelligence agencies to stop what the UN team termed a "preventable" murder.

At the same time, the report implicated PPP insiders. The UN's perusal of video tapes found that the backup security vehicle – which carried Rehman Malik, Babar Awan, Farhatullah Babar and Tauqir Zia – was nowhere on the scene when Benazir was killed. Even if the four men did not hear the loud explosions from the area, Rehman Malik had told reporters after departing from Liaquat Bagh that Benazir was "all right."

Zardari's failure to investigate the men and the career elevation of three of them – Rehman Malik as minister of interior, Babar Awan as minister of law and Farhatullah Babar as PPP spokesman – has left dark shadows around his government.

Interestingly, the Joint Investigation Team, headed by Minister of Interior Rehman Malik, would, like Musharraf's earlier JIT, hold FATA militants responsible for Benazir's murder. But in

February 2011, a wider FIA investigation found Musharraf guilty of the conspiracy to kill Benazir. A Pakistani court has since issued a warrant of arrest against the former military president, who lives in London.

Despite her fears Benazir had, after her return to Pakistan resolutely thumbed her nose at the powerful spy agencies and pushed through her populist agenda. The bullets that went through her head and brought her down left the image of a fighter – an image that is seared into the consciousness of the Pakistani people.

A Mourning Federation Catapults the PPP to Power

The skeletal iron framework that binds the federation of Pakistan groaned with the stress of Benazir's murder. People wept on the streets in unprecedented scenes. In Balochistan, already in the throes of an insurgency, the administration shut off electricity and blacked out cell phones. It fanned more fears and rumors. Violence spread in Sindh and Balochistan as people vented their anger by damaging railway tracks, breaking government offices, banks and institutions of state.

Benazir's assassination was a defining moment for Sindh where the Bhutto family – Prime Minister Zulfikar Ali Bhutto and his sons Shahnawaz and Murtaza – are buried. Benazir had seen her father executed by Gen. Zia ul Haq's military government and had buried two of her brothers, without their perpetrators ever being brought to trial. Her murder now threatened to sever the province's last link with the federation.

Jeay Sindh Mahaz convenor, Abdul Khaliq Junejo says that Sindhis were shocked by television images of the brutal shooting of an unarmed, defenseless Benazir, as though she was an "orphan." Despite being critical of her PPP, Junejo says the images were enough to make the peaceful, mystical people of Sindh take up arms against the military and support a violent struggle for secession.

At that defining moment, the nation watched as Asif Zardari, in his new role as widower – his hair pushed back, a shawl wrapped across his chest – stepped into the shoes of his late wife. While bitter Sindhis cried out *"Pakistan Na Khappay"* (We Don't Want Pakistan), Benazir's widower responded to the rallies with PPP's federalist slogan *"Pakistan Khappay"* (We Want Pakistan).

Although Asif named their son Bilawal as the party's future successor, the young man made a brief debut and then departed to Oxford University in Britain to complete his education. The mantle of leadership fell to Asif, who was named in Benazir's will to lead for the "interim period."

While doubts swirled about the authenticity of Benazir's will, her lawyer Mark Siegel attested her handwriting was genuine in the will – an excerpt of which is reproduced below.

Figure 13 Excerpt of Benazir Bhutto's will.

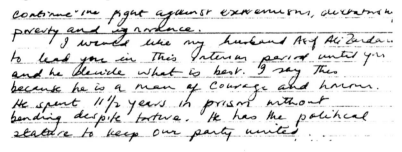

Benazir's murder was the signal for the nation to defeat President Musharraf's Pakistan Muslim League (Q) in the February 2008 elections. The two political parties PPP and PML (N) – which had been in the woods since Musharraf's military coup in 1999 – spoke of impeaching him. Musharraf, a commando at heart, carried on as president, even as he worked to deflate the overwhelming public perception that blamed him for Benazir's murder.

But by 2008 Musharraf's chief US patron, George W. Bush, too had lost public support because of the flagging economy and the unpopularity of the wars in Iraq and Afghanistan. The upcoming Democratic Party distanced itself from Gen. Musharraf, who in any case had lost his vital importance after he shed his uniform.

Musharraf's resignation gave a green light to Asif Zardari to use his personal charms to do what he does best. He made political deals with former rivals like the PML (N) and the MQM and in August 2008 succeeded in being elected as president of Pakistan. The PPP nominated another party loyalist, Yusuf Raza Gilani, to become prime minister.

Ironically, the Charter of Democracy – which Benazir Bhutto initiated with Nawaz Sharif and which culminated in the eighteenth amendment – would clip the wings of her widower. Making no mention of the irony, President Zardari addressed the joint houses of parliament on April 5, 2010 to laud the constitutional package as Benazir's brainchild. Party loyalists wasted no time in telling the world that Zardari was the first president to voluntarily give up his presidential powers.

Chastened by Benazir's murder and years in exile, Sharif worked with her widower to do away with the ordinances passed under former military rulers, Generals Zia ul Haq and Pervaiz Musharraf, that had strengthened their despotic rule.

Meanwhile, the Awami National Party too worked to fulfill the aspirations of their Pashtun voters when they changed the name given by the British, namely "North West Frontier Province," to "Khyber Pakhtunkhwa." Still, the province's minority ethnic Hazara community has challenged the name in the Supreme Court.

Whilst the eighteenth amendment formally clipped Zardari's presidential powers, the army let him know quite early on who would remain the real boss. Zardari's interviews to the media that the Indo-Pakistani peace process should not be "hostage" to Kashmir and his description of Kashmiri militants as "terrorists" sent ripples of consternation ran within the army circles. Given that in Pakistan, the term *"masla-i-Kashmir"* (problem of Kashmir) is a metaphor for an intractable problem, civil society knew right away that Zardari would suffer the consequences of his remarks.

Shortly thereafter, in November 2008, there was a terrorist attack in Mumbai's Taj Mahal hotel, in which over a hundred innocent people were killed and over three hundred injured.

India blamed the attack on the Lashkar-i-Tayyaba (LET; also known as the Army of the Riteous), led by Hafiz Saeed Mohammed, claiming it had trained for the attack in Pakistan. India conducted an investigation and handed the results over to Pakistan. But Pakistan's courts claimed that with only one surviving terrorist in Indian custody, they did not have enough evidence to imprison the LET chief. Saeed was released due to lack of evidence.

The Mumbai incident put Indo-Pakistani relations into deep freeze – one that, despite the PPP government's best intentions, is proving difficult to thaw. Moreover, given that the terrorist attack happened at a time when NATO leaned heavily on the Pakistan army for its war strategy in Afghanistan, the US preferred not to lecture Pakistan about harboring militants.

As the PPP government dug its heels in, President Asif Zardari was left with the unenviable task of carrying a sword against the Islamic militants as he walked the tightrope between America and the Army.

The Swat Operation

By the time Zardari took over as president, the Tehrik-i-Nifaz-i-Shariati-Mohammedi (TNSM) had established a parallel Taliban state in parts of Malakand division, where it ostensibly practiced *"Nizam-i-Adl"* (Order of Justice; essentially Sharia law). Awami National Party's Senator Afrasiab Khattak told me that his new government was taken aback to find it had inherited an ill-trained, ill-equipped police force that was no match for an increasingly ferocious Taliban militancy, which, in Swat, was headed by Maulana Fazlullah.

In Khattak's words, the situation had deteriorated so rapidly because "Musharraf's duplicity had suited the Bush administration."

Toward the end of 2008, a massive suicide bomb attack at the Marriot Hotel in Islamabad had destroyed the myth that parliamentarians, diplomats or even armed personnel were safe. Islamabad grew even more strongly fortified. A wide cordon was thrown around

Figure 14 Paramilitary personnel patrol a road in Bajaur tribal agency on February 28, 2009 (*Dawn* photo).

the parliament buildings and cars were investigated at checkpoints set up at every few yards. The besieged political leadership traveled in groups and only to fortified locations.

In Swat, residents were too terrified to speak up against the Taliban militants after the group had burnt down hundreds of girls' schools and beheaded the law enforcement personnel they had kidnapped. While TNSM chief Sufi Mohammed was imprisoned for fighting against the US forces that invaded Afghanistan in 2001, his son-in-law Fazlullah had joined hands with TTP chief Baitullah Mehsud to eliminate hundreds of tribesmen and political opponents in FATA.

Fazlullah's spokesman, Muslim Khan told me with aplomb that it had become necessary to behead political opponents and that the practice fell well within the dictates of Islam.

Under these circumstances, the Zardari government was relieved when TNSM chief, Sufi Mohammed pledged to follow the pacifist road and confine the enforcement of Sharia law to Malakand division in return for a ceasefire and the release of

Taliban prisoners. It was ostensibly a throwback to 1994 when Sufi Mohammed and his tribesmen had blocked the Swat Mingora road for one week to demand the enforcement of Sharia. Then, Benazir's government had buckled into supporting the TSNM chief's demands for a superficial enforcement of Islamic law.

In February 2009, the ANP government signed the controversial Swat peace deal with Sufi Mohammed, pledging to release 300 Taliban prisoners in return for Fazlullah's promise to disengage from the Tehrik-i-Taliban militancy.

But the TTP promise turned out to be an exercise in duplicity. Fazlullah's militants, already engaged in shady trade activities in Malakand took advantage of the cease fire to deploy Taliban militants to take over government owned emerald mines in Mingora and spread out in FATA to demand *jaziya* (tax for non-Muslims).

As Washington watched with alarm, Pakistan's civil society was the first to speak out against the Swat peace deal. Talk show hosts in television and radio, print journalists and bloggers expressed alarm as a video surfaced of a girl who was flogged on suspicion of marital infidelity. Fazlullah's spokesman, Muslim Khan defended the flogging as he told incredulous television anchors, "It is the girl's good fortune that Qazi courts had not been set up, otherwise she would have been stoned to death."

In April 2009, the Taliban advanced to nearby Bunair, where they sealed the civil courts and announced that they would be converted to Islamic courts. Sufi Mohammed issued a *fatwa* against Pakistan's courts, embarrassing even for the Jamaat-i-Islami, who admitted that the Taliban had gone too far. As the Taliban forces rampaged through the Margalla hills, the ousted leader of the opposition and JUI (F) chief Maulana Fazlur Rehman told the National Assembly with the confidence of an insider that the Taliban would soon be knocking on Islamabad's door.

For the incoming Obama administration, the situation in Pakistan was a rude awakening to Bush's failed foreign policy. As Secretary of State Hillary Clinton testified before the House Foreign Affairs Committee on Capitol Hill that Pakistan posed a "mortal threat" to the rest of the world, Congress authorized a flurry of diplomatic activities to Pakistan to convince the new army chief, Gen. Ashfaque Pervaiz Kiyani, that the Taliban could take over the government in Pakistan.

In May 2009, the Pakistan army sent thousands of forces to battle Taliban fighters in Swat. It triggered the largest and swiftest exodus in recent history. As the army imposed curfew and flushed out the Swat militants, the UN set up tented communities in Mardan and Swabi to support over 1.5 million Internally Displaced Persons (IDPs). Still, as the numbers of the displaced grew dramatically, over half the IDPs stayed with their relatives – with the generous hospitality provided by locals in Khyber Pakhtunkwa proving to be the saving grace for the government.

The Army Takes On the Pakistani Taliban

The ferocity with which the Taliban had emerged in the Swat and Malakand division jolted the US into realizing that eight years after the 9/11 attacks – and despite the deaths of thousands of people and billions of US dollars spent – the Afghan-Pakistani border region was more unsafe than before.

Only months after taking office, US President Barak Obama demonstrated the sense of urgency when he began to work with Pakistan's new army chief, Gen. Kiyani. His administration would use a carrot-and-stick policy to pressure Pakistan's military into turning away from its traditional anti-India attitude and instead focus on battling against the insurgents.

In March 2009, Obama declared his strategy was to crush Al Qaeda and Taliban militants in Afghanistan and Pakistan. He went on to announce plans to deploy 30,000 additional US troops in Afghanistan in 2010, before drawing them down to allow Afghan forces to run their own security.

It was a policy that would put the secular PPP government and its like-minded ANP allies in Khyber Pakhtunkwa in the front lines of blowback from rampaging "Talibanization" in the region.

As the Obama administration prodded Pakistan's military to fight the very militants that the US and Pakistan had coddled for decades for *jihad*, there were scores of major attacks against security forces. The most brazen attack was against the army's General Head Quarters in Rawalpindi, where the militants killed six soldiers before they were overpowered. Afterwards, a state-sponsored militant group active in Kashmir, Jaish Mohammed (Amjad Farooqi group) claimed credit for the attack.

With Pakistan's existence at stake, on June 19, 2009, the army began its six-month "Operation Rah-i-Nijat" (Operation Good Riddance) in South Waziristan. It would force thousands of tribesmen to relocate to the settled areas of Tank and Dera Ismail Khan.

As the US and Pakistan combed the hills of Waziristan, Baitullah fled like a trapped animal turned loose to escape drone missile attacks. In the last two years, the Pakistan-based militant had become dispensable. The Musharraf administration had, in 2007, repeatedly named him in assassination attempts on Benazir Bhutto. For the US, which had also unsuccessfully tried to use Baitullah to break the Taliban, his refusal to serve their interests and mobilization instead against NATO forces in Afghanistan had led to a PKR 430 million (USD 5 million) bounty being placed on his head.

Having made enemies on all fronts, Baitullah was finally killed in a drone missile attack on August 2009 on the rooftop of his remote home in South Waziristan. For a while, the TTP refused to acknowledge his death. He was succeeded by Hakeemullah Mehsud, who resorted to subterfuge to survive. Media reports that Hakeemullah had been killed in a US drone attack were not refuted by the militant group, allowing the new TTP leader to lay low and escape to a safer location.

Despite the TTP's new leadership, there was no let up in their attacks in 2009. Like bees out of a nest, militants attacked congregations of religious minorities, crowded market places, aid organizations, mosques, refugee camps, funerals and mourning processions. The combined tally in violent incidents during 2009 left a gruesome 12,632 people dead, according to figures compiled by the Islamabad-based Institute for Peace Studies.

As Pakistan grew into the new epicenter of terrorism, people were furious not only at Taliban militants but also at the US for "bringing the war home." National surveys found that by 2011, the terrorist related violence had claimed some 40,000 lives and caused billions of dollars' worth of damage to the economy. Even before the floods hit, the Swiss Agency for Development and Cooperation discovered that almost half the people did not have enough food to eat.

The Obama administration accompanied its war policy with a PKR 640 billion (USD 7.5 billion) aid package authorized by the Kerry Lugar Berman Act of 2009 to "win the hearts and minds," of the people of Pakistan. Desperate to show that the partnership with the US could benefit the people of Pakistan, in March 2010 Foreign Minister Shah Mahmood Qureshi arrived in the US with a 54-page shopping list that included requests for power generation, rebuilding of roads and to boost industry and employment.

But whilst the US promised to devote PKR 10.7 billion (USD 125 million) to refurbish thermal power plants, boost Pakistan's educational system and build its destroyed infrastructure, US media reports indicated that even by 2011, most of the promised civilian aid had not moved out of Washington. Even before the floods devastated Pakistan, US aid packages seemed to be designed to further the superpower's goals. It entailed the construction of roads in the FATA belt – where the army conducts its operations – and the reform of government educational schools in southern Punjab that breed a jihadist mindset.

With the US stuck in an increasingly unwinnable war in Afghanistan, Pakistan's military emerged as its largest beneficiary. By early 2011, the US had given nearly PKR 1.11 trillion (USD 13 billion) for security related items. Gen. Pervaiz Ashfaq Kiyani was the real guest of honor in the "Strategic Dialogue" between the two nations. It led to the US training Pakistan's fighter pilots, equipping them with state of the art F-16s, providing it with naval boats, unarmed, unmanned aerial vehicles and promising the transfer of drone technology in exchange for logistical support and enhanced cooperation against the militants in the region.

In April 2010, the Pakistani army held its biggest war-games in two decades – "Azm-i-Nau" – at Bahawalpur. It was an event watched by parliamentarians and foreign military observers.

The arms display was a message from Pakistan's army that notwithstanding its troop involvement in Afghanistan, it had the capacity to give a fitting response to India and its war games – among them "Hind Shakti" – held a year earlier.

No Stops on the Democracy Train

For people who knew Benazir Bhutto and her spouse Asif Zardari in the 1980s, the suggestion that Benazir would be killed and Asif would carry on Bhutto's populist legacy of "food, shelter and clothing" would have been dismissed as surrealistic. Benazir's cheerful husband was a businessman with a penchant for kickbacks, which put him in and out of prison and occasionally provoked his wife to undertake damage control by keeping him out of the public domain.

But in the outpouring of grief that followed Benazir's assassination, Asif appeared a palliative for a wounded nation. The PPP's home base of Sindh held on to him as an heir to Bhutto's legacy, who would represent them in the federation. Expectations ran high that after the ousting of military ruler, Gen. Pervaiz Musharraf, the default President would turn around a nation hurt by terrorism, deteriorated law and order, inflation and unemployment.

From day one, Asif stamped the PPP with his new style of governance. It reversed Benazir's style of 1988 – when she allotted tickets to party loyalists who suffered under Gen. Zia ul Haq and made sacrifices for democracy. Some 20 years later, PPP feudals faced off against feudals from other parties. Middle-class people told me that parliamentary and senate tickets were "sold" at exorbitant rates to ensure a mindset that catered to the wealthy and "wannabes."

It was an approach that Asif Zardari had taken in 1993 when his wife made her second bid for relection. That year, I attended a luncheon for prospective PPP candidates – amongst them, feudals with twirling long moustaches and parliamentarians, known for strong-arm tactics. Seated next to Asif, I asked him point blank why he had allotted party tickets to known *patharidars* (sponsors of dacoits) and corrupt businessmen. The question took him by surprise and he scrambled to answer,

"Look at her, she looks so sweet. But look at the questions she asks."

Asif accepted allegations of corruption with as much aplomb as a compliment about his warm personality. After Benazir's brother, Murtaza, was killed, I visited Asif in Karachi Central Jail, where he was charged for abetting in his brother-in-law's murder. As we walked from the barracks, where he seemed to do well as a VIP prisoner, the man who is today Pakistan's president flashed his irrepressible grin and told me with disarming frankness:

"I may be corrupt but I can never be involved in murder."

For both Benazir and Asif, Chief Justice of the Supreme Court Iftikhar Chaudhry embodied the person they feared would open a Pandora's Box for the future PPP government. While Benazir worked furtively to cover up her NRO deal with Musharraf, her widower reacted in a manner that would expose the deep insecurity of his fledgling government.

Having replaced Musharraf as Pakistan's president in August 2008, President Zardari spent months delaying the reinstatement of the chief justice. In early 2009, as the opposition and civil rights activists threatened a long march to pressure for the reinstatement of Iftikhar Chaudhry, President Asif Zardari sent police to round up and harass them. Among those targeted was Islamabad-based human rights activist, Tahira Abdullah, who had stood with Benazir as she rallied outside Chaudhry's home to declare, "He is our chief justice."

The PPP government was pressured to restore the chief justice through a notification issued on March 22, 2009, which has not been ratified by parliament to date. Nine months later, Iftikhar Chaudhry reopened corruption and crime cases against 8,000 people, including President Asif Zardari. The National Accountability Bureau was ordered to investigate secret bank accounts of corrupt politicians including Zardari's PKR 5 billion (USD 60 million) fortune – which Musharraf's attorney general, Malik Qayuum had helped to unfreeze from Swiss banks in 2008.

The PPP government cried foul, alleging that these were "politically motivated" cases, including several that were dismissed by the courts for lack of evidence. President Zardari claimed immunity by virtue of his position. His law minister, Babar Awan offered large sums of money to bar associations in lieu of support for the government. The government appointed their former loyalist in the Sindh Assembly, retired judge Deedar Hussain Shah, to chair the National Accountability Bureau.

In this cat-and-mouse game between the Supreme Court and the PPP government, the nation has grown polarized. Opposition parties have arrayed themselves against the government. The media has often sided with the Supreme Court. They claim to represent people caught in the grip of terrorism, daily violence, inflation and unemployment. Indeed, the chief justice's declaration that "even if the heavens fall," he plans to bring President Asif Zardari and his coterie to answer for the billions of dollars in kickbacks they have stashed abroad, has resonated with the people.

And yet, like any suspenseful screenplay, Pakistan's politics are far more nuanced. Zardari owes his rule to his wife, Benazir Bhutto, who lost her life in the pursuit of democracy. In this backdrop, political circles and even independent political commentators argue that the chief justice is "wired" to political circles. They argue that in Pakistan, the establishment reins in politicians by using legal cases against them.

Zardari's failure to prosecute members of his inner circle, named by the UN for their involvement in Benazir's murder, has done little to win confidence. PPP insiders, who have been critical of Asif Zardari's failure to prosecute Benazir's killers, have been shunned aside. When asked who may have killed Benazir, government leaders have gestured to indicate the "angels of death," or "hidden hands" – code words for military intelligence.

Today, a fragile PPP government survives as a mediator between the US and the Pakistan army. Despite the events of 9/11 and Pakistan's prima facie alliance with the US, the army has retained its policies of "strategic depth" in the region. Under this policy, the army maintains its hostile stance with India over the Kashmir issue, even as it prepares for a hegemonic role in

Afghanistan. As the army grows in strength, so does its ability to spawn militant groups that may be used for its regional interests.

Whilst the US government mulls over an exit strategy from Afghanistan, the Pakistani army too contemplates regional strategy. Although it has permitted the US to operate drone missiles in the tribal areas – targeting Al Qaeda's foreign fighters – and has provided logistical support so that NATO troops can cross in through the Khyber Pass, it has held off going after the Afghan Taliban in North Waziristan. Its contacts with Taliban leaders – while an open secret – have also contributed to a thorny relationship with the US, causing the CIA to intensify its covert operations in the region.

As the face of the democratic government, Prime Minister Yusuf Raza Gilani has made some populist gestures to tackle burning problems. But the PPP government remains far too involved with bare survival issues to overhaul the system – by reducing population, improving literacy and education, empowering women and searching for new sources of energy and clean drinking water.

Political analysts say that the establishment wanted to deliver a government minus a Bhutto, because the specter that Benazir threatened – of unleashing populist forces – did not suit the status quo. Today, the Zardari government is shorn of that type of leadership. Without the public interfacing skills that Benazir possessed, its leadership faces the serious challenges of terrorism and a crippled economy. While it is threatened externally by global powers – who see its inability to deliver – internally it is challenged by those who resent Zardari's inability to brook criticism.

Still, decades later, a civil society of academics and professionals keeps tabs on the government – be it civilian or military. The unprecedented freedom in the media and the bold decisions made by the courts are, in themselves, evidence that people do not leave the task of governance to the politicians alone. Democracy is a noisy business in Pakistan, but it is a form of government that the majority of the people have chosen to go forward.

EPILOGUE

Pakistan's Epic Monsoon Floods

Pakistan's catastrophic monsoon floods of 2010 – which scientists link to climate change and global warming and which has mostly hurt the farmers who eke a living along the Indus River – have turned into a defining moment for the nation.

The world watched with disbelief as the torrential rains, which bloated the Kabul and Indus rivers, swept away hundreds of people, homes and livestock in the north of Pakistan. As bridges and hotels collapsed in the scenic Kalam and Swat valley, the northern areas of Gilgit and Baltistan were cut off from the world. Despite this, crisis-ridden Islamabad appeared unaware and unprepared for the most devastating natural disaster in its history.

Only then – as the Indus River, swollen to nearly 12 times its normal size, wreaked havoc on villages and towns in its southward journey to the Arabian ocean – did the government wake to the existential threat to Pakistan.

"It's like partition," said a dazed PPP Prime Minister Yusuf Raza Gilani, who compared the sheer scale of the devastation caused by the 2010 floods to the events of 1947, when Pakistan was carved out of India.

Prime Minister Gilani, who has stepped into the late Benazir Bhutto's shoes, had the unenviable position of answering to millions of people who voted for the PPP because of its founder Prime Minister Zulfikar Ali Bhutto and his daughter, Benazir's pledge to provide "Food, Clothing and Shelter" to the people.

The government came under global scrutiny as the media zeroed in on shirtless villagers stranded on highways, hands outstretched with vessels for food and drinking water. Modestly draped mothers, clutching their infants, waded through waist-deep currents, farmers sloshed through the waters with sheep on their backs and people waited for rescue helicopters on islands along river beds that looked like *chapattis* (an Indian flatbread) floating in gravy.

Adding insult to injury, Pakistan's President Asif Ali Zardari chose the occasion to visit his family's chateau in France. His meeting with President Nicholas Sarkozy was ill-timed, given that French prosecutors prepared a case against Sarkozy for funding an old political campaign through kickbacks from the submarines provided to Pakistan. Zardari is also named for receiving kickbacks, although he was in prison when the French engineers building the submarines were killed in 2002.

But in July 2010, President Zardari was en route to London to coronate his eldest son, Bilawal Bhutto Zardari, as the party co-chairman. It was a program arranged ahead of time. As hundreds were swept away by the deluge and their sufferings appeared in the world media, his ill-timed foreign tour would send a message of disconnectedness with the people.

The US quickly demonstrated the importance it attached to Pakistan, becoming the first nation to respond with USD 50 million aid, helicopters, boats and halal meals. Helicopters were sent to the Gilgit Baltistan area to rescue stranded people. As torrential rains rushed down the denuded Koh-i-Suleman mountain range, the US coordinated with Pakistan's federal National Disaster Management Authority (NDMA) and the army to save villagers fleeing the rising Indus waters in southern Punjab and Balochistan.

Early into the disaster, US Secretary Hillary Clinton took to the airwaves in Washington DC to appeal to the American public to come forward and donate to the flood victims. It was a commendable move, laced only with the irony of being issued while President Zardari fiddled in London.

The UN Secretary General Ban Ki Moon's visit to flood-ravaged Pakistan and his declaration that he had before never seen such devastation gave pause to those who were listening. As the UN declared that the disaster was bigger than the 2004 Indian Ocean tsunami, the 2010 Haitian earthquake and Pakistan's 2005 earthquake combined, the world reached deeper into its pockets in a gesture on a scale that seemed like it might just fulfill the humanitarian needs of the flood's victims.

But as weeks went by and the world media depicted poor, ill fed and homeless people displaced by floods, it did nothing to win global confidence. The UN's first fund appeal for PKR 40 billion (USD 460 million) fetched 70 percent of its target with great difficulty. That forced the UN to launch a second appeal for PKR 171 billion (USD 2 billion). Still, as winter set in, UN officials working hard for flood victims in Pakistan reported that they had already run out of essential supplies.

In his visits to Washington, Foreign Minister Shah Mahmood Qureshi told the world that if it did not help Pakistan in the flood relief efforts, the nation would fall prey to militants. It was an argument repeated like a mantra. Indeed, where the PPP government had fallen short of providing for the enormous needs of flood ravaged Pakistan, Islamic fronts for jihadist organizations had emerged to dispense relief aid.

If the world needed proof that floods had not washed away the militants, they did not have to wait long. Barely had the floodwaters stopped ravaging communities in the north of Pakistan and the Punjab than the suicide bombers began detonating. A succession of suicide blasts on religious processions in Lahore, Quetta and against security officials in Khyber Pakhtunkhwa would convince the world that the bombers were alive and ticking.

As the Indus River made its south ward journey toward the riverine areas of Sindh – wiped clean of the marshy jungles cut down at the height of the dacoit menace in 1992 – it threatened the thickly-populated towns of upper Sindh. The PPP government issued flood warnings in its home turf – Sukkur, Shikarpur, Jacobabad, Shahdadkot, Dadu, Badin and the southern town of Thatta – forcing millions to evacuate their homes.

Still despite trains and bus services run by the government for the flood affected to go to Karachi, the victims preferred to take temporary shelter with relatives or simply move to higher ground. Indeed, with floods coinciding with the ethnic flare-up between Pashtuns and Mohajirs in Karachi, the rural Sindhis, already battered and robbed of their life savings, took chances with the vagaries of nature rather than a tense ethnic situation in the city.

There was high drama in Bhutto's birthplace of Larkana, where the government worked frantically to prevent damage from breaches in the Kirthar canal to save the graves of Zulfikar Ali Bhutto and his children – Benazir, Murtaza and Shahnawaz. PPP officials rushed to create a four-kilometer-long embankment around Garhi Khuda Baksh in Larkana to save the graves of the Bhuttos, whose murders have come to symbolize the eternal sufferings of the people of Pakistan.

Sindh and southern Punjab swirls with tales of feudal lords, including those from the ruling party, who arm-twisted irrigation officials to breach the dikes and save their lands. A pattern emerged where the most influential managed to protect their assets at the cost of the weakest. It would increase resentment in an environment where millions lost their crops and livestock and became internally displaced persons in their own territory.

In October 2010, a survey conducted by the World Bank and Asian Development Bank said that Pakistan's floods caused an estimated PKR 831 billion (USD 9.7 billion) damages to homes, roads, farms and personal property. PPP officials called the figures grossly underestimated. There were fears that in an agriculturally based economy like Pakistan the damage to the crops alone could be as high as PKR 3.69 trillion (USD 43 billion) – 25 per cent of its Gross Domestic Product the year before.

About two thousand were killed in Pakistan's floods – dramatically lower than the estimated eighty thousand casualties caused by the earthquake five years before. Still there was more bad news ahead, as hundreds of thousands fell victim to acute diarrhea, respiratory infections, skin disease and malaria. Children who saw their parents being washed away were traumatized and put up for adoption.

Under world scrutiny, Pakistan made payments of PKR 20,000 (USD 233) in four installments to each family. The United Nations and civil society networks injected a modicum of transparency that involved disbursing aid after verifying the national identity cards of flood victims. Still, double payments occurred, as did complaints from families that they had received no money. With food supplies running out, the UN was faced with the difficult choice of staggering the aid or giving people less than their nutritional requirements.

For the US government, the biggest concern is that the economic devastation created by the floods will fuel militancy. The army operation against the Taliban in Swat, for example, resulted in massive losses of infrastructure and livelihood for 2.9 million residents of Malakand division. Barely had government surveys reported that the division would need PKR 85.7 billion (USD 1 billion) for recovery, when the floods struck.

Awami National Party's Minister for Information, Mian Iftikhar Hussain touched a note with the people when he declared, "First we were devastated by the terrorists. Whatever was left was finished by the floods." For the ANP minister, it was a particularly emotional time, when just prior to the floods the Taliban had killed his only son.

The US would prioritize its aid programs to Pakistan with a view to thwarting potential militant attacks. In September 2010, the Obama administration diverted PKR 71.2 billion (USD 831 million) set aside under the Kerry Lugar Berman act for Pakistan's developmental needs like energy and water and earmarked it instead for humanitarian assistance in FATA and Khyber Pakhtunkhwa.

With the US and Europe waging their own financial battles for recovery, the US Coordinator for Economic and Development Assistance Robin Raphael urged Pakistan to pass meaningful reforms, including expanding its tax base. There was a muted response from the government. The feudal ruling elite has traditionally shunned land reforms, even as the urban industrial class is hostile to suggestions that it should pay more taxes. There was consensus to raise sales tax, which would have the consequence of raising prices for already stressed consumers.

The fact that the floods struck in the post-9/11 scenario and not when the world was busy somewhere else should give pause to Pakistan's observers. With aid coming in, the civilian government has gone into autopilot – leaving flood recovery and civilian development to foreign and international organizations. As people watch to see if the leadership cuts back on their extravagant lifestyles, the international community too has put Pakistan under a microscope to see if it is able to get its act together.

SELECT
BIBLIOGRAPHY

Abbas, Hassan. *Pakistan's Drift into Extremism: Allah, the Army, and America's War on Terror*. New York: M.E. Sharpe, 2005.

Ahmad, Eqbal. *Confronting Empire: Interviews with David Barsamian*. Cambridge, MA: South End Press, 2000.

Ahmed, Leila. *Women and Gender in Islam*. New Haven: Yale University Press, 1993.

Bearden, Milton and James Risen. *The Main Enemy: The Inside Story of the CIA's Final Showdown with the KGB*. New York: Random House, 2003.

Bhutto, Benazir. *Daughter of Destiny: An autobiography*. Florida: Touchstone Books Ltd, 1990.

————. *Reconciliation: Islam, Democracy, and the West*. New York: HarperCollins, 2008.

Cohen, Stephen Philip. *The Pakistan Army*. Karachi: Oxford University Press, 1998.

Coll, Steve. *Ghost Wars: The Secret History of the CIA, Afghanistan and Bin Laden, from the Soviet Invasion to September 10, 2001*. New York: Penguin Books, 2004.

Duncan, Emma. *Breaking the Curfew: A Political Journey through Pakistan*. London: Arrow Books Ltd, 1990.

Frotscher, Ann. *Claiming Pakistan: The MQM and the Fight for Belonging.* Berlin: Nomos Publishers, 2008.

Goodson, Larry P. *Afghanistan's Endless War: State Failure, Regional Politics, and the Rise of the Taliban.* Seattle: University of Washington Press, 2002.

Haeri, Shahla. *No Shame for the Sun: Lives of Professional Pakistani Women.* New York: Syracuse University Press, 2002.

Hughes, Thomas R., ed. *Memoirs on Sind – Selections from the Records of the Bombay Government* (vol. 1 and 2). Karachi: Allied Books Company, 2005.

Jaffrelot, Christophe, ed. *A History of Pakistan and Its Origins.* London: Anthem Press, 2002.

———, ed. *Pakistan: Nationalism without a Nation?* London: Zed Books, 2002.

Jones, Owen Bennett. *Pakistan: The Eye of the Storm.* New Haven: Yale University Press, 2002.

Lamb, Christina. *Waiting for Allah: Pakistan's Struggle for Democracy.* London: Hamish Hamilton Ltd, 1989.

Levy, Bernard-Henri. *Who Killed Daniel Pearl?* Hoboken, NJ: Melville House, 2003.

Mernissi, Fatima. *The Veil and the Male Elite.* Cambridge, MA: Perseus Books, 1987.

Moghadam, Valentine M. *Modernizing Women: Gender and Social Change in the Middle East.* Boulder, CO: Lynne Rienner Publishers, Inc., 1993.

Mumtaz, Khawar and Farida Shaheed, eds. *Women of Pakistan: Two Steps Forward, One Step Back?* London: Zed Books, 1987.

Musharraf, Pervez. *In the Line of Fire: A Memoir.* New York: Free Press, 2006.

Nawaz, Shuja. *Crossed Swords: Pakistan, Its Army, and the Wars Within.* Karachi: Oxford University Press, 2008.

Newberg, Paula R. *Judging the State: Courts and Constitutional Politics in Pakistan.* Cambridge: Cambridge University Press, 1995.

Niazi, Zamir. *The Press in Chains.* Karachi: Karachi Press Club, 1986.

———. *The Web of Censorship.* Karachi: Oxford University Press, 1994.

Rashid, Ahmed. *Descent into Chaos: The United States and the Failure of Nation Building in Pakistan, Afghanistan, and Central Asia.* New York: Viking Press, 2008.

————. *Taliban: Militant Islam, Oil and Fundamentalism in Central Asia.* New Haven: Yale University Press, 2000.

Singh, Khushwant. *Train to Pakistan.* London: Chatto & Windus, 1956.

Suskind, Ron. The Way of the World: A Story of Truth and Hope in an Age of Extremism. New York: HarperCollins, 2008.

Talbot, Ian. *Pakistan: A Modern History.* New York: St Martin's Press, 1998.

Wolpert, Stanley. *Zulfi Bhutto of Pakistan: His Life and Times.* New York: Oxford University Press, 1993.

INDEX

Lightning Source UK Ltd.
Milton Keynes UK
UKOW040616090513

210411UK00001B/14/P